BEST FRIENDS

BEST FRIENDS

The True Story of the
World's Most Beloved
Animal Sanctuary

SAMANTHA GLEN
Introduction by
MARY TYLER MOORE

KENSINGTON BOOKS
http://www.kensingtonbooks.com

KENSINGTON BOOKS are published by

Kensington Publishing Corp.
850 Third Avenue
New York, NY 10022

All Kensington titles, imprints and distributed lines are available at special quantity discounts for bulk purchases for sales promotion, premiums, fund raising, educational or institutional use.

Special book excerpts or customized printings can also be created to fit specific needs. For details, write or phone the office of the Kensington Special Sales Manager: Kensington Publishing Corp., 850 Third Avenue, New York, NY, 10022. Attn. Special Sales Department. Phone: 1-800-221-2647.

Kensington and the K logo Reg. U.S. Pat. & TM Off.

ISBN 1-57566-735-5

First Printing: February, 2001
20 19 18 17 16 15 14 13 12

Printed in the United States of America

Dedicated to:

No more homeless pets

ACKNOWLEDGMENTS

Once in a rare while in your career you might get lucky and connect with something or somebody . . . and magic happens. Little did I know when I accepted a spontaneous invitation to accompany a special friend to Best Friends Animal Sanctuary (thank you, Meredith Meiling), that it would be the beginning of a wondrous journey.

Like everyone who visits Best Friends, I too was touched by the many furred and feathered creatures, pleased to observe their playful well-being, and awed by the spectacular scenery of Angel Canyon. But it was the quiet tranquility of the land, the pervasive feeling of goodwill, and the kindness of the people who lived and worked at the sanctuary that tugged at my emotions.

I was taking a break from writing and had no intention of starting a new project when I emailed our tour guide, Cyrus Mejia, a few days later to ask, "Has anyone ever suggested writing a book about Best Friends?"

"Many," he shot back, "but I'll pass this on to Michael."

Michael Mountain, editor of *Best Friends* magazine, called that night. We talked a long time, the conversation ending with an agreement that I would revisit to meet everyone.

And so it began. As the work progressed and I got to know the men and women who founded the sanctuary, I felt as if I were being enfolded into a large, loving extended family. Now, I am not a Pollyanna kind of woman, and as the months went on, a part of me looked hard for the discrepancies, the phrase or action that didn't quite ring true. They were not to be found. Instead, I found normal, everyday human beings with an uncommon difference: these were people who truly lived and breathed their ideals and commitment to the well-being of the creatures of this planet and the land we all share; people who really "walked their talk" that kindness is the answer; people who made it a pleasure and a privilege to write their story.

One person in particular went above and beyond the call of duty in his tireless input to the manuscript. Thank you, Michael Mountain, for your endless hours of talking through the narrative, your attention to details, your often brilliant suggestions for more vivid portrayals. I shall never forget that you were always there for me when I needed clarification, were always a friend when I'd spent too many hours alone in a room staring at a computer screen. I will forever recall with gratitude your calm insights when frustrations arose.

Then too, I shall always thank my "simply the best" agent, Meredith Bernstein, for her advice when I first started writing. "Write about what you love—the animals. That's where your passion lies." Her words changed my direction and began the journey to this book.

Different, but no less genuine words directed that I work with the marvelous Tracy Bernstein as my editor. At the end of our first conversation she said, "Samantha, I know other major houses want this book. I want you to know that, whoever you choose, I wish you the best of luck and success. Best Friends is a wonderful project." My decision to go with Kensington Books was made in that moment.

I also wish to gratefully acknowledge the patient and perceptive advice of veterinarian Jim Lane of Incline Village and Katie Stevens of Reno Animal Control, and the input of my dear friend Mary Pesaresi.

Almost last, but never, ever least, thank you to my husband, Alan, and his infinite understanding when I just wasn't available.

And, perhaps most of all, my gratitude to the so-very-special furred and feathered beings that bring so much joy and comfort into our lives. My heartfelt wish is that every one of you will be part of a loving family—that one day there will be no more homeless pets.

CONTENTS

Part Three: Reaching Out, 1991–1997

INTRODUCTION

When I look into the eyes of my dog, Shadow, I see such love, such acceptance. Animals may not be able to communicate in our language, but their goodness transcends the barrier of words in a way that to me is spiritual.

Even as a child I felt this way, and over the years this love of animals has brought me into contact with many very special people, including Best Friends.

I'll never forget when Bernadette Peters and I were starting our own organization—**FIDO**NYC—to help homeless pets in New York, Francis Battista of Best Friends was one of the first people to call. "Our sanctuary is out near the Grand Canyon," he said, "but we have a lot of members in your city. I'm sure that several of them would love to work with you, too."

Francis suggested a kickoff benefit, and that was where I began to connect with a whole grass-roots network who felt the same as I do about animals.

The benefit was a huge success for our fledgling **FIDO**NYC and the beginning of my friendship with Best Friends. So when I heard about this book, I knew I'd be fascinated with the tale of how a group of men and women who wanted to make a difference took a piece of raw land in the wilds of southern Utah and turned it into one of the most beloved animal sanctuaries in the world.

If you're like I am, get ready to laugh and cry, be deeply touched, and fall in love with all the delightful creatures whose stories emblazon the pages and trumpet the belief of Best Friends that kindness is the answer: to the animals; to one another; and to the planet we all share.

Best Friends is a wonderful book. I wish you joy in reading it.

—Mary Tyler Moore

In the summer of 1982, a group of young men and women pooled their resources and bought 3,000 acres of high desert in the wilds of southern Utah. Nineteen years later they had brought into being the most beloved animal sanctuary in the world—The place called, simply, Best friends.

This is their story.

PROLOGUE

The Brothers

The woman hugged her fleece vest tighter as she peered into the shadowy quiet of the alley. It was going to be unseasonably cold tonight; she could tell by the persistent twinge of arthritis in her left knee. She glanced over her shoulder one last time before venturing into the narrow passageway between the huge apartment buildings. Her husband had told her a million times that the streets of downtown weren't safe after dark anymore.

The rank odor of garbage almost made her gag as she moved deeper into the gloom. "Kitty, kitty, kitty," she called softly. As if they'd been waiting, a dozen apparitions materialized from the shadows. Quickly the woman slid a Tupperware container full of food from her backpack and spooned the daily rations onto the ground. She smiled as she counted the hungry felines. Not many left now. She'd trapped most of the colony and miraculously found homes for them. But something was wrong. Two were missing. The brothers were always here by now. Where were Tommy and Tyson?

The woman skirted the feeding cats and hurried along to the front of the alley. She paused as she stepped out to the sidewalk, adjusting her eyes to the sudden onslaught of light from passing cars. Where *were* Tommy and Tyson?

Suddenly she saw them: two little cats, black as ebony, tails entwined like furled flags, picking their way across the street with agonizing slowness. She could hardly bear to watch. She wanted to run and grab them, but knew better. Tommy and Tyson had never felt the touch of a human hand. Any such gesture on her part would frighten them back into the street.

The woman felt an uncommon sense of relief as Tyson, two steps in front of his brother as always, nudged his sibling's front paw onto the safety of the curb. She remembered the first time she saw the two cats: skittish bundles of fur hugging the brick wall of the alley, freezing at every movement as they felt their way into alien territory.

She'd wondered why they walked so close together, attached like Siamese twins. It was only after observing them for a few weeks that she realized the smaller cat was blind and his brother was his guide.

Slowly the woman retraced her steps. This had gone on too long. It was time to call Best Friends. It was the only refuge she knew where the lame, the blind, the old and the ugly, those reject animals nobody else cared about, could live out their lives in a safe, loving environment.

She felt rather than saw the movement behind her as Tommy and Tyson melted into the alley. She scooped out the last of the food for the blind cat and his brother and walked out the way she'd come. She would call Faith in the morning.

The weary basset mother lay on her side, belly swollen like a pregnant pig, four pups suckling hungrily on her pendulous nipples. Faith Maloney noted with satisfaction that the filmy glaze clouding the dog's eyes had cleared up since yesterday. The family could be moved out of the clinic to Dogtown in a couple of days. Through the half-open door of the operating room she could hear Dr. Allen nattering to himself as usual. Faith smiled, took a last look at Mama Basset, and hurried to join him.

"You're going to be much happier without these big things getting in your way, you know," the veterinarian earnestly assured a huge Rottweiler that lay sedated on the immaculate table in the middle of the room. The animal lay as dead, oblivious to the soothing patter of the man preparing to neuter him.

"You'll wake a bit groggy, but guess what?" Rich Allen hummed loudly as he picked up a gleaming scalpel. He held it to the light and critically eyeballed its razor edge, then continued his one-way conversation. "We're going to introduce you to the prettiest little girl. But no more unwanted babies," he chided as if expecting the dog to argue with him.

"Morning, Doc," Faith said.

The veterinarian looked up and smiled at the pleasing comfort-of-a-woman before him. Dr. Allen was very fond of Faith. The director of the sanctuary was the quintessential earth mother. Irish-born, with chestnut hair framing honest hazel eyes as quick to genuine empathy as to laughter, Faith was a female to whom you could pour out your heart. One of Rich Allen's treasures was the mandala that she'd painted to welcome him to the sanctuary. Her artwork reflected Faith's special spirit.

"You're just in time, my dear." He nodded toward the formica-topped cupboards snuggled under a rectangle of windows. "I'm missing my music this morning. Would you mind?" The veterinarian held up his rubber-gloved hands in explanation.

Faith rummaged through the clutter of dressings, boxes, and bottles crowding the counter and unearthed an old boombox from beneath a mound of bandages. She pressed "play" and Dolly Parton's sweet contralto quavered achingly into the sunlit space of the operating room. "Don't leave me darlin', I'll die if you do."

"Ah-h," Dr. Allen sighed. "Can't beat a little country to soothe the soul." He leaned over and lifted his patient's left eyelid. "Out like a light," he drawled with satisfaction. He turned his attention back to Faith. "You want to scrub up and help me? Nothing like warming up with a neuter or two."

Faith shook her head. "Not this morning, Doc. I just popped in to look at Lucy next door, and to tell you I'll be bringing Rhonda for her final checkup this afternoon."

"You mean someone's going to adopt that plain little mutt?"

"She's not plain," Faith objected, then caught the teasing in Rich Allen's eyes. "Okay. Okay. A member, Dr. Sharyn Faro . . ." The annoying buzz of an intercom interrupted her in mid-sentence.

"Faith, are you there?" The girl's voice sounded urgent.

"I'm here," Faith answered quickly, her fingers muting Dolly's closing notes.

"Oh, good. I've got Lydia on hold from L.A. She says the blind cat Tommy's looking real bad. She doesn't think he'll last another week on the streets."

Faith scrolled through the Rolodex of her mind. Lydia? Of course, Lydia Rice. She and Francis Battista were good friends. He was Lydia's liaison in Los Angeles for the feral cats program. Faith picked up the phone. "Hello, luv. What's up?"

Lydia had never been so glad to hear Faith's calm English accent. "I know it's early but . . ."

"No problem. What's with Tommy?"

Faith listened while the woman who saved cats recounted watching Tyson lead his brother through last night's traffic. "I'm sure that Tommy's totally blind now," Lydia finished.

Faith didn't hesitate. "I think we can find room for both little ones, Lydia. Do you think you could trap them?"

"Well," Lydia said, "I've had zero luck so far." She paused. "Maybe if I let them go hungry for a few days. Oh, I'd hate to do that."

"Could you give them just a little food for a night or two, then bait a trap with tuna?"

"I'll think of something," Lydia replied.

Faith cradled the phone, then stood lost in thought as Dr. Allen bent over the Rottweiler, suturing the incision with practiced speed. "Something wrong?" he asked without looking up.

"We're about out of room at WildCats Village until the new addition's finished, and I'm expecting two very special newcomers."

"They're all very special, and you always find a place."

The director of Best Friends Animal Sanctuary smiled as she walked to the door. "We always do, don't we?"

Faith paused for a moment outside the clinic. The familiar essence of sage and piñon, perfumed with the earthy scents of horse, dog, cat, goat, and bird, wafted sweetly toward her. The sky above was so brilliant a blue, it almost hurt her eyes. Once again, as she did every morning, Faith gave thanks to whoever was up there for leading her to this place.

She strode the red-dirt paths that crisscrossed the sprawling enclosures of Dogtown, happy with what she saw. Dogs, dogs everywhere. Canines of every shape, size, and character barking their greetings as she passed. Even Ginger, the aging Chesapeake who guarded her stash of tennis balls with gallant zeal, hobbled from beneath her favorite juniper tree in welcome. Faith petted the grizzled head and acknowledged the slow licks to her hand as permission to navigate the last few yards to the kitchen.

The usual carpet of snoozing canines lay sprawled outside the pink-washed adobe building. As Faith approached, a small reddish terrier mix extricated herself from the mass of fur. With the built-in radar of the loved, the dog with the deep, strong eyes and soft, white muzzle padded purposefully toward her Big Mama.

After eleven years at Best Friends, Rhonda had earned the right to hang out with the old dogs around the kitchen. She even had a title—Volunteer First Class Official Greeter—and a job. It was Rhonda's solemn duty to meet all visitors as soon as they arrived, for the explicit purpose of evoking silly smiles and lots of petting before the company was allowed to tour Dogtown.

Faith squatted to receive kisses. "Hello, Rhonda," she murmured, enfolding the common little mutt who was so very dear. "Now you musn't get your knickers in a twist—just listen." Rhonda snuffled a moist nose into her special person's neck.

"I love you. We all love you. But we know things haven't been the same for you since your mate died." Faith rocked the terrier like a baby as she talked.

"Remember when you first came here I promised that one day I'd find you a lovely home? Well, Rhonda, a nice lady from Atlanta read all about you in the magazine and wants to give you just that—a wonderful home. She has an enormous garden, three older dogs for you to play with, and . . ." Faith wasn't doing too well with the stiff upper lip bit. She buried her face in the scratchy ruff of fur tickling her chin.

It never changes, she thought. *We get so attached, especially to the most needy.*

"Come on, Rhonda," Faith groaned as she straightened up. "My thighs are killing me. Let's save the good-byes until later."

Lydia was stiff. She sat with her back against the Dumpster, knees hugged to her chest, wondering what she'd come to. Three nights now she'd waited. Three nights Tommy and Tyson had paused at the lip of the trap, then turned away.

It was frustrating. The usual cage baited with food at the rear wasn't built to trap two cats bonded like Siamese twins. Lydia thought she'd been very inventive in fashioning a tight-woven net like a party tent over the mound of tuna bait. If the brothers would just venture inside, all she had to do was pull the light thread that held up the retaining pole and they were hers.

She'd fed the other regulars and shooed them away. Tommy and Tyson should be here soon. Was that them? Yes! Two blended bodies, blacker than pitch, were wending their way down the alley.

Lydia held her breath, afraid they would intuit her presence by the very air she breathed. But something was different. Tyson had no hesitation this night. The bigger brother drew abreast and turned two glowing yellow eyes in her direction. If Lydia didn't consider herself a pragmatic woman, she'd say the little feline was sending her a message: that he knew—that it was time.

Tyson guided his brother toward the food they'd rejected for three nights, into the trap waiting to be sprung. They screamed when the net fell upon them. Lydia rushed forward, carrier and gloved hands at the ready. She had an edge: Tyson, with Tommy slowing him down, could not move fast enough to escape the enveloping mesh. She had them. "It's okay. It's gonna be okay," she soothed the yowling felines as she sprinted toward her car.

Lydia had it all planned. Las Vegas was an easy shuttle from Los Angeles. She'd take the first flight, grab a rental, and, if all went well, be at Best Friends the same morning. She smiled as she eased the cat carrier onto the back seat of her car. Tommy and Tyson would never be in harm's way again.

By 6:00 A.M. Faith had stopped asking herself why a blind cat and his brother would keep her up worrying half the night. She knew. Faith could name every one of the over eighteen hundred animals at the sanctuary, and she carried their histories and quirks like biographies in her head. They were all special in some way.

She thought of Rhonda for the hundredth time that morning. Yes, they were all special, yet there were always those who took your heart, those whose bravery, spirit, sweetness, even irascibility made you smile and promise they would never be hurt again. It was the same for everyone at Best Friends. All the humans had their secret favorites among the animals. The happiness when one went to a good home was always tinged with regret at losing it.

She would miss Rhonda. It had been a joy to watch the forlorn little mutt discard her doggie depression. Eleven years was a long time. Come to think of it, eleven years was longer than her three marriages had lasted.

Faith Maloney laughed. The universe had funny ways of working things out sometimes. Rhonda was gone, and in a few hours Tommy and Tyson would arrive.

Faith stood and stretched out the kinks in her back. She tightened the belt around her thick flannel bathrobe and, taking a cup of her favorite decaf with her, padded barefoot through the trailer. Eight old dogs rose stiffly in greeting as she slid on her slippers past the door. Smiling, Faith bent and stroked each one back to dreamland. Tiptoeing carefully over the last snoring bloodhound, she let herself outside.

A warm shed abutted the sixty-footer Faith called home. She had but taken a step inside before a dozen felines were curling their bodies around her ankles, purring with pleasure. Faith repeated the petting routine, assuring each it would be fed soon, before opening the door to the outside compound.

Faith scanned her own personal sanctuary. In the adjacent enclosure a fat, white sheep snored, head on his hooves in the thin winter sunshine. Three hens roosted comfortably on his broad back. As always, there would be chicken poop to wash off later.

In a big hutch next door, seven rabbits snuggled in their straw-plumped bed. Six tiny hamsters snoozed in a spacious neighboring cage, safe, yet close to the bunnies for company. Nothing stirred in the emerging dawn. All was well.

Faith sipped her coffee slowly. She loved this time of morning: the palpable quiet that wrapped her in a cloak of serenity. All she could hear was the swish of a hawk's wings flying low, a raven's caw, the chattering of a creek as it wended its way to the Grand Canyon that seemed to deepen rather than shatter the tranquility.

She stood silently, watching the dawn sweep the shadows from the valley floor, higher and higher until the naked cliffs of the red-rock gorge were brushed with the delicate pinks and blues of a Monet painting. No wonder the Anasazi Indians had gathered here to beg plenty from Mother Earth.

A distant barking told her the sanctuary was awakening. Faith stepped back to the trailer, turning her mind to what must be done this day.

*   *   *

"I'm at a pay phone outside of Kanab. I'll be there in twenty minutes," Lydia was almost shrieking with excitement.

"Stop by the Welcome Center and get directions. You'll find me outside Building Three at the WildCats Village," Faith said.

As usual, the feral cats' habitat looked like a disaster area first thing in the morning: overturned water bowls, toys flung everywhere, scatters of granules around the litter boxes betraying nighttime toiletries. Faith smiled as she surveyed the damage. *Partying all night, the lucky pussycats.*

To a casual observer there was not a feline to be seen, but Faith knew to look up at the redwood joists. She counted twenty-one pairs of wary eyes watching her every move.

A serious young man pushed a cart laden with bowls into the room. Judah grinned when he saw Faith and waved "hello" before proceeding to ladle vittles from a red bucket.

Within seconds the room erupted in a flurry of fur. Down from the roof joists they scurried, jumped, or climbed with dainty precision. From behind litter boxes, from carpeted climbing trees and shocking blue sleeping tents they emerged in full meow, tails swishing, all wariness abandoned. The cats knew Judah. They knew feeding time.

Faith felt the vibration against her hip. She pulled the cell phone from her jacket. "Lydia's just left the Welcome Center. She's on her way."

"Please let Francis and Dr. Allen know, and Michael needs to talk to her, too," Faith instructed.

A minute later, Faith stood assessing the woman she'd talked with many times but had never met. Lydia Rice was slender, with dark hair cut short and chic. Light wrinkles fanned from intelligent eyes. More than anything, Lydia radiated a sense of confidence and reliability as she stood beside her rental car, appraising Faith in turn.

Faith closed the gap between them and the two women hugged in wordless conversation. "I've wanted to come here for so long," Lydia finally offered.

They both turned as a white Jeep slid to a stop behind them. A tall, lean man with a shock of red hair unfolded himself from the driver's side and strode toward them. "Michael Mountain," he introduced himself. Faith smiled as she saw Lydia take in his impeccable khakis and matching vest, the crisp cotton of his precisely pressed shirt. Michael was always immaculate, and always so intensely British.

"Michael is our president and editor of our *Best Friends* magazine," she explained.

Lydia's eyes lit with pleasure. "Of course. I've got to tell you I devour every issue. I love that it's so upbeat. I can't stand to read any more horrible things done to animals."

A faint blush diffused Michael's cheekbones. "Thank you."

"Hello, Lydia," Francis Battista smiled as he joined them.

"Francis," Lydia exclaimed, obviously happy to see the familiar bearded face beneath the soft felt hat. "I tried to call you in L.A. but couldn't reach you."

"I was traveling," Francis explained. "How're you doing?"

"Great, now that I've got the cats here."

Before she could say more, a battered Dodge Ram diesel fishtailed to a halt in a cloud of red dust beside them. A round-faced man with an outrageous handlebar moustache bounced out of the vehicle, rushed over to Lydia, and pumped her hand. "I'm Dr. Allen. So pleased to meet you. This is a fine job you've done. Fine job. Where are the little ones?"

"They're right here." Lydia was enjoying the action. "In the backseat." She opened her car door. "They're quiet now, but boy do they have some vocal cords!"

"Let me," Michael offered and disappeared into the car's interior. He re-emerged with a large black cat carrier. "Ah, matches the cats," he said with a little smile, leading the way to Tommy and Tyson's new home.

They all lapsed into silence as they followed Michael, who bore the brothers' carrier before him like a precious gift.

"Oh how lovely," Lydia exclaimed, eyes huge as she took in the sunny window, toys, and carpeted kitty condos of the quarantine room. Michael set the carrier on the floor and cautiously opened its door.

Dr. Allen was already ushering everybody out. "Let's give them some space."

The five humans bunched together outside the quarantine room, unable to tear their eyes away from the small glass aperture that afforded a view into the interior. Nothing. The brothers stayed as silent as mutes in their former prison. Not a movement. Not a meow. Faith could feel the rising tension in the woman beside her. "Easy," she said. "Remember, they're terrified. They may not stir for hours."

"It's good Judah put tuna out for them," Francis observed.

Minutes passed. Half an hour. Forty-five minutes.

"How's your day?" Faith whispered to Michael.

"Nothing that can't wait," he replied.

Some of the residents of WildCats Village decided that breakfast done, maybe it was time to play—or nap, whichever came first—and wandered in from taking the air of their outside play area. One glimpse of the knot of people, staring as if all the answers to life's questions lay beyond one door, and they scattered like buckshot.

Faith shifted position for the umpteenth time and thought of all the things she should be doing. Michael waited, motionless. Dr. Allen's cherubic smile said that all would happen in its time.

"They're coming out," Lydia whispered.

"I can't see any movement," Faith said.

"They're coming out."

Two paws emerged first. Tentative, kneading the rag rug in front of them as if to ascertain its safety. A small, dark head appeared, nose twitching, sniffing this alien territory. One solitary step and the cat froze, eyes fixed on a bowl a foot away.

"It's Tyson. He smells the tuna," Lydia whispered.

Another step and a second face appeared, seemingly glued to the haunches of its protector. But the lead cat wasn't sure. He backtracked his brother into the carrier. "Damn," breathed Lydia.

"They'll be out soon now. Tyson's just testing for any reaction," Faith soothed.

As if not wishing to prove her wrong, Tyson emerged once more . . . curious . . . hungry!

And then what the five humans had been waiting for: the bigger feline stepped purposefully into the light, stopped for a second, and licked the little head beside him. Tommy swayed unsteadily against his brother. Two skinny, tiny bodies trod tentatively in lockstep . . . forward.

Then they saw what Lydia had tried to explain. Tyson would

not walk fast. He couldn't. His tail was entwined like a garland around his blind sibling's. The cats walked as one, tails high, Tyson leading the way—truly his brother's keeper.

"You see what I mean?" Lydia did not try to hide her tears.

"I've never seen the likes of this," Dr. Allen murmured. He put his arm around her. "You did good, woman. You did very good. Now just from looking, they need nourishment. But unless I find something bad, they've got some good years ahead of them. We've got many special-needs cats here. Tommy will fit right in."

Lydia buried her face in his chest. "I'm not a silly woman. It's just . . . thank you."

Faith took Lydia's hand. "Let's go outside for a minute."

"Why don't you all go," Dr. Allen said. "I want to observe a little longer."

They strolled into the sunshine, Michael and Francis chatting animatedly with Lydia. Faith wandered over to a piñon tree whose trunk, thick and wide, said it had seen many things. She leaned back against the smooth, silver trunk and closed her eyes.

Into her mind floated the classical tale of the man walking by the ocean, throwing back the starfish beached after a storm. One at a time you save them. One at a time.

That's the way it had always been for the men and women of Best Friends. Most of them had known each other since the 1960s. Even when they'd been scattered over the globe with everyone "doing their own thing," they'd stayed connected, bound by their passion for animals and the belief that kindness was the answer— to each other, to the environment, to the creatures with whom they shared the planet.

To rescue animals was as natural to them as waking up in the morning. It was the notion that they could make a difference that encouraged half a dozen of them in the late seventies to pool their monies and buy a small ranch in Arizona as a place of refuge for more of the animals they saved . . . one at a time.

Yet it wasn't until Francis Battista had found this place that their ideas could blossom—that Best Friends could truly become a force for change.

June of 1982: That's when it all *really* began.

The day Francis found the canyon.

PART ONE

The Canyon
1982–1986

CHAPTER ONE

Montezuma's Treasure

It was just sweet serendipity, Francis said. Yet he believed nothing extraordinary happened by chance. And this, after all, had been foretold.

On a late June morning in 1982, Francis left the ranch in Prescott, Arizona, heading north for Salt Lake. He drove steadily through the afternoon, stopping only once as he neared the Utah border to rifle through the jumble of U.S. Geological Survey maps he carried everywhere. With his real estate background, Francis was always on the lookout for that perfect piece of land where they could build the animal sanctuary of their dreams.

The small ranch a few of them had bought four years earlier was already too small for the increasing number of animals that he, Faith, and the half-dozen other permanent residents rescued and cared for. When any of their far-flung coterie of friends came to stay, sooner or later the talk turned wistfully to everyone's vision of a place where hundreds of animals could be safe, loved, and allowed to live out their natural lives.

Francis checked in at the Parry Lodge in Kanab that night. He was the first customer in the dining room the next morning, ordering his customary black coffee—the stronger the better.

As he waited for his breakfast, Francis casually studied the map of the southernmost slice of the state, but his attention kept wandering to the framed pictures and movie posters that adorned the walls: signed sepia photos of Tom Mix, Clint Eastwood, and

Ronald Reagan, in full cowboy regalia flanked by advertisements for *The Lone Ranger, MacKenna's Gold,* and *The Outlaw Josie Wales.*

The high-school waitress was full of information as she poured his coffee. "Oh yes, they used to shoot a lot of westerns around here in the old days. In Kanab Canyon, just outside of town. Ronald Reagan had his own room right upstairs," she confided, as if she'd known the President personally.

The waitress looked down at Francis's map and pointed to a large block of land about eight miles north of town. "There, that's Kanab Canyon." For a moment her young face looked sad. "But nothing much happens there nowadays. Nobody seems to know what to do with the place anymore."

After breakfast, Francis cruised slowly through the one main street of Kanab, but nothing particularly caught his interest. He passed the canyon the waitress had mentioned, but didn't pay it much mind. He had the impression that the terrain hereabouts was mostly inhospitable desert favored by rattlers and needled with wind-chiseled rocks.

What Francis didn't realize as he left the town behind was that he was entering the golden circle of Grand Canyon, Zion, and Bryce Canyon National Parks. He was not prepared for the stark beauty of red-rock cliffs, majestic cottonwoods, and soft, summer greens of whispering willows that gentled his way as he pressed on toward Salt Lake City.

He had no reason to turn around that morning, but forty miles up the highway he made a U-turn. Half an hour later he eased onto the rutted road of Kanab Canyon and stumbled onto destiny. By noon he was on the phone to Michael.

"Michael, I've found it."

"Did I hear a 'Hello, how are you?' I'm fine. Thanks for asking."

"I've found our place, Michael."

The two men had been close for years, working together in London, New York, Los Angeles, and New Orleans. As well as he understood anyone, Michael thought he knew Francis. Yet he couldn't ever recall hearing such suppressed excitement from his normally pragmatic friend. He stopped joking. "Where are you?"

"Kanab."

"Kanab?"

"It's a town north of the Grand Canyon in southwest Utah."

"What are you doing in Utah?"

"On my way to Salt Lake. But listen, remember that dream you had about an oasis in the desert? You won't believe it, but I've just stumbled on a three thousand-acre oasis."

"Three thousand acres?"

"Along with all the federal land we can lease with it. It's the size of *Manhattan;* that's how big it is."

Michael tried to visualize the immensity of a piece of land the size of Manhattan.

"And it's filled with junipers and willows, and there's this tributary of the Colorado that runs through it, and these incredible red cliffs that embrace the whole place. . . ." Francis paused. "And they have over three hundred and twenty days of sunshine a year."

Francis definitely had Michael's attention. For a man who had endured, as he liked to complain, twenty long years of terminally gray British winters, the promise of sunshine was like manna from heaven for Michael.

But Francis wasn't finished. "Are you ready for this? There's an ancient legend that when the Aztec King Montezuma was executed, his followers fled with his treasure and buried it right here in an underground lake. Are you hearing me? Red rocks! Treasure! The old man's prediction!"

Michael felt a chill. He knew exactly what Francis was referring to. He'd spent some time on the Yucatan Peninsula in the late sixties with a dozen friends, sleeping on the beach because the boarding house in the fishing village at which they'd stopped refused to rent them rooms. The landlady wouldn't allow their dogs, and, as far as they were concerned, if their dogs weren't welcome neither were they.

A brown-skinned man, bent with age and leaning on a stick, a yellow dog by his side, had appeared out of nowhere and directed them to a Mayan ruin on the seashore where they might stay. Michael had looked for the *señor* the next week to say thank you and invite him to eat with them. But nobody in the village knew of the old man.

This seemed strange given the close-knit nature of a place of less than fifty souls. But at the time, Michael shrugged it off. Mexico, after all, was the land of the mystic writer, Carlos Castañeda. Three months later, as Michael was about to leave, the old man appeared again.

"You will be back," he said.

"I don't really plan on that."

"Not here." He raised a withered arm and pointed his stick toward the United States. "You will go where our people went with Montezuma's treasure, a place of big, red rocks." He smiled. "There is where you'll find what your heart is looking for."

The memory washed over Michael like a vivid dream. "I'll meet you tomorrow," he told Francis. "We need to call Faith."

"She's next on my list."

CHAPTER TWO

Coming Home

Michael Mountain and Faith Maloney flew into Las Vegas—the closest airport to Kanab—the next afternoon. Francis was waiting for them, a bundle of nervous energy.

"You've gotta see it. You've gotta see it," he repeated as he sped down Interstate 15.

Francis hadn't been idle while waiting for his friends. For the next three and a half hours, he regaled them with what he'd found out around town. It seemed that about half of Kanab had chipped in to buy shares of an outfit called Golden Circle Tours. Collectively, the locals owned much of Kanab Canyon, as well as the Parry Lodge and several other motels. But the stockholders weren't averse to selling the canyon property. "I got the feeling they think the land's a bit of a white elephant. But it's ideal for what we want," Francis finished.

Michael had a question. "You haven't told us how much this is all going to cost."

"I'll get to that in a minute. There's one thing I haven't mentioned." Francis paused.

"You mean there's something you've left out of this perfect picture?" Michael inquired mildly.

Francis was too intent on not missing the turnoff to catch Michael's wry humor. "There's one guy, Norm Cram, lives in a house not too far in once you get off the highway. We'll see it soon. He might not be too keen to sell."

"Why?" Faith asked, bracing against the backseat as the Toyota bumped onto the dirt road of the canyon.

"For one thing he's got a nice little deal peddling tour maps of old movie locations and Indian ruins. This used to be the land of the ancient Anasazi people." Francis paused as they approached a crude wooden gate that blocked their way. "Then he's got four cabins he rents out when he can, and he's lived here for twenty years. But I think the others will override him and . . ."

Michael spoke softly. "Can we sit for a moment?"

Francis turned off the engine. "Be my guest."

Michael closed his eyes. He'd only half heard what his friend had been saying. Almost from the moment they entered the canyon, a powerful feeling of peace had settled over him. As he listened to the wondrous silence surrounding them, a pervasive tranquility, the kind that clears your head and heals your heart, seeped into every pore of his being.

A voice suddenly intruded on the moment. "You planning on going anywhere?"

A slender young woman in a blue cotton shirtwaist reminiscent of the fifties sauntered toward them from a trailer parked beyond the gate. She leaned in the driver's window. "Don't I know you?" she asked saucily.

"Hello, Bonnie. I was here yesterday," Francis reminded.

The girl lifted her granny glasses. "Oh, yes. You wanted to speak to Norm." She pointed ahead of them. "He's up the road past his house a ways. I told him someone's been asking for him."

"Thank you," Francis pulled a five-dollar bill from his shorts.

Bonnie grinned. "This one's on us." She strolled back to open the gate. "It's all yours," she called as she waved them through.

No one spoke as Francis steered them past meadows lush and green with summer's clover, past Norm Cram's dwelling. Soon they were leaving the canyon floor behind and climbing the narrow spiraling road to the mesas.

Before they'd gone too far, a John Deere tractor trundled around a curve toward them. A gaunt cowboy-looking fella, complete with spurs on his boots, ground the machine to a halt as they drew abreast. Slowly, deliberately, he tipped the brim of his Stetson and took their measure.

"Hi, there," Francis greeted him.

"Howdy," Norm Cram answered.

Michael climbed out of the car and walked to the tractor. Francis and Faith followed. Norm Cram didn't move.

Francis broke the impasse. "I was in town this morning. Your partner Dale said this place was for sale."

"Anything's for sale at a price," Norm Cram said carefully. "But this property ain't much good for anything. Not enough water for ranching. Certainly can't put a subdivision on it, if that's what you got in mind."

"That's not what we've got in mind," Faith said.

Norm Cram considered her with the gaze of an inquisitor. "So what do you want it for?"

Michael had the distinct impression that the man was not too pleased about their interest. Maybe "suspicious of strangers" would better describe his attitude. "This is a special place," he said, trying to diffuse the tension.

"Special don't pay the rent. And you won't find nothing here except some falling-down barn from an old Ronald Reagan movie. But even the Hollywood folks don't come any more. I'd look elsewhere if I was you." With that, Norm Cram grumbled his John Deere to life, tipped his Stetson to Faith and went on his way.

"The dragon at the mouth of the canyon," Michael murmured.

"What?" Francis said.

"In the old legends, hidden treasure is always guarded by a dragon at the mouth of a canyon."

"Oh, Michael," Faith said with affection. "You do love your legends, don't you?"

The three friends were quiet as they explored, awed by the spectacular beauty surrounding them. As the afternoon shadows lengthened into dusk, Francis brought them to the foot of a red-rock cliff. "I've saved the most incredible till last—but it's a bit of a hike."

The day before, Francis had scoped out deer paths that traversed hidden landings to make the climb easier. Still, they struggled through an underbrush high with horsetail, mullein, squaw bush, and nettles.

Michael was concerned for Faith. She'd forgotten to bring a

hat, and her face was taking on a pinkish tinge without protection from the sun. Besides, he could see she was tiring. "How much farther?" he called.

Francis stopped and clasped Faith's hand. "We're almost there. Trust me and close your eyes. I'll lead the way. You too, Michael." Carefully he filed them around a massive boulder. "Now."

They opened their eyes to a green sweep of land. Arched above the grassy carpet like a great domed amphitheater was a striated pink rock overhang, ribboned with brown desert varnish. "Turn around," Francis said, guiding their gaze to the east.

They looked out to a vista that old Western painters must have known. High desert mesas stretched into infinity. Imperious red-rock cliffs, sculpted by the hands of the gods, thrust skyward into clean, calm air. Below them, the muffled rush of a river swollen with seasonal rains pulsed through a broad expanse of emerald meadow.

Michael stood silent beside two people he considered his true family. He was not unaware of what they were about to undertake if they bought this land. The men and women who shared their passionate love of animals were city folks, every one. Few of them had any practical building skills. He himself couldn't even replace a fuse. Yet they were contemplating acquiring this utterly impractical piece of acreage with no water, sewer, or electricity, not one livable building.

It didn't matter. Walking the property this day, he'd experienced a sense of timelessness—of returning to something very basic, very real. A transforming perception of something "so right" overwhelmed him from a deeper consciousness, and Michael knew in that instant that at last he'd "come home." This was a place of sanctuary for both people and animals. This was the land for which they had all been searching.

Michael was so absorbed in his own vision, he was unaware that Faith had slipped her hand into his. She squeezed gently when she felt him return to them.

"Yes," she said, and the word was enough.

They were quiet on the hike back to the car.

"We need to get everybody together," Faith said as they drove out of the canyon.

"To see who wants in," Michael affirmed.

"Yes," Faith acknowledged.

"The Arizona ranch is the logical place to meet," Francis said. Michael and Faith nodded agreement. "Back at the ranch it shall be, then."

CHAPTER THREE

Commitment

It took a month to coordinate everybody's schedules, but on a weekend in July, twenty-seven men and women came to Arizona to hear about the land in Utah. It was rare for all of them to gather in any one place at the same time, but Michael wasn't surprised.

These were people who had drifted in and out of each other's lives, supported each other for over fifteen years. Any place they settled became a refuge for an eccentric assortment of wonderful and lovable creatures that were, for the most part, unadoptable. These were people who got inordinate pleasure from nursing four-legged or feathered friends back to health, training them, or spending time to make them "person friendly," because the greatest joy was placing a rescued little one in a happy home.

The Arizona ranch had been good for this dedicated group of animal lovers. In the four years they had owned the land, they'd managed to save so many more animals whose luck was about to run out, all the while pursuing the "no-kill" philosophy in which they all fervently believed. Now they had a chance for a piece of property on which they could truly create an animal Eden.

Michael stood a little apart as he listened to Francis describe the canyon, and tried to guess who would be part of the new venture, and who would demur.

Steven Hirano would come.

Michael had met the Japanese-American poet/physicist in Los

Angeles when they were both in their early twenties. Traveling in Europe, they'd been sickened by the spectacle of bullfighting in Spain. They had gone on to Sicily, but couldn't get the senseless slaughter out of their minds. In their naiveté, they determined to protest to the Pope, but by then they were woefully short of money.

Michael would never forget that day in the railway station at Palermo: He and Steven stranded, broke, with only empty pockets to fuel their quest. A small man in a faded navy stationmaster's uniform patrolled his platform with somber vigilance. In a confusion of broken Italian and Spanish, Michael explained their predicament.

The conductor was not young, not old, with skin that looked as if it had been pockmarked by insects. He studied the bell-bottomed, long-haired youths before him. His eyes held the Sicilian weariness of having seen it all, yet there was a curious belief in their depths. "Wait here," he said.

The stationmaster took off his conductor's cap and accosted a knot of passengers waiting for their train. He talked volubly, gestured, and pointed at Michael and Steven. The travelers stared. The conductor shook his cap impatiently under their noses. They quickly rummaged in their pockets, producing notes and coins.

It took but a few minutes before the stationmaster returned. He scooped the money from his cap and pushed it into their hands. "Go with blessings from all of us," he said. "Tell His Holiness that we, too, want no more slaughter of the bulls."

Steven Hirano would come.

Maia Astor-Drayton would come, too. Michael smiled as he watched the petite, dark-haired woman hang on Francis's every word. Maia had a sense of the absurd that Michael loved. She'd earnestly joined the Beatles entourage when they visited Maharishi Mahesh Yogi in India. When the "Fab Four" bought the guru a Lear jet, the English tabloids had a field day screaming about movie stars and heiresses conned into giving money to dubious causes. As a joke, Michael put a one-line advertisement in *The London Times:* "Wanted—heiress to back worthy cause."

Maia Astor answered.

"The whole Maharishi trip was such a hype," the granddaughter of old John Jacob sniffed. "My cats have more spirituality."

"The ad was just a gag, you know," Michael said.

Maia Astor scrutinized the men and women assembled in Faith's flat. "Didn't you say you wanted to publish an anti-vivisection book?" She spread slim, pale fingers in question. "So what's stopping us?"

Maia Astor-Drayton would come.

Diana Asher would also be with them. She already lived at the ranch, taking care of all things cat. Michael looked across the room at the attractive blond woman who had once been his wife. She caught his eye, nodded toward Francis, and gave a thumbs up. Momentarily he was back in a Safeway parking lot three years earlier.

He had accompanied Diana to pick up twelve mangy cats from the Prescott Humane Society. The unhappy creatures were feline leukemia positive, and the rattiest, dirtiest, most miserable bundles of fur that he'd seen in a long time.

On the way back to the ranch, they'd stopped to pick up some food at the supermarket. To Michael's surprise Diana insisted he stay in the car. "Somebody might steal the cats," she said as if he should know better.

Diana Asher would come.

Tall, taciturn Paul Eckhoff sat beside her. Everyone always teased the architect that the *pièce de résistance* of his career was the prison he'd conceived for the London County Council. Yet they all knew what a fine designer he was. Paul had made their Arizona ranch animal-friendly.

Paul Eckhoff would come.

Michael's glance shifted to the open, interested face of Virgil Barstad. The violinist/composer from Alabama could bring forth tears with his playing, yet he loved nothing better than to be working the land, riding up high on a backhoe or bulldozer. And the bigger the machine, the better he liked it.

Virgil Barstad would come.

Jana and Raphael de Peyer sat studying the pictures Francis had taken, their heads touching, Jana's waist-length hair a dark cascade to the floor. The endearing photos that the husband-and-wife photographers snapped of the animals brought to the ranch had been invaluable in placing so many in good homes. Michael hoped they would be part of the dream in Utah.

His reverie was disturbed in that moment by the sensation of being watched. He looked at Anne and Cyrus Mejia, snuggled close on the sofa, with her head on his shoulder; he, the artist in his signature head-to-toe black, absently winding a strand of her long, brown hair around his finger.

Anne was staring intently at Michael as if she wanted to talk to him. When she caught his attention she turned and whispered in her husband's ear. Cyrus nodded. Anne extricated herself from under his arm and came to Michael's side. "Do you remember my family bible?" Anne's blue eyes held Michael's, forcing the memory of her story.

She had come home from high school in Toronto one day, and an inner voice directed her to open to the back of the family bible, where she would find an appendix listing all the saints. She was to write down the names to which she was drawn. It wasn't Anne's habit to hear voices, yet this was an oddly persistent message. She did as she heard. Since no more instructions were forthcoming, she put her list in a safe place and forgot about it.

Six years later, in 1972, Anne was volunteering after work at an animal shelter when Cyrus walked in. Her heart skipped a beat at the dark, handsome man who'd come to help. They were married a year later.

"You might find this hard to believe, Michael, but I was clearing out my mementos chest a few weeks ago, and found the list I made in nineteen sixty-six. I counted twenty-one names." Anne looked around the room. "All of them are here tonight. And I didn't tell you before, but I wrote Cyrus's name down in the corner as the person who would be the most important in my life."

For the second time in less than a month Michael felt a chill. He was a practical man, a thinker who'd studied political science. He was more comfortable planning and implementing than he was in the metaphysical realm. And yet . . .

The majority of shareholders in Golden Circle tours voted to sell their property in Kanab Canyon. But Norm and Mary Cram had lived there most of their lives and elected to stay on their front thirty acres.

The down payment on the canyon was $60,000. Before the summer was over, seventeen men and women pledged with Michael, Faith, and Francis to buy and commit to the land and all it might need in the years ahead.

All twenty names were on Anne Mejia's list.

CHAPTER FOUR

The Welcoming
Committee

Their battle plan was simple.

Michael, Francis, Steven, Cyrus, Gregory, Paul, and Virgil—the "upper body brigade" as Francis nicknamed them—would go ahead to Kanab Canyon and start building. The Arizona ranch would be put up for sale with Faith and Diana Asher staying behind to take care of the animals until a buyer came along. As the sanctuary came together, the rest of the group would phase into the operation as needed.

The men argued that the two women should come with them, but Faith would have none of it. "Get real, guys," she said firmly. "You don't even have a dog run. I'm not chancing our animals being coyote fodder. You get some simple accommodations on that land and we'll be there."

Yet seventeen long months would pass before all the "upper body brigade" could wind up their respective business affairs and leave for Utah. Then again, everyone had hoped the Arizona ranch would sell quickly, but with no offers forthcoming it was deemed prudent to bank enough seed money to take them through at least a couple of years.

Finally, on a cold February 1, 1984, a little after midnight, Francis Battista's old blue ranch truck, pulling an ancient trailer and followed by Paul Eckhoff and Virgil Barstad's equally aged green and yellow trucks filled with seven eager men, left Prescott, Arizona for good to begin the journey to the canyon.

* * *

The drive to Utah was uneventful except for Michael's threats to wring Francis's neck every time he took a rut in the road at seventy miles an hour, sending Michael bouncing into the ceiling like a pogo stick.

Steven Hirano, squashed between the two of them on the front seat, just shook his head. He was used to the banter between his so different friends: Michael, built like a beanpole, with an angular, aristocratic face that seemed to betray his Oxford education even before he opened his mouth; Francis, a few inches shorter, quick to thought and action—a true product of his Italian genes and New York upbringing. The funny thing was, they complemented each other perfectly.

The brigade arrived in Kanab as a pale dawn sun struggled through a sky threatening snow. Not a soul was about as the convoy rumbled down Main Street. Substantial red brick storefronts, reminiscent of a bygone era, shone dim yellow lights onto empty pavement. It was as if the whole town had decided to stay in bed this chilly morning.

Still, nothing could dampen the men's enthusiasm as they rattled over the rough road of Kanab Canyon, past Norm Cram's house and cabins, past the dormant meadows, winding ever higher toward the flat-topped mesas.

A winter's landscape of austere beauty awaited them at the crest of the butte. The valley below curved and bowed between sandstone cliffs that gleamed like white cathedrals under a hard night's frost, not yet melted. Willows and cottonwoods, long stripped of their greenery, were dark sentinels along a meandering twist of creek.

All around them, the highland stretched to infinity, thick with sage and juniper. Francis bumped his truck off the road and followed a deer path into a clearing before killing the engine. For a few minutes everything was quiet. Then the silence was shattered by the stomp of seven pairs of boots crunching onto rock-hard ground as seven cramped bodies hit the earth.

Everyone was smiling, all tiredness forgotten.

Cyrus Mejia was not to be contained. He threw back his head and flung his arms wide like Zorba the Greek. "Yes, yes, yes!" he whooped. "We're here, we're here!" He stopped. "This is too stunning. Where's my pad? I've got to sketch this right now."

"It's not going anywhere," Michael assured him.

"All right, everybody. How about we eat, then explore some?" Francis suggested.

Paul led the way. He had made several trips to the canyon in the past twenty months, figuring where they might build, where the power and electric lines might go. Now he pointed out the advantages of different sites, showing his friends the possibilities.

The men hiked until exhaustion overcame the ebullience that had kept them going. Still, they were too wound up to nap. Someone had thought to pack some beach chairs. They unfolded them against the side of Virgil's truck and sat, knees scrunched up against the cold, tired beyond words.

The distant clank of an engine in need of an oil change was like a slap in the face of the afternoon's tranquility. "We expecting anyone?" Cyrus asked.

"Nobody knows we're here," Michael said.

A truck to rival any of theirs in age and wear rumbled over a rutted track across the mesa. The vehicle jerked to a stop in front of them and a wrinkled elf of a man jumped down. In his right hand he gripped a shovel almost as big as himself.

"Afternoon, Francis. Taking it easy I see," he said with obvious disapproval.

Francis pushed to his feet. "Even God took a break. How you doing, Kelvert? Guys, this is Kelvert Button. He's the man for all our water questions."

Kelvert's woolen-capped head bobbed in greeting as each of the men felt obliged to stand.

"Kelvert, this is Michael Mountain. . . ."

Kelvert thrust out a sandpaper-skinned hand. "You were here last year."

"That's right."

"Cyrus Mejia," Francis continued.

"Mejia," Kelvert turned the name over. "That be Mexican?"

"Colombian," Cyrus grinned.

"Never been to Colombia," Kelvert pronounced.

"Paul Eckhoff and Gregory Castle. They're Brits. Virgil Barstad,

Steven Hirano and myself are the Yankee contingent," Francis finished.

Kelvert gave a satisfied nod. "Regular United Nations, eh?"

Francis smiled. "So, Kelvert, how'd you know we arrived?"

"Norm Cram saw you come in."

"Good watchdog," Michael observed.

"Norm likes to keep an eye on things."

Steven was staring at Kelvert's truck. "I don't mean to be rude," he said, "but is that a goat in the front seat?"

A wide grin split Kelvert's flinty features. "That's my girl. Goes everywhere with me." He slapped his thigh as if calling a dog. A Nubian goat immediately jumped delicately to the ground and trotted over to her master.

It was the prettiest goat Michael had ever seen. The glossy gray fur on its body shone from daily brushing. Long basset-like ears framed sweet almond eyes that surveyed the group with the guileless quality of a Bambi. Soft, velvety down covered a nose that twitched with curiosity in their direction.

Michael had a compelling urge to touch the beautiful creature. He strolled over and squatted beside the nanny. "May I?" he asked, hand extended to pet the goat's head.

"I'd be a bit careful; she hasn't had her supper yet," Kelvert warned.

Michael jerked back his arm. Too late. The goat lifted her upper lip and a set of healthy incisors chomped down hard on the red-and-white plaid of her admirer's sleeve.

"Girl, you know you shouldn't do that," Kelvert scolded. The nanny continued chewing, and Michael could swear she was smiling. "Ah well," Kelvert sighed. He fished a carrot from the depths of his overalls and gently tapped his pet on the nose. The goat immediately transferred her affections to the more edible treat.

"Thank you," Michael said gravely, glaring at his friends, who were having a hard time keeping straight faces.

Kelvert composed his features and shifted his shovel over to his left hand. "I came to see what you're up to," he said.

"Deciding where we're going to build," Francis answered.

"You should plan where there's lots of water—in one of the meadows, like Norm Cram."

"We'd rather stay higher up; we love the view," Michael said.

"And we don't want to spoil the beauty of the canyon with a lot of buildings and dog runs," Cyrus explained.

Kelvert's weathered face puckered into a frown. He shifted his shovel back to his right hand. "Lots of buildings? Dog runs? What you planning to be doing here?"

"An animal sanctuary."

Kelvert ruminated on that one. "Animal sanctuary? That's not what I heard." A sly grin cratered the little man's features. "Rumors are Clint Eastwood's coming back. Gonna build some kind of fancy retreat here."

Francis shook his head. "Kelvert, Kelvert. We're not fronting for Clint Eastwood, or any other Hollywood folks." Kelvert looked decidedly unhappy.

Michael nudged their spokesperson. "Maybe that's one rumor we should help along," he murmured.

"What'd you say?" Kelvert demanded.

"Nothing," Michael replied, all innocence.

"There's just going to be eighteen ordinary people here," Francis insisted, frowning at Michael.

"Ladies joining you, I hope?"

"Of course, and we'll need places for people to stay, and shelter for the dogs, cats, horses, maybe even a goat or two."

Kelvert had visibly perked up at the assurance of ladies. "Still think you should build below. The wind howls like a banshee up here, and the sun'll give you no mercy come July."

Since Michael had spent time exploring the canyon the summer before and found the weather to be perfectly agreeable, he suspected that Kelvert Button had a propensity to exaggerate—especially to people he imagined might not know any better. "We'd rather stay up here."

Kelvert leaned on his shovel. He looked from his goat to Michael, as if confirming their similarities. "Well, mad dogs and Englishmen," he said finally. "Think I'd better give Francis here a hand, then. Looks like he's going to need it. Follow me." Kelvert picked up his shovel and stomped away.

For an old man, Kelvert was all wire and energy. With his nanny goat gamboling ahead, he marched the men like a drill sergeant until they reached a sloping plateau. Here he stopped, crossed his arms over his concave chest, and smiled with right-eous satisfaction as they exclaimed over the spectacular view.

Kelvert let them enjoy the sight for a few minutes before his next pronouncement. "Now about water," he began. The men gathered closer, an expectant congregation waiting for the words of wisdom from their preacher man. "I know you'll be thinking you see it all over the place trickling down these cliffs, and you can sink a well anywhere, but up on these mesas it be different. Before you drill you gotta find a good, deep seam—and that ain't as easy as you might figure."

The water expert held forth to his captive audience. "You be needing a dowser, and when you're ready I have just the man. Cox can find water in a horse's ass. Let me tell you about the time. . . ." Kelvert rattled happily on about the exploits of Cox, the best dowser in the state. His nanny, meanwhile, no doubt hungry for her supper, butted her master a couple of times in the rear.

After repeated hints, Kelvert fondly scratched the back of the goat's neck. "My girl here says we gotta go," he announced. Without another word, the little man swung around and tromped back the way they had come. The newcomers fell in line and dragged wearily behind.

But Kelvert Button wasn't finished with his day's advice. He paused as they reached his truck. "You'd best tell me when you're ready to build, too. I'll steer you right on who to hire."

Paul Eckhoff spoke quickly. "We all really appreciate your sug-gestions, but we plan on doing most of the building ourselves."

Kelvert smothered a laugh. "Please yourself." He opened the passenger door and his goat jumped inside. "Let's go, girl," he said, still laughing. "These folks got a lot to do."

"Was that the official welcoming committee?" Michael asked as the vehicle jolted out of sight.

"Kelvert's good people," Francis said. "Just curious. Kanab was known as the most isolated town in America before they pushed the highway through in nineteen sixty. I mean, how would you feel about a mess of people descending on *your* terri-tory?"

"I think we're going to get along just fine," Cyrus declared.

"Maybe I should call Clint Eastwood and invite him to visit. Then we'd be in like Flynn!" Michael deadpanned.

"Okay you guys, knock it off," Francis said. "Let's make something to eat and turn in early. Tomorrow's another day."

They fell asleep to the music of coyotes howling in the night.

CHAPTER FIVE

Angel Canyon

Daybreak greeted them with a thin frosting of snow. The men layered on sweaters and jackets against the cold, then took their steaming bowls of oatmeal outside. The winter foliage of a giant sage bush caught Steven's attention. He rubbed a silvered leaf between thumb and forefinger, cupped the crumbled fragments in his hand, and inhaled deeply.

"Smell," he said, sharing the burst of fragrance with the others. "Isn't it wonderful?"

Francis was scanning the distance to the plateau Kelvert had shown them the day before. The land on this mesa rolled and undulated in mounds and hollows to the cliff's edge, every yard as far as they could see thickly carpeted with scrub, piñon, and juniper. "We need to clear a road," he stated.

"I've been thinking about that," Gregory Castle said. He spoke softly, as befitted the quietest member of the group. Gentle of demeanor, Gregory was their English philosopher, a calm pillar of strength in the often rambunctious world of his colleagues.

"It might work just to run the trucks back and forth to the site a few times. The tires can lay down tracks, flatten the smaller plants, and we can cut out the bigger obstructions."

"Let's get to it," Francis said.

They macheted brush all day. By noon they'd worked up enough of a sweat to take off their shirts, exulting in the bite of chilled air against their skin. They didn't stop until it was too dark to see.

They slept in town that night. Before leaving Arizona they'd rented, sight unseen, the cheapest house they could find in Kanab. As Steven had sagely pointed out, "Seven guys in one trailer can get a little too close for comfort."

Cyrus cooked, finding the energy from somewhere to whip up a tofu quiche and green salad while his companions struggled to keep their eyes open. The crew was asleep by eight o'clock.

It was a routine that became habit as the months passed: awake at sunup; bang nails until dark; then back to the house with the leaking roof, or to one of the three local restaurants if Steven or Cyrus, the designated chefs, were too beat to cook.

The men grew to cherish the simplicity of laboring with their hands and the satisfaction of exhaustion at day's end. They found that, in spite of their inexperience, they could do this work.

Sometimes their lack of knowledge was even in their favor, as when they desperately needed power and a phone. Frozen ground made the hand-digging of trenches for cables an impossibility. Gregory came up with a simple but perfectly adequate solution: "We'll just drape the lines on top of the ground until it gets warmer."

Their faces became familiar at the hardware store. The bakery knew of Virgil's love of pastries, and their vegetarian preferences were discussed at great length at the grocery.

They were regulars at Nedra's, Chef's Palace, and the local Italian restaurant run by a former boxer from New Jersey—until one night there was a "CLOSED" sign on the door.

The guys thought they were making some small progress in being accepted when it was revealed to them in Duke's Sporting Goods that the former boxer had left his wife that morning to run off with a very young girl from the nearby polygamous community of Colorado City.

But they couldn't seem to make much headway with their only neighbor at the mouth of the canyon. They would wave or shout "hello" when they spied him, but Norm Cram would either watch them go by or turn around and stomp back into his house.

Grant Robinson was another matter. Cyrus was puzzled by the buzz of a chainsaw one afternoon and went to investigate. About a mile away he found an old man, easily in his late eighties and bent like a gnome with arthritis, cutting limbs off a tree.

"Me and my Effie homesteaded this place," he said. "I sold it fifteen years ago, but . . ." He winced and carefully shifted his saw from a clawlike hand to his equally disfigured other. "Can't seem to leave the place alone."

The old man nodded to the sapling, stripped of limbs and growing straight as a plumber's line to the sky. "You might find a use for these one day. They make the best barn posts."

"Feel free to come any time," Cyrus said and was pleased to see the old man's eyes light up with pleasure.

Grant Robinson took Cyrus at his word. The guys came to look forward to his appearances. They ate up his stories of the old days of pioneers and sheepherders and how the canyon was scoured by a hundred-year flood, and they listened to his wisdom on the land. It was Grant who warned them never to go anywhere without a shovel and jack. "Some places this soil gets like quicksand, and your truck will sink in up to its axle."

"So you dig it out?" Michael sounded doubtful.

Grant chuckled. "First you let the air out of the tires. Then it's easy."

"Now I understand Kelvert and his shovel!" Paul exclaimed.

After their initial push, the men allowed themselves a respite on Sunday afternoons to explore their land or just do nothing. Still, they were consumed with the urgency of finishing at least one livable building and some shelter for the dogs—they sorely missed having their animals underfoot. There was no pressure from their friends, but they were all too aware that Faith and her team were holding down the Arizona ranch while others worked in the cities to contribute their share of expenses.

So it was a happy crew who, in the first days of July, passed the word that 1,800 square feet of bunkhouse stood rough but ready for visitors.

Faith was the first to call. "Michael, I can't wait. It's so exciting. Is it hot? I'm bringing dogs, and Diana's following right behind with some of the cats. We've got Jasper, Brooke, Monica . . ." Faith rattled off the names of each of their pets.

"Everything's under control. We even picked up another trailer through the *Thrifty Nickel* for the feline leukemia cats."

"*Thrifty Nickel?*"

Michael laughed. "It's a free sheet. You know, a paper where it costs people nothing to advertise stuff they want to sell."

"Michael, that sounds great. We've got more and more animals coming in. I'd like to bring some of the unadoptables if possible."

"We can handle that, Faith. When are you coming?"

"Diana and I plan on being there late Saturday afternoon."

"We'll be waiting."

Francis's Afghan, Jasper, was the first to hurl his golden body out of Faith's old Ford Econoline when she arrived. "Oh baby, I've missed you so, so much," Francis said, happily accepting slobbering kisses. The Afghan couldn't make up its mind whether to bark with joy or rush around and bestow an equally crazed greeting on his other persons.

The rest of the "upper body brigade" were engaged in mutual love-ins with their own dogs. Seventeen canines jumped, squealed, and licked in joyous reunion with their equally ecstatic owners. The cats were the next to be unashamedly kissed and cuddled.

When men and beasts finally settled down, the women were proudly shown the bare-bones bunkhouse with its concrete floor, unpainted walls, and secondhand furniture. Diana particularly liked the wire enclosures that Francis had built so the cats could go outside and get some fresh air.

"There is one small thing, though," she said.

The men waited.

"Window ledges. You know what I mean? This place needs some nice, fat window ledges for the cats to lie on and look outside."

Francis laughed. "And I imagined I'd thought of everything. Consider it done." Francis loved cats every millimeter as much as Diana.

"I've got something to show you," Steven said. "Come on."

Faith and Diana followed him out of the bunkhouse.

Steven led them down the slope to a small clearing protected by a sapling fence. "You know, I've tried never to live anywhere without a garden. What do you think?"

The women were quiet, looking at what Steven had wrought. More than a vegetable plot, he had fashioned a Zen garden that might have been transported from the old country.

A statue of the Buddha blessed a tiny pond surrounded by budding edible flowers. Wind chimes hung from a gnarled juniper that shaded early lettuce and radish. None of them knew it then, but they were looking at the inspiration for a place to which one day thousands would make the pilgrimage to say good-bye to animals they'd come to know and love.

"Where did you get the Buddha?" Faith asked.

"I asked my parents to ship it to me," Steven said.

"This is what Steven did on his time off on Sunday afternoons," Michael said as he joined them.

"It's so special," Diana murmured.

Michael saw that her eyes were creased with fatigue. A hank of long hair had worked loose from its ponytail and stuck damply to the back of her neck. "You look a little wilted."

"I think my clothes are permanently glued to my body after driving all day. I need a shower, and some food would be nice."

Michael grinned. "I was just coming to get you."

Cyrus and Steven went all out on the meal that evening. Cyrus complemented his famous tofu pot pie with a simple green salad from Steven's garden, tossed with a special low-fat mayonnaise for Faith. He knew how she loved to smear it over everything, especially her beloved banana sandwiches. His fellow cook contributed tempura vegetables and apologized for the store-bought peach pie. All was satisfyingly washed down with the State of Utah government liquor store's best red.

It was in this sated after-dinner contentment, with dogs lolling at their feet and cats on their laps, that Kanab Canyon lost its name.

"Kanab Canyon? " Michael sniffed as if he'd just smelled something rotten. "It doesn't say a thing about what we're trying to do here."

The others nodded agreement.

A cooling breeze wafted the cinnamon scent of nightflowers through the screened front door. Fireflies danced in the darkness outside. The guardian presence of a hooting owl was the only sound in the night.

"Angel Canyon," Cyrus said. "It should be Angel Canyon," he repeated, not knowing where the name came from, but knowing it was right.

"Of course," Steven whispered. "Of course."

CHAPTER SIX

Goldilocks

Faith and Diana left for Prescott Thursday morning. Nothing the men could say would dissuade them. "You know we have volunteers lined up for adoption day in Phoenix on Sunday," Faith admonished. "You don't think we're going to let them down, or miss a chance to find a kind home or two for our little ones?"

It was a good thing really, because Faith was becoming increasingly irate when she returned from town. "Do you know I counted six different signs in windows? Litters of dogs and cats, for anybody who wants them! Don't these people know about spay and neuter?" She slammed her groceries on the kitchen table. Ignorance where animals were concerned was one of the few things that could get Faith's dander up.

Yet she was pleased to meet the man who had befriended the guys over the last few months. He introduced himself when she stopped for gas on her last afternoon in Kanab. "It's so nice to see ladies," Kelvert Button said.

"Thank you," Faith replied, strolling over to his truck. The goat's gentle face nudged into her hand, and she felt the softest touch of velvet under her fingers. "That's the most beautiful goat I've ever seen."

Kelvert watched closely. His nanny, perfectly content to be stroked, made no attempt to eat Faith's blouse. He nodded approvingly. "I'd like to invite you to church services this Sunday. Can't do much with those boys of yours, but ladies have better sense, don't they?"

Faith smiled. "Kelvert Button, you're as full of the blarney as any Irishman I ever met. But I'm a Catholic gal. It doesn't seem right to worship in your church."

This seemed to inspire Kelvert to even greater persuasion. He took a deep breath. "I understand, but I'd like to explain—"

"You know, Kelvert," Faith interrupted, thinking this was a strange conversation to be having in a gas station. "I'm leaving tomorrow, so I couldn't come Sunday anyway. But I really respect your religion because it's full of teachings about kindness to animals. Maybe we can discuss it further when I come back." Her words had the softness of dandelion puff concealing the stubbornness of steel. Kelvert retreated before her conviction.

Francis was also thinking about religion as he drove back the next week from buying construction supplies in Las Vegas. The nearby towns—even St. George—were woefully lacking in some of the necessities. Now that they were starting a bigger building project for the sanctuary, he was having to make the seven-hour round trip ever more frequently.

As the highway blurred past, he was musing on the many religions in which they'd all been raised. Jewish, Catholic, Protestant, Buddhist, Baptist—their group pretty much covered the spectrum. It amazed him how they had all been searching for a better way to live their lives, and how simple was the basic philosophy they had adopted: live with kindness and compassion toward all living things. It was as godly and spiritual to them as any of the recognized faiths.

He thought next about money and Michael's concern that the ranch hadn't sold, how they would need to raise funds when everyone finally came to Angel Canyon.

Most of all he considered the fact that there was no veterinarian in Kanab. A mobile vet came once a week if they were lucky; otherwise, the nearest clinic was in Panguich, sixty-seven miles north. What would they do in an emergency? Certainly they weren't ready to rescue any animals yet.

Francis was so preoccupied, he almost missed the rest stop. He pulled the steering wheel hard right, and the blue truck screeched into the parking area.

The semis were lined up like tankers at a dock as Francis

cruised through looking for a free slot. The place was crowded at 10:00 P.M., with truckers taking advantage of the few degrees' relief from the searing heat of the day to stretch their legs. Francis didn't envy the truckers' lot: the hours of endless blacktop, the loneliness. He knew that some of the drivers were husband-and-wife teams, and he wondered if any of them took a pet on the road.

A vacant spot beckoned between two eighteen-wheelers and he pulled in, then hurried to the facilities. Coming out, he punched up two Coca-Colas from the vending machine, nodded to a couple of guys sitting on a bench smoking, and climbed back into his vehicle.

Francis took long swallows of his Coke, quenching his thirst. He was bemused by the kaleidoscope of lights flashing into the darkness beyond as one truck eased in and another maneuvered out.

It didn't register at first, but after the fourth or fifth time he realized that two golden eyes kept blinking in the headlights. Was it a fox? A coyote? He didn't want it to be a dog, although he knew only too well that rest stops were favored areas to dump animals in the hope that somebody might pick them up.

Francis sighed. He finished the Coke, got out of his truck, and walked slowly toward the eyes. Of course, they disappeared behind a Dumpster as soon as Francis got within a few feet. *Must be a wild animal scavenging for food,* he thought gratefully. He walked around the Dumpster just to be sure. From out of nowhere, a body flung itself against his legs. Francis stopped, startled. At his feet was a shivering, shaking, filthy little dog.

Francis bent and quickly picked up the pitiful creature. He tried to hold the dog at arm's length, but the small canine had already desperately wrapped its paws like a child around its savior's neck. Francis could feel the little heart beating as fast as a hummingbird's wings against his chest. Instinctively he knew the dog had to have water.

The chance of the trembling animal belonging to anybody at the truck stop was slim to none. Judging by its condition, the matted creature must have been there for at least a week. But Francis had to try. He walked into the lighted picnic area behind the facilities where a half-dozen truckers were taking a break.

First he cupped water from the fountain and watched the dog gulp thirstily. Then he soaked a paper towel and squeezed the excess over the animal's head and body to cool it down. *Looks like a cross between a terrier and a poodle,* Francis thought as patches of curly hair emerged. "I don't suppose anyone knows anything about this dog?"

Heads shook in unison. "No."

"It's not the first mutt I've seen here," one man said.

"Maybe they figure if they take them to the shelter they'd just get put down," offered another.

"Or they're too damn lazy," opined a third.

Francis looked down at the terri-poo. The dog had Velcro'd its wet body against Francis's leg and was trembling uncontrollably. Francis knew they were pressed for space to accommodate all the animals Faith had brought in from Arizona, and more were on the way. Nobody needed to bring in anymore at this time . . . but he knew what he would do.

He gathered the mutt in his arms and felt the dog's panting breath hot against his cheek. He hesitated, debating for a minute before turning to the watching men. "There's a place, the locals call it Kanab Canyon, only an hour from here, eight miles outside of the town on the way to Zion National Park. It's an animal sanctuary." *Was he crazy?* "If you see a dog or cat like this here again, and you're going that way, stop by. We'll take the animal."

Six tired faces studied his. The first man stubbed out his cigarette. "Might do that. I got a soft spot for dogs."

When Francis got back to the bunkhouse, the starving canine inhaled three large cans of dog food. "What a beautiful little thing," Michael exclaimed as a gentle bathing revealed softly curling golden hair and a sweet, pointed poodle face.

The terri-poo was a she, and Francis named her Goldilocks. As far as Goldilocks was concerned, she'd found her man. She shamelessly flirted with Francis's big Afghan, Jasper, until he relented and acceded snuggling rights on the bed of their mutual person. Daytime, while the other dogs sprawled sleeping under chosen trees, Goldilocks would sit wherever her person was working, patiently following his every move with her golden eyes.

Goldilocks became Francis's barometer on the world—even, he

joked, picking out his future wife. He liked to say she was so intelligent that if she had known of Angel Canyon, she would have found her own way to him.

For Francis, the saving of Goldilocks was nothing extraordinary—to him it was just a routine, everyday extending of compassion to a vulnerable creature. But in its way, it heralded the birth of "Best Friends." This was the first rescue for the fledgling sanctuary. It would be far from the last.

CHAPTER SEVEN

Sun

Maybe it was the morning the farmhand drove up and unloaded a cowering black Labrador pup, which he declared he would have to shoot if they didn't take him. "Word is you're accepting unwanted animals, and this one's gotten to like eating chickens."

Maybe it was when Francis was asked if the men would like to let Bucky and Jazz out to pasture on their land in return for which they could ride the two former rodeo horses. Or when they were tipped off about Sparkles, who had been one of a dude string in the Grand Canyon but was abandoned to starve when he got too old to work.

Michael was not alone in seeing that their plan to build more shelter for both people and animals before taking in any more critters was mere wishful thinking. The animals were coming—and much sooner than anyone had expected. Michael knew that meant his time, thoughts, and energy would be taken up even more by this place that he now knew would be his home forever.

That may have been why he was thinking about his family in England lately. His father had died when he was two, his mother when he was sixteen. The rest of the clan had been expecting him to come into the family businesses, of which the crown jewel was Granada Television.

But the family's way was not Michael's, and when he dropped out of Oxford University, dashing all their hopes and plans for him, the break was deep and bitter. His preferring to work with animal groups was the final insult as far as the family were concerned, and they washed their hands of him.

Distance, and the passage of years, had mellowed Michael. If he could, he wanted to heal the breach with his family—to make things right before embarking on what he considered to be the most important work of his life.

Francis had a favor to ask before he left. "You're coming back through New York, aren't you?"

"That's my plan. Why?"

"I've kept in touch with some friends who work at the local shelter. They're very upset about this woman who breeds show dogs."

Michael grimaced.

"I know, I know. My friends have been trying like crazy to find a home for one of this breeder's Dobermans. He's a gentle, sweet animal, but the woman complains he's not performing well. She doesn't want to keep him, and they can't find a home for him."

Michael knew what was coming.

"The woman is willing to meet you at Kennedy with a kennel and money to ship the dog. I said we'd help out."

"Francis, we're not set up yet. Besides, that's not the kind of animal we said we'd take. It's healthy, a purebred. *She* should try to find a home."

"*She's* talking of putting it to sleep, or taking it to the city pound." Francis had that stubborn bulldog, "I'll-argue-til-you-capitulate," look on his face.

Michael sighed. "You're such a soft touch."

"Only when it comes to the four-leggeds."

Loitering on Row B2, Level 5 of the parking garage at Kennedy Airport on a Saturday in August wasn't exactly what Michael had in mind when he agreed to bring the Doberman home with him.

He had been waiting like a sweating idiot for over an hour for the breeder to show, and his feeling of suffocation was fast turning into claustrophobia. Michael didn't even like being in a room with the door closed, let alone shut up with a million cars in a building where he couldn't even breathe the air.

The roar of yet another sports car blasted his ears as it screamed up the ramp and flew down the aisle toward him.

Michael winced and jumped back hurriedly as a Corvette accelerated into the parking space next to him.

Try to get a little closer, fella, he scowled, almost gagging as the acid bite of gasoline fumes hit the back of his throat. He'd kill Francis for this one. Where was the woman?

He looked at his watch for the tenth time. She couldn't have missed him. Francis had told her to look for a tall, skinny Englishman with big, curly hair. Well, he supposed she couldn't guess he was English.

He turned as a fire-engine red Porsche Carrera rounded the far corner and burned rubber toward him. The driver hit the brakes and the Porsche screeched to a stop. A window opened in a billow of perfume and a woman with a chic, short Vidal Sassoon haircut stuck her head out. "Michael? Michael Mountain?"

"Melissa?"

The woman smiled. "The traffic, and it's so humid. . . ." she stopped as a glossy, pointed brown head reared up from the floor. Michael and the Doberman eyeballed each other. The dog made up its mind and flung itself across the woman to get at the stranger.

"Sun, Sun, it's okay. Be nice, he's a friend. He's going to take you to a wonderful place." Her words had about as much effect on the dog as telling a New York cabbie not to honk in traffic.

Michael watched with interest as the woman struggled out of the sports car. She was hanging on for dear life to a leather leash that barely restrained the hyperactive beast.

What had Francis said? That this was a show dog that wasn't performing well? A gentle dog, trained, easy to handle? Ha! More likely he tried to eat the judge.

He noticed the woman had a nervous tic that kept twitching the left side of her cheek. She was trying, with little success, to smooth the folds of her immaculate linen skirt and hold the creature at the same time. Suddenly she shoved the leash into Michael's hand.

"He's really a good dog; has the best pedigree—just a bit overexcited at the moment." She was jabbering as if terrified the savior would change his mind at the last minute. "He'll be fine in the airport, you'll see." Before Michael could stop her, she jumped into the Porsche and gunned the engine.

"His kennel . . . his ticket," he yelled as she sped away. Too late. Michael was left choking on a cloud of exhaust fumes—again. He looked at the straining, whirling animal at the end of the leash. He had not expected such a frenetic dog. What happened to the planned delivery of a nice, well-behaved animal in a crate that he could then simply give over to baggage?

Michael suddenly realized he had less than forty-five minutes to catch his plane. "Heel," he urged, pulling the dog toward the elevator. To his surprise the Dobie's cropped ears stiffened, his head lifted in haughty obedience, and he pranced alongside Michael—the perfect Westminster show dog.

This was better. But Michael was still stuck. Obviously he couldn't just leave the Doberman, and no way was he going to put such a hyper animal in a crate for five hours. Well, he'd just have to figure something out when he got into the airport.

Michael and the dog had barely made it through the automatic doors when Sun suddenly stopped. The dark, wet nostrils twitched. Food! In a nanosecond a ravening, overwrought monster was dragging a helpless Michael through the airport.

Michael didn't pump iron, but he was no weakling. Still, he could hardly restrain the Doberman. He was aware of open-mouthed stares as they tore by. He yelled a quick "sorry" as three people tripped over themselves trying to get out of their way.

Maybe if he fed the creature he'd calm down. Michael jerked the leash and accomplished a momentary halt in the dog's head-long rush. He pulled two sandwiches he was saving for his own snack out of his carry-on. "Hope you like veggies," he grimaced. Sun took both sandwiches in one gulp. "Guess you do."

Out of the corner of his eye Michael saw a newsstand. But it wasn't a magazine that excited him. Stacked in three pretty rows in the window were the biggest, baddest, black sunglasses. A terrible idea dawned.

"Heel," he ordered again, and steered Sun into the shop. "I'll take those," he said pointing to a square-framed pair. Michael walked out of the shop holding his arm stiffly ahead of him, allowing the Doberman to lead. Sun twirled in circles the entire way to the check-in counter, then plopped his haunches on the cool tile floor and looked around curiously.

"One fifteen to Las Vegas," Michael said staring ahead unseeingly as he deliberately handed his ticket into thin air. An attractive redhead gently pried the coach class reservation from his fingers. "Forgive us, Mr. Mountain, we had no idea you'd be needing special consideration."

Nicely put, Michael thought. He felt a movement by his feet. *Be good, you crazy animal*, he prayed. *Keep still for once.*

"You're all set, but you'd better hurry. I'll let them know you're coming." She signaled a hostess, who immediately came over and took Michael's arm.

Michael jerked Sun's leash. "Come," he commanded. Sun took him at his word and lunged forward, pulling Michael behind him.

"I thought guide dogs always had harnesses," the hostess puffed, running to keep up with them as a galloping Sun flew ahead.

"He was homesick and chewed through it," Michael shouted. "I had to buy him a temporary."

The hostess opened her mouth, but thought better of pursuing this line of questioning. She hustled them through security and delivered them to the boarding area. "They're all yours," she said archly, handing man and dog over to the two waiting flight attendants.

"Mr. Mountain, you almost didn't make it. We were just about to close the gate. What a handsome dog. I've never seen a seeing-eye Doberman before," the younger of the two women gushed.

Michael forced a smile. Sun decided he liked the pretty female and jumped up and down like a yo-yo against her leg. "Sit," Michael ordered through clenched teeth.

They were half-way through First Class when the worst happened. Sun smelled food from the back galley. With a deep-throated bark he lunged again. Michael felt the leash slide through his fingers.

"Oh no," the attendant gasped as Sun hurtled down the aisle.

Shrieks filled the plane as people saw a huge, drooling animal bounding toward them. Instant anarchy ensued. Passengers leaped onto seats. Children wailed. Men cursed and tried to grab the dog. The scene on the plane was straight out of a Mack Sennett movie. Michael stood in the middle of the uproar, trying hard not to laugh hysterically at the absurdity of it all. *I'll get you for this, Francis.*

Sun didn't like the screaming. He looked disconcerted for once and decided to jump onto the nearest empty seat. A woman let out a high-pitched cry. Sun leaped to the next row. Passengers panicked, scattering to get out of his way. "Keep calm. Keep calm," the attendants called as they dashed after the Doberman.

Michael decided he'd better do something quickly or he and the dog would be thrown off the plane. He pushed forward. "He's just finished training. This is his first flight," he yelled. "Let me through."

Passengers parted like the Red Sea. Michael rushed down the aisle to see a happily slobbering Sun dominating an empty back row. "Where is my dog?" he said, suddenly remembering he was supposed to be at least partially blind.

"Here," the younger attendant guided Michael to a seat. Michael noticed that she was trying hard not to laugh. Then she winked. He pretended not to see.

"You *can* control your animal now, Mr. Mountain?" she said, failing miserably at a stern demeanor. "You know he can't sit there for takeoff." She put her lips to Michael's ear. "And if we don't get off the ground NOW, we'll have to put you off the plane."

Michael grasped the Doberman's neck in a vice-like grip. One mighty heave and the dog was on the floor. Sun proceeded to howl and squirm. "Maybe these will help." The attendant pushed packets of peanuts into Michael's hand. "Thank you," he said gratefully.

Fortunately Sun was a perfect angel for the rest of the flight, although he did insist on sitting on Michael's lap the whole time.

The attendants hadn't had so much fun in years. They kept sneaking filet mignon out of first class. "For the dog," they said sweetly as they brought Michael the usual bland coach fare.

On the drive from Las Vegas, Sun decided that Michael's thigh was the only place to put his head, snoring all the way. Michael passed the time by lecturing the sleeping dog on his wretched behavior, and how he would keep Sun in a run all by himself, and how nobody would ever, ever adopt such a silly, silly animal. The Doberman would show his terror at these threats by occasionally waking and licking Michael's hand.

The saving of Sun *(what else could you call bringing home that mis-*

erable creature?) was thoroughly unlike the rescue of Goldilocks. And yet both in their way showed to what lengths and with what good humor the men and women of Angel Canyon would go for any animal in need.

They would need all the ingenuity and humor they could muster in the years to come.

CHAPTER EIGHT

Good Days/Bad Days

There were good days and bad days, and sometimes they both came on the same day.

When Mary Cram arrived at the bunkhouse with a fresh-baked apple pie, it was a good day. No explanation was given, but the gesture broke the ice, and the men were pleased to have a nod of recognition and an exchange of pleasantries with Norm Cram when they passed his wooden house.

It was both good and bad in the summer of 1984 when the rains came—sudden downpours that in seconds turned their dusty dirt roads into ankle-deep mud slides. The benign river that meandered slowly through the meadows below was suddenly a raging torrent of water that reminded them all too clearly of how the canyon was created. It was no wonder the descendants of the Kanab oldtimers still told the tale of the great flood of the 1890s.

But of more immediate concern to the men in Angel Canyon was the deluge of saturated red earth that threatened to inundate their new home. They scrambled like ants to shove logs up-slope from the bunkhouse to stop the slow ooze, toiling two precious weeks to build a retaining wall. They spent more valuable hours laying two-by-fours on the paths to the county road so that their trucks wouldn't sink, hopelessly mired until the rains ceased.

But the rains taught them to build their future Catland and Dogtown on the highest ground of the mesa, well out of the path of flash floods, as well as giving a brief but gave blessed relief from the summer's heat.

When Steven Hirano was reunited with his first love, it was very good. "I received a letter from Mariko," he confided.

Michael was surprised. Mariko had been Steven's childhood sweetheart, but she married another when Steven went to London. He hadn't mentioned her in years.

"She's divorced," Steven continued. "I'm going to Los Angeles to see her over New Year's."

Mariko came to Kanab the spring of 1985. By the time the last of the potatoes were dug, the canyon's first wedding was planned. It would be at the newly christened Angels Landing, the spectacular amphitheater to which Francis had first taken Faith and Michael three years before.

The ceremony was Buddhist, the vows simple. Mariko was radiant in white chiffon, and parents from both families snapped many photos to remind them of the day. Mariko's loving energy was embraced by all. Steven smiled more; he seemed lighter somehow.

By the fall of 1985, they were ready to begin construction on the sanctuary's headquarters. The Village was Paul Eckhoff's first chance to show his genius as an architect. He designed a sparkling white Spanish-style structure with a central meeting room, offices, and two wings of living accommodations. For this major project, Paul hired a contractor from town, but Steven Hirano would be the supervisor on the job.

On this fateful morning, fourteen-foot beams were painstakingly erected in place, framing a panoramic view of the red-rock gorge and endless mesas so loved by all.

The men stood, quietly proud. The air was still, without a whisper of a breeze. Suddenly, as if from nowhere, a wind ripped, hard. The builders watched helplessly as the wall leaned, shuddered once, and slowly tumbled away down the hill.

"Oh, Steven," Mariko comforted.

But Steven and the rest had already collapsed with laughter.

Word of the sanctuary in the canyon was getting around. The trickle of animals was picking up momentum: litters of kittens; dogs dropped off with the repeated refrain, "We'll shoot them if you don't take them." One day rangers from the Grand Canyon stopped by with a pup that had been dumped at the lodge. "It's part coyote," they said. The little dog looked more like a chubby shepherd mix than a wild predator, but Michael named him Coyote—what else? So it was a good day when Diana Asher left Arizona and moved into the bunkhouse. There were just too many critters to care for while the men were busy building.

Everybody was happy when seventeen-year-old Judah Nasr came for a visit and decided to stay. Francis Battista's son had inherited his father's love of all creatures great and small, especially cats. He built his own dwelling, and became invaluable to Diana.

Faith's son David Maloney had naturally adopted her love for animals and the environment. The teenager shared his mother's passion for dogs, and loved nothing better than to hike in the wilderness. After spending the summer in Angel Canyon, he declared that, he too, would stay on the land.

Judah and David were the first of family and friends to make the trek to the sanctuary. People discovered that exploring the golden circle of National Parks—Zion, Grand Canyon, and Bryce Canyon—was somehow more satisfying when they could spend a few days scooping the poop, feeding, or just socializing with the animals.

Early one Saturday, the crunch of car tires and the infectious peal of a woman's laughter disturbed the breakfast rituals in the bunkhouse.

"That's got to be Jana and Raphael," Virgil Barstad exclaimed, opening the door so the dogs could check out the visitors. The men smiled and followed their animals outside. A woman was bent over the passel of dogs that had gone wild in greeting her. Beside her a tall man, blond hair waving to his shoulders, smiled indulgently at the show.

"Hi, guys," Jana called.

Jana and Raphael de Peyer had moved to Nevada earlier in the year from Atlanta, Georgia. Jana wanted badly to be closer to the fledgling sanctuary, but at the same time she and her husband needed a place to continue their photography business. Las Vegas was the logical choice.

Jana had an idea for the sanctuary this weekend. "Raphael and I brought our cameras with us," she told Michael and Francis.

"We thought we'd take photos of the adoptables and see if any of our contacts in Vegas might be interested. If we can find good homes, we'll take the animals back with us on our next trip."

"Absolutely. That's a great idea," Michael said.

"And you might as well tell me what supplies you need, Francis," Jana continued. "Raphael and I can bring the stuff back on our next visit. By the way, we haven't checked in yet. Is there anywhere besides the Parry Lodge that's halfway decent to stay?"

Francis laughed. "There isn't much choice."

The men walked out of the bunkhouse the next morning to see Jana on her knees, planting desert flowers. "You got up too soon," she chided. "I wanted to surprise you." She leaned back and studied her handiwork. "I picked them up at a roadside stand on the way here," she said. "Makes the bunkhouse more livable—a bit of color, don't you think?"

Jana and Raphael took photos of the animals and went back to Las Vegas the next day. Two Sundays later, Jana had another surprise for the people of Angel Canyon. This time the men came outside to witness her staggering from her car under a huge flat of bedding plants. "Don't worry," she laughed a sound akin to chimes in a breeze. "I got the flowers donated."

The pink impatiens, yellow daisies, and sunflowers were not all Jana and Raphael had brought. "You tell them," Raphael said to his wife as they sat around the Formica kitchen table after dinner.

Jana smiled broadly. "I was 'tabling' at the airport and met Wayne Newton, Cher . . ." she began. Everyone smiled. They had all taken their turns sitting behind tables in front of supermarkets and similar locales to raise money for different charitable causes. But Jana explained that the Las Vegas airport was an awesome place. "So many winners." Then a mischievous look crossed her face. She bent to rummage in the large carryall beside her.

Suddenly a small raccoon dressed in a black tuxedo and bedecked with gold necklaces popped his head above the table. "Hello," said the cheeky puppet. "My name is Rocky Raccoon. What's yours?"

Jana's hand walked over to Paul Eckhoff and stuck the puppet's nose into the architect's shirt pocket. "Oh dear, nothing here, sorry." The puppet moved on to Gregory Castle. "Ah ha!! I smell money. Now let's have a look, Mr. Castle." Without further ado he pulled Gregory's wallet from his jeans and extracted three one-dollar bills. The disappointed slump of the puppet's body had everyone around the table crying with laughter.

"I don't know how you do that," Diana said wiping the tears from her eyes.

"Well, I usually strike it a little richer than three dollars," Jana giggled.

"Jana and Rocky have no shame," her husband declared. "That raccoon has been known to pout until he gets a respectable sum."

"With Rocky, people drop ten-dollar chips, fifty-dollar chips, and twenty-dollar bills." Jana grinned at her husband. "Your turn."

With the casualness of a rich uncle about to bestow a great fortune on a favored child, Raphael plucked a white envelope from his pocket and laid it on the table. "For the animals," he said, smiling. The envelope contained a deposit slip for a few dollars short of $1,000.

"This is incredible," Michael said. He and Francis both knew how the influx of animals had strained their budget to the maximum. Jana's contribution was a godsend.

"We cashed the chips and put the money in the Foundation's charitable account as soon as Jana came home," Raphael said.

"This is truly incredible," Michael repeated wonderingly.

Jana de Peyer blushed with pleasure. The friends had long ago set up a charitable foundation to be able to solicit funds for those causes dear to their hearts. Jana's "tabling" efforts had been mostly directed toward raising money for terminally ill children. Now she was doing it for the animals.

It was a good day when Jana and Raphael moved to Las Vegas.

The week before Thanksgiving, they received the great news that the Arizona ranch finally had a buyer. The up-front money was frustratingly small, but monthly payments would cover the mortgage on Angel Canyon, and Faith and the rest of the animals could at last move to Utah. It was celebration time.

Francis, however, was worried. "We're holding sixty animals and taking in more all the time. Faith has got to be bringing in close to a hundred. We can't keep caring for that many without a vet close by."

Michael shared Francis's concern. They had gotten pretty good at taking care of any minor problems that might arise with the animals, but for anything more serious, there was no resident veterinarian in Kanab, and Francis had become increasingly frustrated with the erratic schedules of mobile vets who came to town maybe once a week. He and Diana had made the three-hour round trip to the nearest clinic so many times with a sick cat or dog, they could do it with their eyes closed nowadays.

Michael knew the constant anxiety and travel had to be taking its toll on their energies. He was also aware that their budget wouldn't stretch to building even a bare-bones facility, let alone hire a vet. Yet there was nothing anybody could do at the moment.

"We've got to get a veterinarian," Francis fretted.

"I'll have a talk with the great conjurer in the sky," Michael said, poker-faced.

Francis just glared.

CHAPTER NINE

Dr. Christy

The air had a tart bite that foretold early snow as Francis drove into Kanab the following Saturday. He wasn't in the best of moods. Francis still had the troublesome habit of trying to cram seventeen chores in a fourteen-hour day, and he was really pushing the envelope this week. Faith, Maia Astor, Anne Mejia, Jana, and Raphael were coming in for the holidays, and he had a million things to do before they arrived.

Busy as he was, Francis always made time to stop by and see Lorelei, the local animal groomer. Besides, she had some eye medicine for Monica, his cat. He just hoped she wasn't busy this afternoon. Francis parked in front of the now defunct White Pines Motel, whose rooms had been taken over by a variety of small businesses, and knocked on the corner room next to the florist.

"Door's open," a parrot's raucous squawk informed him. In spite of himself, Francis smiled as he walked in. Lorelei was an animal person, and along with the talkative Yellow Nape, he'd have to say hello to the two large mutts that kept her company all day.

Lorelei's room was small and poorly lit, but well equipped with a spotless chrome table, towels, electric clippers, and all the accoutrements to make a house pet smell and look good.

"Make yourself useful. Make yourself useful," the parrot ordered as two dogs burst out from under the table and threw themselves joyously upon Francis's chest.

"Down, down. And all of you be good," Lorelei chided her menagerie. Francis thumped the two dogs on their rumps and they plopped to the floor, panting happily.

"How you doing today, Francis?" Lorelei wrinkled her nose as she smiled. She gestured to a slight young man leaning his elbows on her grooming table. "Do you two know each other?"

Francis's eyes traveled up from a pair of dirt-encrusted boots from which the left sole was coming apart, to torn Levis, a plaid shirt, and a friendly, tanned face under a shock of unruly, strawberry blond hair.

The young man straightened, stepped forward, and stuck out his hand. "Bill Christy."

"*Doctor* Bill Christy," Lorelei said proudly.

Francis offered his hand and felt a surprisingly firm grip. "Francis Battista."

The doctor nodded. "Kelvert Button's spoken of you."

Francis wondered why the man who so loved his goat hadn't mentioned Dr. Christy. "New in town?" he asked.

"Just moved to Panguitch a couple of months ago. Came down to see some of my patients."

Francis was puzzled. Why would a doctor come sixty-seven miles to make house calls. "Patients?"

"Cows, pigs, horses. I'm principally a large animal vet."

Francis couldn't believe what he was hearing. A veterinarian who came to people's houses. Then he realized that the doctor had said his practice was farm animals. Still he had to ask. "Do you come to Kanab very often?"

"As often as I'm needed."

Francis looked at him. "I don't suppose—I mean . . ."

"That I might be interested in having a look at your dogs and cats?" The veterinarian laughed at Francis's surprise. "You know how small this town is?" he said by way of explanation.

Francis joined in the laughter. "There are no secrets. But would you really consider coming out to our place?"

"He's the best vet," Lorelei interrupted. "Just graduated from Colorado State. We love him around here."

"Why haven't we met before?" Francis asked, exasperated.

"I hear that property of yours keeps you pretty busy, but I planned to come by sooner or later." Dr. Christy dragged a cracked leather wallet from his jeans pocket, pulled a crumpled white card from a mess of receipts, and handed it to Francis. "Call me. I'd like to see your operation."

"Call me. Call me," the parrot mimicked.

Francis forgot Monica's eye medicine. If the police had been vigilant, he would surely have gotten a ticket for driving eighty miles an hour back to Angel Canyon. He couldn't wait to share the news. There was no way to know how soon he would be calling the good doctor.

CHAPTER TEN

━━━━━━━━━━

Burnt Offering

"Hot cider, everybody. Come and get it," Jana de Peyer announced, stirring the contents of the big iron pot simmering on the stove. Michael bent over the bubbling amber liquid and sniffed appreciatively. "Get out of here. You'll have your nose in it in a minute," Jana teased as she ladled generous portions of the clove-scented cider into waiting mugs.

Michael grinned and angled to be first in line. He took his mug and ambled through the "everything room," as they called the open area adjoining the kitchen, and gazed out the window that afforded the endlessly enchanting, ever-changing view.

It had hailed during the night—huge stones that pinged like bullets on the roof of the bunkhouse. He had gotten up to watch jagged flashes of fire split the sky between warring thunderheads, bathing the craggy corridors of the canyon in luminous radiance.

Thanksgiving Day had dawned with the fenny smell of damp, dark earth steaming in the morning sunshine, glistening with freshness. Michael had watched Cyrus rush to capture the elusive magic of the scene on his canvas.

Now dusk was filming the afternoon, and in a few minutes they would sit down to a holiday feast of nuts, grains, and vegetables; blackberry and pumpkin pies, and custard.

Francis came over and stood beside Michael. "I think we found Montezuma's treasure."

Michael nodded and thought of all the different definitions of treasure. The true riches of Angel Canyon were certainly very different from what Montezuma's men, or the Hollywood stars who'd come after them, had considered treasure.

Neither Michael or Francis had been listening to Diana Asher on the phone. She padded across the room toward them, her face anxious. "That was Nancy Hartwell."

Nancy Hartwell was one of their favorite locals. The classic image of the little old lady in tennis shoes, Nancy was so excited when she heard what they were doing. She had sniffled and dabbed her eyes with the corner of her cardigan when they introduced her to the animals. "I've been rescuing these critters all my life. I thought I was the only person who felt this way. I'm so glad you've come. God bless you. God bless you all."

"Nancy hates to bother us, but some woman called about a rotten cat in her driveway. Told Nancy her kids have been trying to kick it out of the way, but it won't move. Nancy's beside herself. She's in bed with the flu, otherwise . . ."

Francis didn't hesitate. "Let's go."

"We'll wait dinner on you," Faith promised as the man and woman sped out of the bunkhouse.

Francis parked on a scrubby grass verge outside the address Nancy had given Diana. The almost-full moon shed a silvery glow over the garden. They saw the cat immediately, an inert form curled on the weed-choked gravel driveway.

Diana dropped to her knees beside the feline. "Oh my God." She turned her head away for a brief second at what was now clearly revealed. Someone had doused the tom with gasoline and set him on fire! Three-quarters of his little body was an oozing, suppurating mass of pus and blood. Diana gasped as the strong stench of charred fur and flesh hit her nostrils like an abomination.

Francis knelt and looked closer. Apparently it hadn't been enough fun to torture the animal with fire, an eye had to be gouged as well. Francis lifted a blistered paw. The cat's pads had been burnt to the bone.

No wonder the poor thing couldn't walk or move. He was immobilized with pain. Worse, he must have been lying in that driveway for a couple of days. Francis could see little white maggots wriggling obscenely between the tom's toes.

Instinct made Francis look up at the house. A woman and two children were silhouetted in the living-room window, staring at them. "Let's get him out of here," he said in disgust.

The cat opened a singed eye. All the fear, pain, and torment one small creature could bear was reflected in his gaze. He struggled unsuccessfully to stand, mewing in pain.

"No. No. It's okay. It's gonna be okay," Diana soothed. Together the two friends slid a towel under the tom's little body. Carefully, slowly, they lifted the corners of the material like a stretcher and carried the burnt offering to the truck.

On their way home, Francis stopped at a phone booth. "Dr. Christy," he said. "Do you remember me? Francis Battista?"

"Of course," the veterinarian interrupted.

"We don't expect to see you on Thanksgiving, but if you could tell us what to do . . ."

The doctor listened while Francis explained about the cat.

"I'll be right there," Bill Christy said.

The men and women in Angel Canyon this Thanksgiving night were not quite prepared for the veterinarian who came into their lives, but their first sight of him would forever remain in their memories.

An hour after Francis's call, Dr. Christy dashed into the bunkhouse, trailing the distinctive odor of cow dung and making strange smacking sounds. Eight pairs of eyes automatically dropped to his feet—the source of both noise and smell.

The veterinarian was wearing bright green galoshes over his shoes, but he'd forgotten to tie the laces. The rubber overboots flapped loudly against his calves, shedding flakes of straw and manure with every step.

Oblivious to their stares, the disheveled young vet carelessly flung his jacket over a chair and rolled up his shirt sleeves. Dried blood smeared his rugged blue denim. "I came as fast as I could. Had another emergency before yours. Had my arm up a cow's ass," he announced cheerily.

It didn't seem to bother him that the only surface available was the speckled Formica of the kitchen table, or that his audience consisted of several curious cats and dogs, as well as their persons. Carefully, he lifted the light sheet that Francis had used to cover all but the head of the burned cat. He leaned close, sniffed, and placed two long, tapered fingers gently over the heart. A tiny mew of complaint rasped from the tom's mouth.

Dr. Christy frowned as he tenderly replaced the sheet. "Follow me," he called and wheeled out of the kitchen. Not sure for whom the order was meant, all the people and several dogs dutifully filed behind him.

Dr. Christy couldn't have parked his veterinary truck any closer: the front fender was in intimate conversation with the bunkhouse wall. His van was a typical "vet box," the sides paneled with drawers of all shapes and sizes, the tiny interior outfitted with a refrigerator and the necessary veterinary equipment. He pulled a flashlight from under a bucket of towels and gave it to Diana. "Would you mind shining this over my shoulder?"

The veterinarian couldn't seem to find what he wanted. He jerked out each drawer in turn and rummaged frantically among a jumble of bottles and jars that didn't seem to have any labels. He seemed totally unaware that as he shut one drawer another would jack-in-the-box open.

Michael's British reserve was having a hard time as each drawer would pop out, and Dr. Christy would absently reach over to shut it, triggering another drawer to bounce open. Diana finally took pity and closed each of the recalcitrants behind him. "Thank you," he said gratefully.

The vet loaded his arms with bags, bottles, and syringes and scurried back into the bunkhouse. He dumped his cargo onto the kitchen counter and extracted a large Coca-Cola bottle filled with a blue liquid. "Somebody lift that animal. Careful," he warned even before Francis moved to do his bidding.

Dr. Christy splashed the dark fluid over the Formica tabletop and wiped it down vigorously with a paper towel. "Novalsan," he said. "Best antiseptic in the business. I'll leave you some." He nodded to Francis. "You can put him back down now."

Once again the veterinarian carefully uncovered the pitiful feline. Faith winced as she got a good look at the damage someone with a can of gasoline had done to a helpless creature. The cat was mewing continually now: small, hoarse cries of distress.

Dr. Christy fumbled around in his arsenal of medicines and picked up two small bottles of liquid, extracted an amount from each into a slender syringe, and quickly inserted the needle into the flesh of the tom's right thigh. "I'm giving him a shot of Ketamine and Valium intramuscularly to put him out. He doesn't need to suffer any more pain," Dr. Christy said.

Again the veterinarian groped around in his muddle of medicines. This time he chose a plump, clear plastic IV bag and held it high above the cat's head, letting the four-foot tube the thickness of a cocktail straw dangle to the table. "With burns like these, this cat's got to be dehydrated. We must get fluids into him fast. This bag holds two hundred cc's of lactated 'Ringers,' which should take about ten to fifteen minutes to drip into him."

Dr. Christy looked perplexed as though he'd lost something. "That's funny, I usually have my stand with me. I didn't bring it in, did I? I must have left it at home." He shook the IV bag. "Would somebody hold this?"

Michael obliged.

With familiar ease, the veterinarian briskly attached another needle to the end of the tubing, picked up a sliver of slack from the back of the tom's neck and slid the needle into the fold of skin. He squeezed the shutoff clamp halfway down the tube and a colorless liquid eased into the sedated body.

While the "Ringers" did its job, Dr. Christy deftly extracted three more IV bags and a half-gallon bottle from the heap on the counter. "You can manage this now, right?" he asked his audience.

Everybody nodded solemnly.

"Good, because I'm leaving you some fluiding. If the cat's not eating or drinking tomorrow you've got to repeat this." The veterinarian pushed his IV bags onto Diana. "Give one hundred cc's a day."

Dr. Christy paused and eyed the men and women watching his every move. "Francis, and you, young man." He pointed at Judah. "You two pick those maggots out of his feet. Gently," he said, handing each a pair of tweezers.

The veterinarian turned to Michael. "You can put your arm down now." He smiled at Michael's gasp of relief. "And remove that needle and get rid of the bag, if you wouldn't mind."

Dr. Christy stepped back to the counter and quickly washed his hands in the sink. "Now for the hard part," he muttered.

The doctor worked with total focus, deftly snipping away the blackened skin and dropping it into a bowl Faith had placed on the table.

He turned the cat over and repeated the operation. Finally he was finished. "Pass me the Mountain Dew with the brown liquid in it," he ordered, thrusting out his hand. "And some cotton." Diana rushed to help.

"Thank you," Bill Christy said, twisting off the cap. He suddenly noticed that Diana was staring at his Mountain Dew soda bottle. He smiled, embarrassed. "Don't take any notice of my containers here. I like to consolidate stuff. Makes it easier. This is Betadine soap to wash the skin."

Diana shrugged. "Works for me."

Dr. Christy's attention was already back to the cat. His hands were fluid magic as, little by little, he cleaned the feline's wounds. He reached behind him to the counter and somehow found the tube of antibiotic cream. With utmost tenderness, he smeared a thick coating of the custard-yellow medicine over the tom's mutilated body.

"Furozone. You need to apply this every day," he instructed before finally bandaging the cat loosely from head to toe.

Dr. Christy stood back and admired his handiwork. "Could pass for a little Egyptian mummy, don't you think?" he said, looking at the anxious faces around the table.

The tension was broken, but nobody was ready to smile yet.

"Do you think he'll make it?" Francis asked.

Dr. Christy lifted the cat's singed eyelid. "He's got a chance. And I've got something else that might give us an edge." Yet again he rummaged in his heap of medicines, this time finding a bottle that actually had a label. "This is five percent dextrose."

"For energy?" Francis said.

"Excellent. Now watch carefully." The veterinarian extracted the required amount into a syringe, flicked his finger against the plastic, and watched the bubbles rise to the top. He pressed the plunger gently until satisfied with the droplets of fluid squeezed out of the needle, picked up another millimeter of skin between thumb and forefinger, and glided the needle into the fold.

"Okay, one more," Dr. Christy said. "This poor creature gets everything I've got." For the last time that night he filled a syringe and explained its contents. "I'm using a B complex liver extract blood builder. I'd better order a bunch of this for you, too." He handed the syringe to Francis. "Your turn."

Francis wasn't sure. He'd given shots before, but not to an animal in such critical condition.

"Come on, it's easy," Dr. Christy encouraged. "You've got to learn these things. I might not be available next time."

The veterinarian nodded approvingly as his pupil eased the needle into the skin and pushed the plunger slowly until the syringe was empty. "Perfect," he said. "That's all we can do for now. Oh, remind me to give you some penicillin. He'll need a half-cc daily for seven to ten days. But I'll look in on him before then."

Dr. Christy suddenly appeared to crumble. He slumped into a chair next to the cat and cricked his neck from side to side. The crack reverberated through the small room.

"Are you all right?" Faith asked.

"Tension, that's all. Nothing to worry about. Does anyone have an idea of what time it is?"

"Almost ten," Michael said.

Bill Christy stood wearily. "I'd better wash up and be getting home. I've been gone since seven this morning. My wife's gonna be mad as hell." He smiled faintly. "I'm always doing something like this. She doesn't like it much. Says I love the animals more than her."

Seven o'clock this morning? On Thanksgiving Day? Faith thought. "Have you eaten?"

"Can't remember."

Michael and Francis exchanged glances. It was all too obvious that the doctor had been running on empty for the past few hours.

Diana took charge. "You need some food inside you. We didn't get around to eating much of our Thanksgiving dinner, so there's plenty left. Why don't you lie down in one of our rooms, and we'll call your wife and tell her where you are."

"Just a glass of milk will be fine. And I want to sit with the cat a bit before I leave." Dr. Christy pulled up a chair. He rested his head on the table and closed his eyes. "Just give me a few minutes."

While the others went to bed, Francis stayed up to wake the veterinarian in half-an-hour, if he was still asleep. But when he came back to the kitchen, the doctor was so deep in slumber Francis hadn't the heart to disturb what he suspected was a desperately needed rest. He placed a pillow under their new friend's head, and tucked a blanket around his slim body to keep him warm.

Bill Christy hadn't moved when they walked in the next morning.

However, Sinjin the Pirate, as he came to be called, was struggling to be free of his bandages, meowing loudly into the ears of the sleep-deprived Dr. Christy. Francis opened a can of Fancy Feast and carefully held the cat upright over the food. To everyone's amazement Sinjin devoured not one, not two, but six small cans in rapid succession.

"We think he'll live, Doc," Francis said as Bill Christy slowly came awake.

The veterinarian blinked sleepily, and gulped the hot tea Diana had brewed for him. He stared at the cat, who eyed him balefully out of his one good eye. "Well, I knew that B comp was great stuff, but this is incredible," he said with a grin.

"*You're* incredible," Faith said. "And you're not going anywhere until you've eaten a good breakfast."

Francis always said that nothing extraordinary happens by chance. He was meant to meet Dr. Christy at Lorelei's that afternoon. The veterinarian was to become near and dear to all of them—and a vital force in the progress of the sanctuary.

Sinjin the Pirate also had a role to play. He was to be the charter member of the TLC Cat Club. In the years to come he would welcome many felines with special needs who, like him, required the tender, loving care of the people of Angel Canyon.

PART TWO

Faith
1986–1990

CHAPTER ELEVEN

Becoming Best Friends

Faith snugged the last crate carefully into place. "Not long now," she assured the two dozen cats already secured in the van. A cacophony of indignant "meows" told her exactly what the felines thought of that cheery pronouncement. Faith ignored the protests and took a last check of the interior.

Her eight dogs were behaving themselves amazingly well. They sat silent as sphinxes, eyes following her every move from behind the doggie barrier that separated them from the cats.

Their feline friends, on the other hand, had been loudly voicing their objections for the past half-hour, and Faith supposed they would continue their complaining for the entire journey. No matter. This was the day she had been awaiting for over two years— the day she was going home to Angel Canyon.

Faith paused for a moment before climbing into the driver's seat. There was no reason to delay her departure: most of the animals had been sent ahead over the past couple of months, making the shutdown of the ranch surprisingly smooth.

Yet she felt a strange reluctance to hurry. The rambling house and surrounding acres that had been her base for the past six years looked forsaken in its emptiness. Faith felt as if she were abandoning a precious resource. What did they say in real estate? "Seller's remorse. Buyer's regret." Enough! She had to get going if she were to make the canyon before supper.

To Faith's surprise the felines ceased their caterwauling about an hour into the trip. She tuned in National Public Radio and re-laxed into the soothing strains of *Swan Lake*.

Faith let her mind drift as the van left Prescott to climb the long, steep grade into the Coconino Forest. The black ribbon of road stretched endlessly ahead, and the monotonous drone of the engine had a lulling effect as it ate up the miles. Now and then she glimpsed Brunhilda's big head in the rearview mirror.

Most people winced when they first saw the bloodhound's mashed face where her skull had been clubbed with a rifle butt. But Faith didn't see any ugliness in the gentle dog whose lop-sided, lugubrious expression always chased away her blues. Brunhilda's only fault was that within seconds of meeting any small dog, she would attack. Faith had learned to restrain the bloodhound until the momentary urge passed.

One of the occupational hazards of working with animals was that she wanted to take every one of them home with her. She wasn't alone, of course. All of her friends cheerfully shared their homes with rescued cats and dogs. Look at Francis. How many had he adopted? Eighteen? Twenty? She had lost count. Not for nothing did Michael call him St. Francis.

For no reason Faith remembered the goose. She was eight years old and staying overnight with a school friend. The classmate's mother had allowed the girls to feed the elegant white birds who were so tame they ate out of Faith's hand. After awhile, the woman came to watch. "Sweet things. We raised them from goslings," she said. "Now which one would you like for dinner? Sarah or Jesse?"

Faith was literally sick. Years later she awoke with the vivid recollection of that childhood goose. From that moment on she never ate anything with a face.

She was glad that her children had naturally embraced her love for animals and the environment. David, her nineteen-year-old, had lived in the canyon for two years now and was never happier.

And Carragh, fifteen last December and a dog lover like her mother, would be joining them for summer recess. Faith wasn't sure if Eve, her blond, blue-eyed middle daughter, would be com-ing. She hoped so. It would be lovely for them all to be together. Besides, she could use help at Dogtown.

Ah, Dogtown! Of course, she and Paul Eckhoff hadn't even decided where to site it yet, but a month ago she had watched a program on an animal sanctuary in California called *Living Free*. She'd fallen in love with the octagon design of their kennels.

The concept was perfect. The octagons housed storage and feeding areas as well as indoor shelter for the dogs. Oversized runs fanned from each of the eight sides with doggie jungle gyms and roomy doghouses in which the fortunate residents could romp and snooze. And Faith really appreciated that from inside the octagons she would be able to see all the dogs at a glance and keep an eye on their activities.

Faith visualized her new Dogtown all the way to Utah. By the time she hit the dirt path to the bunkhouse, she'd planned, fenced, painted, and filled the many pens with happy canines.

The quiet was uncanny as she climbed out of the van in front of the low-slung structure. Nobody rushed to greet her; no shouts of "hello." Even the usual muddle of dogs was absent. The rhythmic thud of hammers hitting nails echoed faintly across the mesa. That's where everyone is, Faith thought, working on The Village.

"Thought I heard a door slam."

Faith turned at the familiar voice and smiled. Diana sauntered toward her from a nearby trailer that she had trucked in to quarantine their feline leukemia cats. "You're early."

"Hi, Diana! Couldn't wait to get here."

The two women hugged. "I've got a room ready for you over at The Village," Diana said, "but let's unload the kids first."

"Good idea. They've had a long drive," Faith slid open the van door. Eight eager canines scrambled past their freshly offended feline companions and immediately ran in all directions to find a place to relieve themselves.

Diana's face puckered into a mock grimace. "Let's get these mewling monsters settled before they lose their voices," she said, grabbing a cat carrier.

The bunkhouse's official greeter was waiting when the women stepped into his domain. As soon as the pirate cat spotted Faith, he leaped onto the kitchen counter, butted his head against the cabinet door, and let out a series of meows that put all his fellow felines to shame.

"He knows we keep the Fancy Feast on the top shelf," Diana

said fondly. "Sinjin's become an expert at inveigling at least one can out of everyone who walks through here."

Faith hadn't seen the badly burned cat since Thanksgiving. Now all she could do was stare at a king-sized, expectant creature whose fur had grown in amazingly black and glossy with only a few patches of scarred, crinkled skin—grim reminders of his ordeal. Sinjin in turn fixed this new person with his one unblinking green eye.

"He's become head kitty around here," Diana said. "Isn't it wonderful?" She walked over to the purring machine and scratched behind his ears. Sinjin immediately pushed his head into her hand. "He's coerced three Fancy Feasts out of us already today. I think he can last until dinner. Let me show you what Steven got together for us." Diana proudly led Faith to a new, shaded enclosure, ready with litter boxes, water, feeding bowls, and cushioned orange crates for the travel-weary felines.

"They're going to love it here," Faith enthused.

The late afternoon sun was shadowing the ridge top before the cats were settled to Diana's satisfaction. By now Faith was tired herself, and more than ready to see her own quarters. She and Diana were leaving the bunkhouse when a flash of sunlight reflecting off a window caught her eye. "What's that? Have I seen it before?" she said pointing to a huge boat of a car parked next to a tiny travel trailer almost hidden by tall scrub.

"That's Tyson Horn's."

"I haven't met him."

"He knows John from Dallas. Came to help out on his vacation a couple of weeks ago. You'll like him, Faith, he's great with dogs." Diana shrugged. "Seems . . . I don't know how to put it exactly, but seems like one of them, if you know what I mean. And I didn't tell you. John's here, too!"

Faith's smile became a grin. She and John Christopher Fripp went back to the London days. He'd regaled her with stories of his two-year stint in the British army. "Almost reenlisted," he confided, his sailor blue eyes rolling at the thought. "They stationed me in Egypt, and I did love that desert."

At the age of twenty-three John Christopher had gone back to school and majored in history. "What a bloody, boring waste!" he said of it. He was good with numbers and figured accountants always made a decent pound or two, so he said good-bye to Napoleon and Henry VIII and took up a more modern vocation. John was the solid elder statesman of the group, the bookkeeper who kept them tightly within their budget, crossing all the *t*'s and dotting all the *i*'s on their charitable foundation's returns. Faith hadn't seen John in ages. She was glad he was in the canyon.

The dogs were suddenly alert, bodies tensed, eyes fixated uphill. Brunhilda assumed big-dog stance at the front of the pack, her bloodhound ears brushing the earth. Strolling toward them was a tall, lanky man. Faith couldn't see his eyes because they were shaded with dark sunglasses and hidden by a wide-brimmed Australian breeze hat. But she did note the passel of dogs that panted at his heels, among them one small terrier.

"Brunhilda!" she yelled, lunging for the bloodhound, but the hound was already on the scent and tearing toward her prey. "Oh no," Faith groaned, puffing after her up the slope.

The lean stranger made a slight gesture with his hand, and his dogs bunched behind him. He squatted to eye level with the oncoming hound . . . and waited. Brunhilda stiff-legged to a dusty halt within inches of the man's face, all the pendulous folds of her disfigured head shuddering with the effort.

Faith stopped. This had to be Tyson. He was murmuring to Brunhilda words that only the dog could hear. The man stretched out his right hand and gently pulled the hound's one floppy ear, caressing the thin skin between thumb and forefinger, calming the big animal to the ground. With his left, he carefully eased his little companion mutt forward, all the time talking . . . talking.

The two canines cautiously sniffed each other from the safety of the man's body. The feisty terrier mutt craned her head closer to Brunhilda's crumpled face, and Faith watched the hound's curious acceptance. Tyson slowly retracted his right hand and Brunhilda rose, shook herself, and lumbered back to Faith.

"Told you he had a way with dogs," Diana said as the man came to meet them. "Tyson Horn, this is Faith Maloney." She paused and grinned. "Chief Dog."

"Ma'am," Tyson said and lifted his hat.

"Call me Faith." She smiled. "You know dogs."

"Seems that way," Tyson said.

Faith could detect no bravado in his words. If anything he was shy. Faith also knew that the dogs who ambled with him so companionably were among the most difficult she'd had to contend with at the Arizona ranch. Yet the animals seemed docile around the man. "How long are you staying?"

Tyson didn't answer straightaway. He gazed into some imaginary distance, weighing his reply. "I work in a bank installing computers, ma'am," he began, his Texas drawl wrapping the words like molasses.

"Faith."

"Faith," he acknowledged. "But it doesn't . . ." Tyson shrugged as if this woman would know what he meant. She did.

"I like what you people are doing," he paused. "I'd like to stay on awhile if you've a mind. Help out some more. You need help," he finished, nodding to confirm his observations.

"You have no idea," Faith sighed, thinking of Dogtown.

"We're on our way to The Village," Diana said.

"I'll take care of your dogs, if you'd like," Tyson offered.

"Thank you, Tyson," Faith said. "I'd like that very much."

Faith was amazed at the progress that had come about during the past six months. The Village had taken the shape of a southwestern structure to rival any in Santa Fe. The whorled, whitewashed walls snaked respectfully around old-growth junipers, Paul's design allowing the ancient trees to dictate the flow of a building whose clean, spare lines rose in perfect juxtaposition to its sweeping, high-desert surroundings.

Hellos were called as they unloaded Faith's bags, but no one made a fuss except John. He held a ladder for Steven and yelled he'd catch her later. In contrast, the dogs, led by Goldilocks, flung themselves on their Big Mama as if she'd been away forever.

Faith's quarters were on the far end of the building from where the men were working. Diana had placed a vase of wildflowers on the table beside the bed in welcome. She left Faith alone to unpack in the sun-splashed quarters that would be her new home.

By the time Faith walked back to the bunkhouse for dinner, the air had taken on the coolness of an early spring evening. Mariko and Steven were cooking a delicious Japanese repast to which Faith wouldn't even try to put a name. After everyone had eaten their fill, the conversation turned naturally to the direction the

sanctuary might take. John appointed himself the group's spokes-
man.

"Chief Dog, Faith, and Chief Cat, Diana, are now here and ac-
counted for," he declared, his ruddy English face alight with the
dry humor his countrymen took for granted. "Let the proceedings
commence. Wait a minute." He held up a hand. "I think our Mr.
Mountain's got something on his mind."

Michael had gotten back to Angel Canyon only that morning.
"To welcome you home," he told Faith. He had been in Phoenix
brainstorming with Richard Negus, of the Fund for Animals,
about a newsletter for Richard's Western territory. Michael hadn't
cracked a smile all evening. He seemed preoccupied, face stern,
arms across his chest, one thumb and forefinger constantly worrying at his dark red beard.

"So tell us what keeps that moody countenance in the midst of
such good company." John wasn't letting his friend get away with
anything this night.

"Actually I do have something on my mind." Michael's clever
eyes slid around the circle. "Has it occurred to anyone that we're
the only animal organization I know of that doesn't have a name?"

"I wouldn't exactly call us organized," John teased.

Michael ignored the remark. "Think about it. We're not playing
games here. We're as much a fully functioning sanctuary as anyone else out there. We're just not very public."

"God forbid," Diana exclaimed. "We can't build facilities quick
enough for the animals coming in already. We'd be inundated
from St. George to Salt Lake if they knew about us beyond Kanab."

"We still need an identity," Michael insisted. "Something that
says who we are and what we're trying to do. Isn't everybody
tired of explaining us?"

"You've got a point, Michael," Steven said.

"Man's Best Friend," John murmured straightfaced.

"Our Best Friends," Virgil picked up the fun.

"Their Best Friends," Cyrus got into the act.

"Now we're being silly." Steven tried not to grin.

Faith wasn't laughing. "It should be just Best Friends. My
friend Hope White always said that Best Friends was the perfect
name for an animal sanctuary."

The voices chorused around the crowded table. "Yes!

"Why not?"

"Perfect!"

"All right!"

"Let's do it!"

Michael smiled at last. "Now it's coming together!"

So it came to pass on the cool evening of May 4, 1986, the sanctuary in the canyon got its name: Best Friends Animal Sanctuary.

It was the beginning of the legend.

CHAPTER TWELVE

Dogtown

They liked being Best Friends. Having a name focused everything they were doing. Everyone on the property was infused with new energy. Michael thought more and more of how the sanctuary would evolve: how Best Friends would coalesce into a coherent organization; where the money might come from five years hence.

The monthly payments from the sale of the ranch had given them a little breathing space. Paul drew plans for a new feline area—Catland. He and Diana decided to locate the cluster of buildings on a high, dry plateau with a view down the canyon, an easy jog from the bunkhouse. "Chief Cat" would get her first "Kitty Motel" as soon as the architect could spare some hands.

Faith spent time exploring, re-acquainting herself with the land, renewing her energy . . . and allowing the canyon to show where her beloved Dogtown should be. Finally she was ready. "I think I know where I'd like to have Dogtown," she told Paul on a Saturday morning. "But I'd like your input."

They were standing in front of The Village. Already, at 7:00 the buzz of saws and the clink of hammers mingled with the country sounds of station KNOY. Faith could hear Virgil Barstad's sonorous baritone trying mightily to drown out Johnny Cash with little success. Virgil did love to sing along.

Paul was thinking. "I said I'd go with Francis to pick up some chicken wire for Diana this morning. But he doesn't really need me. When do you want to do it?"

"How about now?"

"Thought you'd say that." Paul smiled and led the way to the clutter of trucks parked haphazardly along the ridge. He stopped at the last in the line, his old green pickup. Well, Faith remembered it that color. But two years of sun, rain, snow, and red earth had blistered and worn the olive paint job down to the metal body and rusted out a couple of giant holes for good measure.

She hesitated, noting the layer of grime that lay undisturbed over the battered exterior. "You *have* driven this lately?"

"We have a deal," Paul confided. "Green Goddess here threatens not to die before the millennium as long as I take her for a spin every day."

Neither made small talk as Paul bounced the truck over the rutted surfaces of the mesa. "Keep going," Faith directed as he turned south onto the county road that looped to State Highway 89. "About here will do fine, to the right." She indicated where he should stop.

Faith hiked her skirt and jumped onto the giving soil. She strode ahead, gesturing here and there in her excitement as she outlined her ideas for Dogtown.

Paul listened. "That would work. But why here? We're hardly a mile from Eighty-nine, Faith. You want to be that close to the highway?"

A huge smile fanned tiny crinkles of pleasure around Faith's eyes. "Do you know how many people will be coming to adopt?"

Paul wasn't convinced. "The ratio of those dumped to those wanted is not in your favor, Faith. Jana and Anne are the only ones finding any homes, and that's in Vegas and Denver. Not here."

"That will change. People will be coming from all over soon. Just watch." Faith took in the acres of sloping land thick with virgin piñon and juniper. "And the dogs will be in heaven. So much shade and earth to dig in."

Paul couldn't argue with her enthusiasm. "Okay, but we have to finish The Village, and Diana desperately needs a Kitty Motel."

"Paul, I know the cats are crowded, but it's not fair to keep the dogs in the storage areas for much longer. Can't you spare Tyson, and perhaps John, at least to get me started?"

Paul's smile softened the angular, aesthetic lines of his long face. He started to laugh.

"What's so funny?"

"John once built Diana a three-legged stool."

"So?"

"It collapsed when one of her cats jumped on it."

Faith could picture in her mind's eye the clunky piece of furniture that John would have fashioned so proudly, and the way his bushy eyebrows would have pulled together in chagrin when the stool splayed apart under the cat's weight.

"Was it a big cat?"

Paul shook his head, unable to suppress his mirth. "No."

Faith giggled. "So I should absolutely take him off your hands, don't you think?"

Paul made up his mind. "We'll swing it somehow."

Dogtown blossomed over the next few months. Tyson was not only a treasure with the dogs, but he could fence an enclosure quicker than anybody. To everyone's surprise, himself included, John Christopher Fripp developed a talent with saw and hammer.

Faith would see the two men: John, his fair complexion peony red under the pitiless summer sunshine, framing the first octagon; the reticent Texan, shirt wet with perspiration, digging post holes, dropping stakes, nailing the pickets precisely one foot apart, one above the other.

Tyson took it upon himself to assist Faith in every way possible: building, feeding, exercising the dogs, or scooping poop. Whatever she asked, he obliged with a shy smile.

Faith came to understand that the soft-spoken Texan had no fear. Dogs she had kept separate because of their tendency to bite, Tyson took walking together. Somehow he could travel the red dirt byways shadowed by a pack that would fell any lesser human.

One afternoon, she observed an unfortunate black Labrador mutt biting Tyson on the leg. The man promptly bent and bit the dog's haunches in return.

Faith, concerned, had a gentle suggestion. "Dogs don't like sunglasses and hats. Maybe if you didn't wear them?"

"I'm light-sensitive," Tyson explained. "I can't go without shades during the day."

Faith suddenly realized she'd rarely seen the man without his sunglasses. "I'm sorry, Tyson."

After supper that evening she walked the Texan back to his trailer, only half listening as he told her about his new collection of Zippo lighters. Tyson didn't smoke, but he loved to collect, and he would bend Faith's ear all day if she let him.

But tonight her mind was occupied in figuring out a better system of getting water to Dogtown than trucking it in barrels from the bunkhouse. She had about concluded that they would get around to pumping it sooner or later, when Tyson opened his door.

Nine excited curs threw themselves upon their person in joyous welcome. Among them was the ornery black Lab. Man and former adversary greeted each other as if nothing untoward had happened between them. Faith saw that the dog would now live with Tyson in perfect harmony.

Watching the quiet Texan's interaction with the canines, Faith confirmed what she had suspected from their first encounter. Neither shades nor hat made any difference. The dogs accepted Tyson as one of their own. He was an alpha man: one of the pack in human form. Faith wondered if he were truly aware of how important he was becoming to Best Friends. She hoped he would stay when the summer was over.

As July melted into August, more animals found a refuge at Best Friends. At Dogtown, Faith loved the sense of rambunctious freedom that filled her domain with life and energy. Carefully grouped younger dogs, smaller dogs, big dogs, and those that needed special care made themselves at home in their own huge doggie runs that extended from the prototype structure. Several older dogs had the run of the place, choosing mostly to sprawl outside near that first skeletal octagon from which they knew food and doting attention were always forthcoming.

Faith knew that this was just the beginning, that they would be building for years; but already one of her special joys was to watch the animals playing together in their new surroundings, knowing what kinds of situations most of them came from. She counted ninety dogs on the property now and prided herself on knowing each one of their quirks and personalities.

Faith knew, for instance, that Jenny, the sheltie runt, had to sleep wrapped around Simba, the mastiff; but woe betide the giant if he came within three feet of her while she ate. And whereas Sophie, the schnauzer mutt, might be small, she ruled her compound of six canines.

Sophie's subjects had dug an immense hole under a grab of sage, into which they all snuggled for afternoon naps. But Sophie always commandeered her spot first, circling three times to settle herself to her pleasure. Her pack had to wait for a yelp of consent before they dared join her.

Faith wondered how much longer Sophie might be living in Dogtown. Jana had confided that a woman called Kiki had fallen in love with the little mutt's photo and was wanting to adopt. It would be interesting to see who became boss dog when Sophie left.

Sometimes Faith questioned how there could be so many unwanted animals from such a small community, and more coming every week. But even in her short time in the area, she had gotten a taste of the hardships of rural living. Low pay and hard physical work, wedded with a job market that depended heavily on seasonal demand, made for a precarious existence. Just last week she'd heard that the mill in nearby Fredonia was laying off workers and might even shut down. Faith guessed it would mean more animals on their doorstep.

Since coming to Utah, she had continued the early morning habit of taking her decaf and walking with her own dogs. It was a time to be alone with her thoughts. She pondered the probability that word of their no-kill ethic was already spreading beyond the narrow confines of Kanab. She never ceased to be awed by the spectacular beauty and tranquility of this land they had found, but she often wondered why they'd been led to precisely this remote corner of the planet.

She couldn't answer her own musings, but on some deeper level she knew that this place was not just for the people and creatures of Best Friends. Something more was meant to be here—

something greater than themselves. Faith didn't try to imagine what that might be. She was secure in the knowing that events would unfold in their own time.

Right now she had to do something about her living quarters. The Village was too far away from the dogs. Diana could walk to Catland in minutes. Faith needed to be able to do the same. John Christopher tallied every penny spent, so building a house was out of the question; but a trailer would do nicely.

Diana turned her on to the *Thrifty Nickel*. "It's a freebie newspaper. You get the best bargains." She grinned in complicity. "Where do you think our furniture comes from?"

It was as if that certain edition of the *Thrifty Nickel* was printed especially for Faith: on the front page, in black letters, an advertisement for a sixty-footer in Cedar City. The trailer was as old as her youngest daughter—circa 1971—but serviceable. She would have to remove the wood burning stove and replace the shag carpet with linoleum for the dogs, but Faith was jubilant. She hired a guy to load the trailer on a semi, had it brought to Dogtown, and settled in a grove of junipers with a view toward Zion National Park.

Within a week, she had camouflaged the crummy white exterior with army green paint to blend in with the surroundings. Then she persuaded Francis to pick her up some fencing to make a pen for Brunhilda and company.

Her first night in her new home, Faith felt as content as she had ever been in her life. She liked having her own space, being close to the dogs should she hear trouble, and knowing she could get up to check on a newcomer and give comfort if necessary.

As she drifted into sleep, her last thoughts were for the next dog to find refuge in Dogtown. What special needs, what idiosyncrasies and mannerisms would differentiate him or her from the others? As her eyes closed, Faith had not one doubt she would find out soon enough.

CHAPTER THIRTEEN

The Dogfather

"It's for you," Francis said, handing Faith the phone. "She gets more phone calls than we do," he joked to Michael.

"She's like the Queen Mum," Michael quipped. "Younger version, of course," he amended after catching Faith's glare.

It was true. Faith had been in the canyon barely three months and was already the most popular in town. She schmoozed with everybody—the pharmacist, sheriff, gas station attendants, waiters, and grocery clerks. And everybody gossiped with the woman who would incline her head in their direction and *listen* to their trials and tribulations. The person who had asked to speak to Faith was Betty Clark, a checker at IGA Foods.

Faith had corralled Michael and Francis earlier to talk about Tyson, who had asked if he could stay on at Best Friends. They had come to the relative quiet of the bunkhouse to discuss getting the Texan a bigger trailer and moving him to Dogtown.

Michael and Francis didn't particularly listen, but in the cramped confines of the kitchen they couldn't help but hear both sides of the women's conversation.

"I think they just up and left him," Betty Clark said.

"What do you mean?" Faith asked.

"I haven't seen any of the family that lives there for days. There aren't any cars around. The poor thing's out there on a chain with no shade. I don't see any food or a water bowl. . . ."

"Can you go over and give him some water and food?" Faith interrupted quickly. "I'll be right down to pick him up."

"Where does Betty live?" Francis asked as Faith hung up.

"Pugh's Trailer Park."

Francis's face tightened. "That's probably not good."

Faith knew what he meant. For the most part, the mobile homes in Pugh's Trailer Park were a collection of neglected single-wides. Many of the residents had a hard time finding steady jobs, and the weariness of spirit showed in their surroundings. Pugh's was one of the pockets of near poverty of which Faith had become aware since she arrived.

Betty Clark and her husband were an exception. Their home was always painted and clean and their dogs dearly loved. Betty had told Faith she expected to be moving soon to Las Vegas, where her husband could find better paying work.

The cashier was waiting when Faith pulled into the park and rode with her to the deserted trailer. The only sign of life was an Australian shepherd mix who tried to hide under the bottom step as the two women approached. "He hasn't touched the food. Do you think he's sick?" Betty asked.

Faith squatted by the listless animal and slowly lifted his head. Vacant eyes stared into hers. The dog was so thin she could feel its jawbones sharp and brittle through the skin. But what really incensed her was the way the shepherd was tied. He had no collar. A rusting chain had sufficed for his owners, rubbing the neck bloody where the animal had tried to strain farther than the four feet of his tether. "I think he's heartbroken and starving. He's an older dog, and his family has just left him here to die." Faith pushed herself to her feet. "He understands that, somehow. Do you know how long he's been like this?"

Betty's sweet face crumpled. "I don't usually come back here," she said. "You know my place is near the entrance. A neighbor tipped me off. I would have come sooner if I'd known." Betty hovered over the dog, wringing the hem of her cotton T-shirt like a dishrag. Gently Faith disengaged the woman's fingers.

"Easy. It's not your fault. First thing is to get this chain off his neck. I have bolt cutters in the truck. Carry them everywhere."

The dog offered no resistance as Faith cut him free. He was so light it was easy to lift him onto the passenger seat beside her. She took one last look around the depressing line of trailers as she turned the ignition. Betty Clark deserved better. "Thank you so much for caring," Faith said as she shifted into gear. "I hope your husband finds a good job and you get moved soon."

Francis had been waiting at Dogtown. He opened the passenger door and reached for the dog's limp body. The shepherd whimpered and slipped to the floorboards, cowering as far under the dash as he could fit his emaciated frame. "Damn people," Faith said, her eyes tearing. "Some man must have beaten him."

Francis slipped his arms under the shepherd's haunches. "Easy, boy," he murmured. "Nobody's going to hurt you."

Inside Faith's trailer, the man and woman went to work. They comforted the dog on a bed of clean towels on her dining table. Faith cradled the patient's scratchy head against her belly while Francis gave him a shot to ease the pain. Together they bathed the wounded neck and smeared a thick coat of Furozone antibiotic cream over the ravaged skin before bandaging it.

"There, now you can pass for a doggie priest," Francis said to the quiescent animal.

Faith's sense of humor was nonexistent this afternoon. "I don't think he's about to give sacrament," she retorted.

All that was left to help the dog for the moment was Dr. Christy's magic elixir. When the last dose had been carefully spooned into the shepherd's mouth, Francis moved his fingers over the frail form as the veterinarian had taught. "I don't see or feel any damage," he reported, "but some of your special attention would do him a world of good."

Faith nodded. "I'll make sure Brunhilda and the others stay outside and make up a bed on the floor next to mine. This boy needs to know somebody loves him."

Love was what Faith had in abundance to give. For two weeks she hand-fed the dispirited canine until he lifted himself from his blanket to eat of his own accord. She sat with him late into the night, visualizing the dog bright-eyed and strong, eager for life. Faith insisted that David and Tyson visit daily to show the animal that not all men were to be feared.

The first time she took him into the sunshine, the shepherd hugged the steps of her trailer, terrified to hazard beyond a remembered boundary. Faith finally carried the dog into the trees, where he swayed uncertainly on spindle legs, tail plastered to his belly. But he slunk back home after her.

Surprisingly, Brunhilda made no attempt to molest the newcomer, and Faith's other dogs just sniffed and left him alone. Over the weeks the mongrel came to resemble less of a walking X-ray. Flesh appeared between the ribs of his cadaverous form, and his fur took on a healthy sheen in the sunlight. One morning the dog left the security of the trailer steps and plodded after his benefactor along the lanes of Dogtown. The day Faith saw the shepherd's tail, she knew they had turned the corner.

She and Tyson had come back to Octagon Three to wash up after cleaning the dog runs and found the shepherd waiting. "Well, look at you," Faith smiled and bent to scratch his backside. The dog leaned into the pleasure. Slowly he unfurled his tail from under his belly and, as if long disuse had weakened the muscles, wagged it slowly. "Yes!" Faith cried. "Tyson, do you see this? We must go get Francis. He's got to see this."

"Another victory, Faith," Francis said when the dog didn't cower at his approach.

"That's a good name for him. Victor, short for victory. Yes!"

To ensure his doggie confidence further, Faith decreed that Victor be given the run of Dogtown. Every morning she encouraged the shepherd to accompany her about her chores. Victor took the honor seriously. He became Faith's shadow, standing guard, his mismatched blue and brown eyes considering many things as she fed and scooped, petted and conversed with the occupants of the canine paradise.

Sometimes she would observe the dog meandering the paths of Dogtown without her. From time to time he would scuff a bed in the dirt and plop down to contemplate the view. Then, on the last Saturday in September, everything changed.

Tyson had gotten into the habit of walking the rowdier dogs at daybreak. This Indian summer's morn, they padded back past Octagon Three as usual. A few yards ahead, blocking the lane that led to the enclosures, an impassive Victor sat watching. As Tyson and the pack approached, the Australian shepherd rose to his feet.

"Hello, boy," Tyson greeted.

Victor's tail wagged vigorously in acknowledgment, but his eyes were fixed on the dogs straggling behind. The Texan absently ruffled the fur on Victor's backside, as the dog had come to like, and continued his way down the path. Several steps later, realizing the pack hadn't followed, he turned to see what was happening.

The eight dogs were stopped, as if someone had erected an invisible "No Entry" sign. The hackles on their backs rose stiff with fight or flight, but not one moved. Victor stood immobile before them, holding their gaze. He didn't growl, didn't make any threatening moves. Victor just stood.

The standoff lasted a full sixty seconds, then eight tails wagged cautiously in unison. Tyson couldn't believe what he was seeing. It would be too easy for any of these more gregarious dogs to assert its dominance, but strangely, Victor was not challenged. In a language understood only among themselves, each canine backed away and lay down.

Tyson studied the shepherd, remembering what Faith had told him. "Dogs, like people, need a job, need to feel they're useful." It was obvious that Victor, after careful deliberation, had decided on his duties. The shepherd was the gatekeeper of Dogtown's heart, between Faith's home and Octagon Three. From now on, only the hierachy of humans would be allowed to cross his invisible line in the sand. Canines should find appropriate back routes to their respective quarters unless—and this only became clear later—accompanied by a person.

Tyson retraced his steps to crouch by Victor's side. The shepherd panted happily, rolled on his back, and presented his human friend with his vulnerable underside. Tyson rubbed the pale belly in recognition while his subdued pack found another path.

From that moment, the center of Dogtown was Victor's jealously guarded turf. He had established himself as the "Dogfather," capo of canines. Victor did not even have to patrol his chosen territory. He could doze under a nearby tree, not deigning to rouse himself. No dog, no matter what shape, size, or temperament, dared cross his invisible line in the sand unless accompanied by a proper person. Faith declared that if Victor wore a ring, he would raise a paw to be kissed by the lesser dogs on the property.

CHAPTER FOURTEEN

Animal Control

The leaves were turning. The cottonwoods in the canyon spread a vivid canopy of scarlet and ocher along the river, and painted itinerant splashes of brilliant Vermont orange across the mesas. It was Faith's favorite time of year. She loved the earthy, autumnal smell, the bracing shock of morning air. She noticed the squirrels were harvesting piñon cones and leaving the stripped husks beneath the trees—reminders that it would be a cold winter.

Yet nature had fooled them this year. The canyon took on an East Coast palette too soon. A sudden, scorching heat wave sent Faith running to the local thrift store for summer overalls and T-shirts for herself and Tyson.

Faith's daughter Carragh had reluctantly returned to school, and Michael elected to give Faith a hand with the chores. She had been distracted this morning, scanning each compound, lifting up the overhangs of bushes, checking inside doghouses.

"There's someone missing," she explained finally. "Jenny, the Sheltie. I thought she was playing games last night, but she didn't turn up for breakfast."

When Jenny's familiar hungry face wasn't to be seen by lunchtime, Faith was frantic. She enlisted Tyson's aid, and together they searched the canyon.

"I called Lorelei, Kelvert, and Nancy, but no one's seen her," a worried Faith announced to Francis as the day slid away. "I can only think the police picked her up and didn't know she belonged to us."

"They would have taken her to the pound, Francis frowned. Nobody at Best Friends had ever actually been to the pound yet. It was out by the airport, but no one seemed to know much about it.

"I'm going right now," Faith declared.

"I'll come with you."

Kanab's airport was a few miles out of town on the way to Fredonia. "Airport" was perhaps a grand designation for one short runway in the middle of a field. The only building Francis and Faith could see as they drove around the area was a lean-to hard against the inside of the wooden perimeter fence. From what they could glimpse of the structure, it consisted of three sides of chainlink covered with a tin roof.

The sun was low in the sky, gathering its last hour's strength before retreating into dusk as Francis parked the truck. The late afternoon heat rose up from the scrubby pasture like a smothering blanket. Faith stood on tiptoe to see over the fence. "That can't be it," she exclaimed. "The sun's shining right into that thing." But she'd already spotted three small runs attached to the hut and knew better.

Francis scanned the fence. "There's an opening," he said, pointing 100 feet farther along. "Let's take a look."

Even before they got close, Faith was angry. She had guessed right. There was not one scrap of shade under which the dogs could escape the baking sun that poured down on them with pitiless intensity. She started to run. "There's Jenny," she shouted as she reached the pound.

The sheltie lay on the dirt, her tongue lolling, eyes closed. Three other dogs sprawled against her, unmoving. "Jenny, Jenny," Faith called, pulling frantically at the latched gate.

"It's locked," Francis said.

"She's not responding. She's not even lifting her head. She may be suffering from heat prostration. We've got to get her out of here. We've got to get them all out of here."

"Stop this," Francis grabbed Faith's arm. "It's not helping. We're going back to town."

Faith was suddenly calm. "I'm not leaving her here. We'll break the lock."

"We're going back to town," Francis repeated, pulling her away.

Francis drove straight to the police station. A round-faced officer was on duty, his trim, brown moustache looking strangely out of place on his schoolboy face.

Francis got straight to the point. "Our names are Francis Battista and Faith Maloney. You're holding a dog of ours by the airport. We need to get her right now."

The policeman look shocked at the abrupt demand. "Would you mind waiting? I'll be right back," he said and disappeared.

Francis drummed his fingers loudly on the front desk as they waited. Faith stared at the closed office door as if willing the boy to return.

The young officer reappeared ten minutes later. "I'm supposed to escort you," he said. "Why don't you follow me in your truck?"

The rookie had to be the slowest driver on the face of the earth. He took even longer to unlock the gate, fumbling through a large bunch of keys, trying to find the one that fit the lock. Finally the gate swung open, and Faith pushed past him to Jenny. She lifted the sheltie's head and pushed back her lips. The healthy pink of her gums was splotched a deathly gray.

Francis had already twisted on the faucet. He allowed the water to splash full force onto the bare earth until the sun-heated water ran cold. Quickly he knelt and dribbled a cooling stream over each of the dogs' bodies in turn.

Faith's overalls were soaked, but she didn't care. She sat on the dirt next to Jenny, her fingers under the runt's armpit. She nodded to Francis. "Her temperature's dropping." She checked the other dogs. "They're going to be all right."

The officer had waited outside. Faith took a few minutes to compose herself before joining him. "How do these animals get here? What happens to them?" she asked quietly.

The policeman couldn't look at her. "They're usually unclaimed strays. If nobody collects them, the vet comes once a week and puts them down.

Faith breathed deeply. She enunciated each word slowly so there could be no mistake. "I'm taking these animals with me."

The officer finally lifted his eyes, and Faith could see hurt in their brown depths. "I'm sorry, Miss Maloney, but they're government property. I can't let you. . . ."

"He's right, and we're wasting our time here." Francis strode out of the hut carrying a sagging Jenny. "Let's go."

"But," Faith protested.

"Let's go. Thank you, officer," Francis said.

Faith draped a wet towel around Jenny's neck and head to keep her cool as they drove home. Francis's lips were a thin line of anger. "I'm thinking we should take over animal control," he said as they passed Norm Cram's house. "Kanab has, what—three thousand people? How hard could it be?"

Faith stared through the windshield. "If I'd known what that place was like d'you think I'd have waited? We have no choice."

Francis knew that stubborn tone. Soft, yielding Faith was a stranger to all reason when animals were suffering. He knew all too well that nothing would dissuade the lady once her mind was made up. The truck rasped in complaint as he downshifted and headed up the hill. "We'll run it by the others," Francis said. "We need everyone's okay."

The mayor was the one to see. Francis had some passing acquaintance with the man, so it was unanimously agreed that he should be the one to conduct the delicate negotiations.

An hour later Francis found Mayor Jenkins watering his lawn. "Mr. Mayor?" he said.

The mayor jumped as if he'd stepped on a nail, and a gush of water poured onto his shorts and splashed his sneakers. "You startled me!"

"I'm sorry."

Mayor Jenkins wiped his forehead with the back of his hand and resumed his watering.

"Mr. Mayor," Francis repeated, "we've met. I'm—"

"I know who you are."

Francis plowed on. "You're aware, then, of our place in the canyon? Best Friends? We take care of animals?"

The mayor nodded amiably. "I've heard something like that."

"Well, we're volunteering to take the animal control problem off your hands."

Mayor Jenkins didn't miss a beat. "Sure."

"Sure?"

"Yes. Okay. It's yours."

Francis spoke carefully. "Do we need to sign any papers?"

"Not for me."

"Then we can pick up the animals right away?"

"Sure."

It wasn't as simple as that, of course. It rarely ever is. But within forty-eight hours of talking with Kanab's Police Chief Bladesdale, Sheriff Maxwell Jackson, and Marshall Johnson of the nearby city of Fredonia, and obtaining the requisite permits, the dogs were safely at Best Friends. Faith felt especially protective of a reddish terrier mix pup with timid, sorrowful eyes. "You look like a Rhonda," she said to the common little mutt. "Now don't you worry anymore. I'll find you a good home; you'll see."

And so she did—just not in the way anyone imagined.

CHAPTER FIFTEEN

Sheriff of Dogtown

Michael watched the familiar routine with interest. Sun trotted ahead, ears erect, happy to be walking with his person.
The Doberman ignored the three aged canines sprawled in his
path, bounded straight up to Victor, and promptly belly-flopped.

The Dogfather settled on his haunches and gravely surveyed
the visitor. Sun panted happily and made no attempt to venture
farther. Michael strolled up to Victor and smiled down at the dog.
"Hello, old thing."

The guardian of Dogtown rose slowly, tail wagging in greeting,
head lifted for his customary scratch behind the ears. Michael had
to remind himself that Victor wasn't really old, but that being
chained up for the first five years of his life had taken its toll. With
his creaky movements and graying muzzle, the Dogfather was
the epitome of a patriach.

Michael gave Victor one last tickle before crossing the invisible
line down the lane to where John Christopher Fripp was nailing
the roof on a new doghouse.

"She is a plain little thing, isn't she?" Michael observed of the
red terrier mix that lay on the sandy soil of her enclosure, head
snuggled between her paws, one sad eye watching his every
move.

John hit a nail with a satisfying whack. "There, that should
hold for awhile." He dropped the hammer into his carpenter's
belt. "Don't let Faith hear you say that."

Michael laughed. "I wouldn't dare."

The two men watched the muddle of dogs snoring soundly in the summer sunshine. Rhonda lay under a bush, away from the others. She was a delicate thing, the smallest mutt in her run. Even after a year of the safety and freedom of Dogtown, even showered with Faith's special attention, Rhonda was still a sorry specimen. The mutt's rough coat just missed the charming color and curl of a Dandie Dinmont. Her slender tail was no match for the proud, upstanding flag of the scottie, and Michael had never seen her ears not glued to the back of her neck.

The clink of metal on metal rang through the afternoon like a siren song. The doggie sounds of sleep immediately erupted into a cacophony of raucous, joyous barking. One hundred, twenty dogs were immediately awake and alerting their mates: running in circles; rushing the fences; chasing tails. Feeding time!

Even Sun, who had flopped outside Victor's line in happy fatigue after his hike, was up and whirling around in the dirt, panting in happy anticipation.

"Down—down, you silly creature," Michael called. "I've got yours at home."

"Tyson's mixing rations," John said. "Wonder where Faith is."

Faith never missed a feeding. Twice a day, sun or snow, she and Tyson would religiously open the cans, rip open the bags, and stir the wet and dry dog food into an appetizing mixture before spooning the required amounts into stainless steel bowls.

"I think she just got here," Michael said, catching a blur of motion as it flashed by the piñon pines lining the county road. Within seconds, Faith's Nissan bumped into Dogtown.

"I'd better get back to it," John said. "At the rate the animals are coming in, I'll be banging nails for the next fifty years." He grinned and squinted at the flawless blue above him. "Beats crunching numbers any day."

"I'll go give Faith a hand," Michael said. He paused and looked at Rhonda. She was the only dog not rushing around in frenzied anticipation. "John, why don't you hand her over to me. Maybe she needs a little Big Mama time."

Rhonda was a rag doll in Michael's arms as he carried her to where Faith was unloading outside Octagon Three. He set the terrier next to Sun, and she immediately scuttled away.

Faith sighed. "She eats well enough. Loves being cuddled. But she's got no spark. You'd think she'd have gotten used to being with us by now, wouldn't you?" She reached for a sack of ground meal.

"Let me get that for you." Michael hoisted the forty-pound bag. He knew Faith had spent days and nights with the traumatized little dog but somehow hadn't been able to reach that sad place inside. "You'd think so," he murmured, following her inside. Faith put a case of Alpo on the counter. "Hi, Tyson," she said. "Sorry I'm late."

Tyson looked up briefly and smiled behind his dark glasses. "I'm about finished mixing," he said putting his arm around a red plastic bucket to hold it steady before punching down a mass of beefy-smelling wet food into kibble.

"We'll get started," Faith said, opening a cupboard crammed with metal bowls.

"I'll catch up," Tyson said.

On their way out, Michael slipped Sun and Rhonda their supper. To his surprise, the terrier showed no shyness when it came to eating. She slurped with the same enthusiasm as the Doberman, delicate legs squared to the ground in determination.

Michael followed Faith's instructions as they entered the enclosures. "Sadie appreciates hers in the corner. Jenny will eat anywhere. Jamie likes his *under* the sage bush. Paulie will only eat if you spoon it on *top* of his doghouse." Faith rattled off every dog's preference in turn. But apart from informing him where to feed, Faith had little to say.

"Something wrong?" Michael asked as they cruised the Nissan back for a third stack of bowls.

Faith eased to a halt in front of Octagon Three and sat with the engine idling. "Nothing." She abruptly killed the motor and jumped down from the truck. She hesitated as Michael climbed out after her. "Dammit. Yes."

Michael waited.

"I was in Zion Pharmacy today. Kortney Stirland took me aside."

Michael had a mental image of a man about his height with the lean, long-muscled body of a marathon runner, and the aquiline nose of an ancient Roman aristocrat. Michael liked Kortney Stirland, as did Faith.

"He wants to adopt one of our dogs," Faith continued.

"That's great."

Faith looked worried. "I quizzed him a little bit—you know how we do?" Michael nodded. "He doesn't have a fenced yard, so I had to tell him we couldn't."

"You told him why?"

"Of course. I explained that if he didn't have a yard he would either have to keep the animal chained or allow it to run loose. I told him as nicely as I could that chained dogs were usually miserable, and loose dogs in town were roadkill. He wasn't very happy."

Michael knew why Faith was upset. The pharmacist had always been very open and accepting of all of them. They had developed a mutually respectful relationship with him that they liked to cultivate with all the townspeople.

"I told him we wouldn't even adopt to Dr. Christy because he didn't have a fenced yard." Faith absently walked over to Victor as they talked. "Hello, boy," she said, bending to rub the Dogfather's backside. "Did Tyson feed you yet?"

A throaty growl from Sun made Michael and Faith look up. The Doberman stood staring toward the road. A huge, red-coated animal was purposefully making its way toward them. "What a gorgeous malamute!" Faith exclaimed.

The enormous dog kept coming, its powerful muscles propelling it forward like a well-oiled machine. Sun growled again. "Easy, Sun. Easy," Michael cautioned his pet. The Doberman's chest puffed like a pigeon's as he affected a protective stance in front of his person.

"Tyson—Tyson!" Faith called urgently.

From nowhere Tyson was beside her. Without a word, Alpha Man walked slowly to meet the intruder.

The great canine and Tyson halted a few yards from each other. Tyson squatted. The dog padded closer. Michael and Faith could hear Tyson's soft Texas drawl above the last slurpings of the dogs behind them. They saw the malamute listen, cocking his broad head in the man's direction.

Tyson waited, talking, talking continuously. A watchful Sun lowered himself to the ground beside Michael. Rhonda slunk from the shade of a juniper and took a position behind Faith, her brown eyes also watching.

Suddenly the little terrier darted forward. "Rhonda," Faith shouted. Rhonda ignored her. She rushed between Tyson and the animal that dwarfed her like the beanstalk giant and gazed up in adoration. The malamute slowly lowered his head and Rhonda strained to cover the white-furred muzzle with tiny kisses.

The two canines paid no mind as Alpha Man cautiously slid a hand around the perfect wedge-shaped ears and found the malamute's collar. "There's no tags, no name, nothing," he called back.

John had strolled over to see what was going on. "What a magnificent animal," he said, echoing Faith's words. "He won't need much of Doc Christy's attention."

"Look at Rhonda," Faith said with a wondering half-smile. "Look at that little mutt put her curlers in."

The scrawny terrier was preening for the handsome newcomer, prancing back and forth like a showgirl. Suddenly she stopped and barked. The malamute looked askance, his plumed tail fanning a red blur in the sunshine. The terrier yipped again and pawed the earth beside her. Slowly the big dog slid to the ground and rolled on his side.

Rhonda went to work. Her little pink tongue probed the recesses of her new friend's ears, cleaning thoroughly. The immense creature's dark, intelligent eyes were next for attention. Rhonda licked and licked and licked. The malamute yawned in contentment. Rhonda stalked around the sprawled body, sniffing every inch. Finally, satisfied that not one mote of dust had missed her attention, she gave him one final love lick on the nose and paraded back to her persons.

The terrier made straight to her empty feeding bowl and nudged it against Faith's foot. Her doggie eyes stared intently, alternately up at her favorite person and back to the malamute.

"She wants me to feed him," Faith said.

"I'll get it," Tyson offered.

All the lines of worry had smoothed from Faith's skin as she smiled down at the little red dog that had never been happy. Sun just stared, as if he wasn't sure what to make of this strange new behavior.

"I think she's found a friend," Faith said.

"More like she's in love," John pronounced as Rhonda watched the malamute's large white incisors wolf down Tyson's food.

The dog had to weigh at least 145 pounds, powerfully muscled, straight-backed, feet like snowshoes. As they studied him, the splendid animal worried the last scraps from the sides of the bowl, lifted his head . . . and belched.

Faith clapped her hands in delight. She stepped forward and cautiously took the malamute's head in her hands. Gently, she rubbed her cheek against his moist, black snout. She was rewarded with a long, lazy lick. "Oh, you lovely thing, you. Welcome."

Rhonda had one more introduction. She rubbed herself against her new friend's leg and trotted off toward Victor. The Dogfather had seen all . . . and was waiting. Rhonda stopped two feet in front of him, head slightly inclined in deference.

The malamute looked puzzled. He came up beside the little terrier and looked from Rhonda to the Dogfather, as if uncertain of the etiquette to be followed here. Victor lifted his head to meet the huge dog's gaze. The malamute craned forward until his nose was within inches of the gray eminence. Victor didn't budge, a stone statue on its pedestal.

Rhonda whined and snuffled her nose in the dust, glancing sideways at her new love. The malamute cocked his head, then, friendly-like, passed an enormous pink tongue over the Australian shepherd's nose, around his ears, and down his face.

Victor jerked his head back in surprise. He wasn't quite sure about this unauthorized liberty. After all, he had his "capo" position to uphold. Yet this immense creature offered no threat. He could even be an ally. Victor made his decision. With regal dignity he eased to his feet and nuzzled the malamute's great jaw in return—royalty acknowledging royalty. The malamute dropped to the ground, panting happily. Victor settled once more on his haunches, his Dogfather authority intact.

Tyson had made phone calls while the little charade was in progress. "There's only one dog like that around," he informed

Faith. "His owners left town last night. The last the neighbors saw was a truck pulling away with the dog in the back."

Faith's shoulders slumped. No matter where one lived—city, suburb, small town, farm—the story was always the same. Somebody moved and couldn't be bothered to take the animal with them.

"At least they thought to dump him close by," Michael consoled.

"Too embarrassed to bring him in," Faith retorted. Still, she was smiling. "But Rhonda's going to be all right now."

"Faith, once they're here, they all get to be all right," John said. "Look at them."

The four humans studied the scene around them. John, Tyson, and Faith's son, David, had fashioned a small paradise for unwanted canines in the past year. The first octagon—for some reason dubbed Octagon Three—was rough-finished, with comfy rooms for the old dogs to come inside and keep warm in the winter.

The eight-sided building was the heart of a great fan of runs extending like mini-meadows from its windowed sides. Each was close to a quarter-acre, fenced to afford trees and scrub for shade and plenty of red dirt in which canine buddies could dig all day if that was their pleasure.

Two wide lanes separated more spacious enclosures dotted with roomy doghouses that the canines could call home. More than a series of kennels, Dogtown resembled a doggie Boys' Town: a friendly, rustic place where dogs could learn to be dogs again. Which was exactly what Best Friends had in mind.

"So what do you think?" John asked. "Doesn't it remind you of an old cowboy town?"

"You're thinking of all the Hollywood westerns they used to shoot here," Faith teased.

"No seriously. With the dirt lanes, rough wood and all . . ."

"So all we need is a sheriff," Michael joked.

"Maybe Amra will just fit the bill," Faith said.

"Amra?" the men chorused.

"He's a character in the murder mystery I'm reading."

Everyone watched the majestic malamute. Tyson had escorted him past the Dogfather, down the lane, to see his reaction to the other residents. The big animal padded alongside Alpha Man, hips rolling slightly from side to side. He stopped once outside an enclosure and growled at two mongrels fighting over a tennis ball. The dogs glanced once in his direction and broke apart posthaste.

"Amra, Sheriff of Dogtown," Faith declared.

The gorgeous malamute became part of the fabric of Dogtown. Everywhere he patrolled, unearthing hidden tennis balls, confiscating contraband feeding bowls, or just keeping the peace, plain, little Rhonda trotted by his side.

Soon a scruffy "Heinz fifty-seven" variety joined the couple. Feisty Cameron attached himself to Sheriff Amra and Deputy Rhonda, and it was obvious the trio were inseparable.

Rhonda did not divide her affections, however. Only Amra got daily grooming. Only into Amra's eyes did Rhonda gaze like a besotted teenager. Cameron was allowed to assist in their duties, but the Sheriff was her one and only love.

CHAPTER SIXTEEN

New Policy

"Spring is here, and the litters are coming in," Diana said.

"It's the same at Dogtown," Faith concurred.

The two women watched the sizable orange-and-white cat patiently groom a scrap of black kitten that only wanted to cling to his face. Around him tumbled six assorted calico infants.

Diana had her Kitty Motel, basically a cluster of simple plywood rooms with lodgepole pines as the cornerposts for the chicken wire exterior play areas.

The setup wasn't what Chief Cat had envisioned the series of buildings of Catland would eventually look like, but everyone and everything was on a tight budget until they got the final balloon payment for the Arizona ranch.

That was only eighteen months away: December, 1990. Michael had already initiated discussions on how the funds should be invested, and he suggested a couple of business ideas to maximize operating income.

Meanwhile, the felines had plenty of room to roam and lots of tree limbs to scratch and climb, and John Christopher Fripp had conceived the innovative idea of roomy, insulated boxes in which they could curl up when it was cold. To soften the austere appearance of the sleeping quarters, David Maloney had carved fish, birds, and wild animals on their exteriors and painted the compartments in happy purples, emeralds, and bright, lemon yellows. Lined up against the inner walls, they looked like a giant set of child's Lego toys. The cats loved them. On more than one frigid morning Diana had lifted a lid to find a nest of kitties who hadn't moved during the night.

Faith looked at her watch and announced, "Doc Christy's about ready to spay and neuter."

Diana gazed affectionately at the familial scene. "I thought I'd give the kittens a few more minutes with Bruiser."

Bruiser was stretched on his side, his silken fur making a soft carpet on the fine gravel floor where his adopted charges now snuggled against his heavy belly. His large yellow eyes stared unblinkingly at Diana and Faith. One paw lay protectively over the snoozing babies. Five-year-old Bruiser had no nipples on which any kittens could suck, but in every other way he was a surrogate mother to the parade of orphans through Catland.

Diana sighed and picked up the carrying case she had brought in to transport the kittens. "I love that big, old cat."

"Good morning, ladies," Doc Christy's cheerful greeting made Faith and Diana smile.

"Hi, Doc. Francis. Judah," the women nodded to everyone gathered in the kitchen.

The veterinarian looked as disheveled as ever and in need of a haircut. He kept blowing at tendrils of sandy hair that promptly fell back into his eyes as he bent over a sedated pup on the now infamous Formica table.

"Here," Diana said, pulling a bobby pin from her own blond hair. Carefully she pinned back the doctor's tousled strands. "While I'm about it." She smiled and whisked a Kleenex from a box on the counter. Bill Christy held still while Diana wiped away the grain of brown rice stuck to the corner of his upper lip.

"Francis insisted I have breakfast."

Diana nodded. "Thought I heard you come in last night."

"Dispatch called at one-thirty A.M. A dog got sideswiped on Eighty-nine. It looked bad. I had to call," Faith explained.

She didn't have to say any more. Faith got summoned at all hours nowadays—not that she minded. The director of the sanctuary found that she liked her role as unofficial animal control officer. She enjoyed the growing respect of the town, and acceptance as one of their own by the police fraternity. These were perks she hadn't quite expected when she took on the job.

Faith also had to admit she got a secret kick out of seeing the looks of wonder on the faces of Doug Crosby and Tom Cram, the officers who most often accompanied her on a vicious dog call. Faith would stand quiet and still next to the suspect animal. "Now that's a good boy. It's going to be all right," she would soothe while the lawmen lagged behind. Within minutes the "ferocious" animal was wagging its tail. Faith had placed the paws of more than one intractable canine on the passenger seat, heaved its backside up and in, and driven away, smiling to herself as the officers stared at the backs of two heads, sedately side by side in the front of her truck. "She's a regular Mrs. Dolittle," someone exclaimed once, and the nickname stuck.

Faith never disclosed that it was her smell that turned the ravening beasts into her friends. No matter how much she laundered her clothes and cleaned her boots, Faith was around mutts so much that the doggie odor permeated every article of clothing she wore. Within seconds of an animal sniffing her ankles, he recognized Faith as someone to whom he could relate.

Faith would only call Bill Christy if she felt it was an emergency life-or-death situation, and she had offered to drive to Panguich the night before. But the veterinarian had reminded her he was due at Best Friends first thing, so he might as well meet her at the bunkhouse and stay over.

She watched the doctor take the first of Diana's mewling kittens. Faith noticed that the pouches from fatigue under his eyes seemed permanent nowadays. She sighed. Bill Christy looked as haggard as she felt this morning, and he still had a fair number of operations to perform.

"Hello," a female voice called. "Anyone home?"

All eyes turned to the screened door.

"Come in," Faith called.

A stout, grandmotherly woman walked in carrying a cardboard box. Covered neck to ankle in a dun-brown dress, her springy gray hair forced into marcel waves around her face in forties fashion, her appearance immediately placed her as from the polygamous community of Colorado City, fifty miles away. "I'm looking for Faith. Oh, hello, Faith. Didn't see you right off." The woman held out the box. "Rosie's been a bad girl again."

Faith didn't have to open the container. She knew what she'd find. Diana pursed her lips and stalked over to have a look for herself. Six kittens lay on a piece of toweling.

Diana turned on the woman. "I know you, don't I? You've brought in three litters in the last eighteen months."

Embarrassment colored the grandmother's face. "Well, you do tell everybody to bring unwanted animals here."

"And we've asked you three times to bring in the mother."

Francis stepped between the antagonists. "We have a new policy," he said calmly to the grandmother. "We only take newborns if the mother is brought in to be spayed at the same time."

The old face stared at him. "You won't take them if I don't bring Rosie? What if I say I'll drop them in the river?"

Francis put his arm around her shoulders. "You're too good a lady to do such a thing. Did I mention there's no cost?"

"But it's a trouble."

"But Rosie will be so much happier," Francis counseled.

"So you say."

"I'm here till after lunch," Bill Christy intervened.

The woman considered. "Well, for you, doctor," she sniffed.

"That was genius, sheer genius," Faith exclaimed as soon as they heard the woman drive away.

Diana was thoughtful. "It's something we should institute right away. But we can't afford to do it for free."

The veterinarian stitched the last suture on a calico. "I'm willing to cut my fee in half."

"But, Doc," Francis objected.

Bill Christy sat down. "I don't suppose you've got another Coke?" he asked.

"Doc," Francis repeated.

"If I had my druthers I'd be here every day," the young vet stated wistfully. "But I got bills to pay too. So—ah, thank you." He took the soda Faith offered. "Let me do what I want. It's my way of helping out. Okay?"

The veterinarian insisted on spending every Tuesday at Best Friends. "You're getting so many animals, I need a day just to keep an eye on everyone." And invariably he brought his own special gifts: a litter of pups, an old cat abandoned on his doorstep. "They're better off here than anywhere else I can think of," he said.

Best Friends thought it was a very fair exchange.

CHAPTER SEVENTEEN

━━━━━━━━━━

The Silver Bullet

Cyrus watched Sparkles graze the lush grass of the meadow along the river. He sometimes wondered if the ancient dude-string horse ever missed toiling the trails of the Grand Canyon, day after day, hours on end.

Best Friends had decided that, apart from needed exercise, the horses that came to them should be free from the burden of bodies on their backs. Even if they hadn't been abused or abandoned, they had surely done their share of work for the human race. They had earned the right, in their last years, to just be horses. Cyrus patted the old gray neck and slipped Sparkles a chunk of carrot before continuing on his way to the ancient caves.

From the very first months, he had been fascinated by the rich fabric of history that imbued the canyon. Sometimes he tried to envision the massive red cliffs as a shallow sea trod by giant dinosaurs. Cyrus had spent many an hour in the dark coolness of a hidden grotto, running his fingers over the faint petroglyphs carved by Anasazi artisans over a thousand years earlier, wishing he could decipher their meanings.

He had been struck by the absence of any depiction of war, violence, slavery, or any other form of aggression in the rock art. The Anasazi had been a gentle people, and Cyrus felt Angel Canyon itself still carried this same peaceful spirituality.

He sat with his back against the mouth of the cavern and contemplated the ring of stones at his feet. The wall above the rock circle was scarred with the black soot of thousands of fires burned into the porous sandstone, and shards of rough clay bowls had been found buried in the earth.

Cyrus reflected on his wife's last visit. When she wasn't helping Faith or Diana, Anne Mejia loved to hike the secret places of Angel Canyon. She got as excited as a little girl at the profusion of healing and nutritional plants she discovered.

Sundown was her special time. This was when the multitudes of flittering bats, the loping coyotes, and the bobcats would show themselves.

"Every time I come, it gets harder to leave," she'd said on her last afternoon. "As soon as we get the final payment for the Arizona ranch, I'm here, Cyrus."

They sat mesmerized by the shifting waters of the underground lake and discussed the prospect of future tours to Angel Canyon. Cyrus thought that combining visits to the animals with tours of archeological sites could bring needed operating money to Best Friends.

Anne had become increasingly aware of the workload involved in taking care of the animals. "I was helping Faith yesterday," she told her husband. "Did you know we're over three hundred dogs now? I don't know how Faith manages. She really only has Tyson full time. We could hire some help if we could supplement our cash flow."

Still they dismissed the idea for the time being. Everyone valued their privacy too much. Besides, they were far from set up for such a venture. And the possibility of their sanctuary being overrun by inquisitive tourists was daunting.

As Cyrus retraced his steps to the horse field, he pondered the damage that had been inflicted on the canyon in the past few decades. You couldn't see it, but it was there—an invisible psychic wound on the land. Grant Robinson had shared with him that there was a powerful Paiute medicine man on the nearby reservation. Cyrus determined to contact the Indian and ask him to perform a ceremony to cleanse and bless their place.

He heard Sparkles before he saw her: the long, frightening neigh of an animal in pain. Cyrus started running. As he crossed a fallen log over the river, he saw the horse, buckled to her forelegs on the far bank. "What is it?" he called uselessly as he came near.

Faith Maloney communing
with a happy Obiwan,
resident of Dogtown.
(*Photo Credit: Jana de Peyer*)

Diana Asher with Harriet
and her latest charges.
(*Photo Credit: Jana de Peyer*)

A special moment for
Michael Mountain with
Bruiser, comforter of
orphan kittens.
(*Photo Credit: Jana de Peyer*)

Early days: John Christopher
Fripp and Steven Hirano
working on the bunkhouse.
(*Photo Credit:*
Dana Gartenlaub)

Paul Eckhoff contemplating a
building site. (*Photo Credit:*
Best Friends Archives)

Virgil Barstad with longtime
companions Sunnybrook and
Nicolette. *(Photo Credit:
Best Friends Archives)*

Goldilocks with Francis
Battista in his Steven
Spielberg hat.
(Photo Credit: Steven Hirano)

Dr. Bill Christy, first
veterinarian. *(Photo Credit:
Best Friends Archives)*

Raphel and Jana de Peyer
with their Pekinese "family."
(*Photo Credit: Ravell Call for
the* Deseret News)

Sinjin the Pirate Cat.
(*Photo Credit:
Chandra Forsythe*)

Victor, the "Dogfather"
of Dogtown.
(*Photo Credit: Jana de Peyer*)

Tyson Horn on a
daybreak walk.
(*Photo Credit: Harry Munro*)

Octagon Three, Dogtown's first building. (*Photo Credit: Dana Gartenlaub*)

Deputy Rhonda grooming her mate, Amra.
(*Photo Credit: Harry Munro*)

Benton, CEO of Benton's House for special-needs cats.
(*Photo Credit: Chandra Forsythe*)

Anne and Cyrus Mejia with
live-ins, Muffin and Lilly.
(*Photo Credit: Harry Munro*)

Chieftan and Merlin in the
joy of the moment.
(*Photo Credit: Harry Munro*)

Nathania Gartman in her
"Daffydil the Clown"
costume. (*Photo Credit:
Dana Gartenlaub*)

Judah Nasr with three of
the residents of the
TLC Cat Club.
(*Photo Credit: Steven Hirano*)

Carrie Kelley with
Baa Baa Ram Dass and
Baa Baa Ganoush.
(*Photo Credit: Harry Munro*)

Dr. Rich Allen with Citizens
for North Phoenix Strays.
(*Photo Credit: Jana de Peyer*)

Tomato, investigative
reporter for *Best Friends*
magazine, at his desk.
(*Photo Credit: Don Bruce*)

Tammy the Greyhound, Tomato's indispensable sidekick. (*Photo Credit: Steven Hirano*)

Tom Kirshbaum, honorary Doctor of Scoopology. (*Photo Credit: Jana de Peyer*)

Angel Village—Best Friends headquarters. (*Photo Credit: Dana Gartenlaub*)

Ginger, in charge of collecting Dogtown's stray tennis balls, doing her job. (*Photo Credit: Jana de Peyer*)

Mollie the pig.
(*Photo Credit: Jana de Peyer*)

Bruiser and Harriet,
teachers and protectors of
abandoned kittens.
(*Photo Credit: Jana de Peyer*)

Young volunteers
helping prepare the daily
rations for Dogtown.
(*Photo Credit: Jana de Peyer*)

Francis and Silva Battista with their beloved Z.Z. (*Photo Credit: Best Friends Archives*)

Charity Rennie with Mr. Mister who has a special place in her heart. (*Photo Credit: Jana de Peyer*)

Angels Rest—Best Friends Memorial Park. (*Photo Credit: Harry Munro*)

Some of the residents
of WildCats Village
appreciating feeding time.
(*Photo Credit: Don Bruce*)

Sharon St. Joan releasing
rehabilitated falcon back
into Angel Canyon.
(*Photo Credit: Jana de Peyer*)

Dolores and Homer Harris
going to the dogs.
(*Photo Credit: Jana de Peyer*)

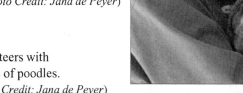

Chandra Forsythe sharing
the softness of Tiger Lily
with a young visitor.
(*Photo Credit: Jana de Peyer*)

Volunteers with
oodles of poodles.
(*Photo Credit: Jana de Peyer*)

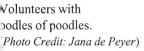

Oscar Heginbotham.
(*Photo Credit: Jana de Peyer*)

Estelle Munro assisted
by office cat Gizmo.
(*Photo Credit: Harry Munro*)

Cyrus with a
recovering Floppy.
(*Photo Credit: Jana de Peyer*)

Sparkles had stumbled into an unseen mudhole. Cyrus winced at the injury. The tendon in the mare's left foreleg was swollen badly, arcing away from the bone like an archer's bow. Cyrus stripped off his shirt and wrapped it tightly around the damaged leg, then somehow shouldered the horse to her feet. "This will have to do until I walk you home," he said. "Just thank God it's Tuesday."

"First she needs an anti-inflammatory shot," Dr. Christy declared. Fortunately, Cyrus hadn't had too far to walk the mare to her barn before driving to the bunkhouse to fetch the veterinarian. Bill Christy jumped into his vet van straightaway. "You come too," he yelled to Francis and Michael.

Now the three men watched the familiar Charlie Chaplin routine with the doctor's drawers. By now however, they knew what to do. As the doctor yanked each compartment open to find his medicine, Michael firmly latched it shut before it could play peek-aboo with the frustrated vet.

"Ah," Bill Christy said with satisfaction, flourishing a bottle of elephantine pills. "Phenylbutazone—'Bute' for short. This will also help the pain." He wrested a formidable-looking aluminum balling gun from Drawer Number Seven and rapidly pushed a tablet into one end.

He offered the scary instrument to Francis. "You've got to get this into the back of her mouth over the tongue. Want to try?" Francis shook his head. Dr. Christy grinned. "Well, I'll let you off this time. But you've got to learn, you know."

The men took mental notes as the veterinarian talked them through the procedure. "You've got to wrap the bandage tight to bind the tendon to the bone. And make sure you put a fat wad of cotton underneath. Like this, see." The veterinarian demonstrated. "Helps ease the pressure. You keep the leg wrapped and Sparkles confined. She shouldn't move around. Not that she'll want to— she's hurting. And give her two grams of Bute twice a day." Dr. Christy took the horse's reins. "Come on, old girl, we need to get you into your stall," he coaxed.

"When can she walk around again?" Cyrus asked.

"Not for ten days. Then you can lead her for a month. But an injury like this takes at least three months to heal."

"Poor old Sparkles, you're going to be lonely," Cyrus nuzzled the gray neck. "But I'll come see you."

"I'll look in on her before the end of the week," Dr. Christy promised, leading the way out of the barn.

Faith saw the "thing" first. While in Zion Pharmacy to get a prescription filled, she thought she glimpsed Dr. Christy's vet van going by. But it couldn't have been the veterinarian's vehicle, because it was pulling this dilapidated Airstream-type trailer, and Faith couldn't imagine what Bill Christy would want with such a piece of junk.

Meanwhile she was a little nervous because Kortney Stirland wanted to talk to her. Faith never knew quite what to say to the man ever since she had refused to let him adopt a dog.

"You know, I've really been watching you people." The pharmacist passed Faith's medicine across the counter. "I see the dedication, time, and yes, the money, too, that you spend on the animals. It's made me rethink my whole relationship with them. You're making a difference, you know."

Faith stared at the tall marathon runner, who was smiling broadly at her confusion. "Thank you; I think that's wonderful," she finally got out. "You've made my day."

"Anytime, Faith. Anytime," Kortney Stirland called as she floated out of the drugstore.

Faith was humming as she drove home, still digesting the full input of the pharmacist's remarks. She wasn't prepared to be blinded by the sun's rays reflecting off some long, metal object as she turned into Dogtown. She hit the brakes.

It was the silver clunker she had seen in town. And it *did* belong to Dr. Christy. The "thing's" front bumper was hitched to his vet box along with a fat Billy that was chewing voraciously on a squat sage bush. *What was the veterinarian up to now?*

The murmur of masculine voices drifted through an open window as Faith gave the trailer the once-over. It really was an ugly, dilapidated piece of equipment, she decided—even older than the mobile homes she had found for Tyson and herself. The "thing" reminded her of a gross silver bullet on wheels with its snub-nosed front end. As for the goat? Only dear Dr. Christy would think to cap the animal's wickedly curved horns with yellow tennis balls to protect the tips while he drove.

A light breeze wafted the unmistakable aroma of moist manure in her direction as Faith strolled toward the trailer. The veterinarian had been working with cows again.

Michael poked his head out of the door. "There you are. We've been waiting for you. Come on up."

Faith mounted the three rickety steps and stopped. The inside of the twenty-five-footer had been completely stripped. In the middle of the denuded shell, Francis and Dr. Christy stood grinning like two guys who had just won the lottery.

"I thought it was about time." Dr. Christy's overboots flapped a welcome as he stepped to meet her. "The interior needs work—paint, basins, power—but we've got our operating table." The veterinarian directed Faith's attention to the end of the trailer. Francis stepped aside, and now Faith could see what looked like an Ob-Gyn table under the window behind him.

"Is that—?" she began.

The veterinarian nodded shyly. "We'll take the stirrups off, of course. Can't see any doggie bitch balancing her paws in those things while I examine her."

"Dr. C's just brought us our new clinic," Michael explained.

Faith suddenly envisioned pristine white walls, counters, shelves, a gleaming metal sink, overhead lights. Their first clinic! No more bunkhouse kitchen. Oh, what a beautiful silver bullet this was! Why hadn't she seen the possibilities immediately? She blinked to hold back the tears. "It is so perfect, Doc. Where did it come from? How did you get it?"

"Let's just say someone's been owing me money for a *lo-ong* time. Thought I'd take some of it in trade. Figured this old trailer could be put to better use here than sitting behind a barn. Now where do you want it?"

The men followed Faith outside. "If we could just maneuver it back a spot," she said, pointing to a grove of junipers a few feet to their left. "The trees would deflect the glare."

"Done," Bill Christy jumped into his vet van, turned the ignition, and started to back up.

"Wait, wait a second. Let me untie the goat," Francis yelled.

"Oh, yes, forgot about him, didn't I?"

Faith held the billy's lead while Michael and Francis helped the veterinarian guide the silver bullet into position. "He's not a very good driver, is he?" Michael commented.

"He gets here, doesn't he?" Francis said.

"There, that should do it." Bill Christy sounded happy. He glanced at his watch. "Looks like I'm late again. Gotta go."

"What about the goat?" Faith asked quickly before the vet could drive off.

"The goat? Didn't I tell you? He's to keep Sparkles company in the barn while she's recovering. Same farmer who owned the trailer was going to have a goat roast this weekend. I said if he threw the goat in the deal, I'd forget he owed me anything."

Faith gave the billy's string to Francis and leaned in the veterinarian's window. She saw the young doctor's face with new clarity: the topsy-turvy, sandy hair that looked like he'd cut it himself without a mirror; the place under his chin where he invariably nicked himself in a hurry to shave; the blond lashes that women would die for, framing eyes that couldn't hide a nuance of emotion.

Dr. Christy looked nonplussed at Faith's scrutiny. She lightly touched the rough growth of two-day beard with her work-calloused fingers. "We love you, you know."

The veterinarian looked down at his jeans and blushed. "See you next Tuesday," he called as he drove out of Dogtown.

CHAPTER EIGHTEEN

The TLC Club

What is it about these creatures that just seeing them, knowing they're all right, makes every petty worry fade? Faith mused. *Is it because they give us back ourselves? That with them we are not judged, need not pretend, can allow the emotions we must hide in order to survive to emerge freely, in all innocence, without fear?*

Faith brooded on these questions as she surveyed her slumbering menagerie. There wouldn't be many more mornings she could bring her coffee and smile at them, still warm with sleep in the wan autumn sunshine. The days were getting shorter. It would soon be time to turn the clocks back again.

Brunhilda the bloodhound lay snoring as usual, her legs splayed, her backside a toasty bolster for her canine buddies.

Wetherby's big woolly body was in its accustomed pride of place hard up against the chicken coop next door. The sheep had gotten fat and happy in the twelve months since a local couple had quit wanting him as a pet. At least they hadn't eaten him.

The only reasonable space Faith had for the black-faced Suffolk had been in with the brood of abandoned chickens found in an orange crate. The first time the wether had lain down, the hens promptly decided his wide, soft back was a perfect roosting platform.

Faith didn't really mind cleaning off the chicken poop, but she wished Wetherby wouldn't butt her every time she collected the breakfast eggs. She supposed it wouldn't be a bad idea to enlarge the coop for the winter. The sheep would definitely want to sleep with *his* adopted kin on frosty nights.

The cats were awakening, the first jug-eared feline sticking a delicate paw from the insulated shed David had built for them. Faith watched the elfin face emerge, screw up its eyes at the sudden assault of daylight, then stretch and yawn. Yes, the cats would be more than warm and cozy on the old sleeping couches she had provided—along with Wooster, of course.

Faith had put Wooster, the rooster, in with the cats because the hens had been rescued with a grumpy, old male of their own, called the Colonel. The newcomer wouldn't have lasted five minutes if Faith had put him anywhere near the Colonel's harem.

What had surprised her was to find the rooster at daybreak on the sofa, contentedly dead to the world in a nest of kitties. Faith shook her head at the improbability of animal bondings.

Now Wooster was awake. She watched him strut out of the shed, chest puffed, beak open, cock-a-doodle-dooing to the world that it was time to get up. "Beat you to it," she called, and the rooster made an immediate beeline toward the fence and the handful of chicken scratch Faith always scattered for him. Wooster had certainly come a long way from the bloodied, feather-torn bird she had rescued from a pack of dogs this past summer.

The sun suddenly went behind an ominous black cloud bank, along with Faith's smile. Why would anyone deliberately loose a chicken on a back street where it was easy dog-kill, when one call to Best Friends would have scooped him to safety?

It wasn't as if nobody knew of them. Faith couldn't even go grocery shopping nowadays without someone accosting her in the aisles and complaining about a barking dog, or the yowling ferals that mated in their yards at night. "So what are you going to do about it?" was the all too familiar refrain. Then again, Faith blessed the courage of the crying child who had sobbed into the phone that "They're killing 'im in our front yard."

Faith recognized that her tolerance for the unthinking behavior of her fellow man was beginning to fray at the edges. She had always been emotionally involved with the animals under her care: it came with the territory and had never been a problem. It was the face-to-face dealings with people and their everyday callousness and indifference toward the helpless and the innocent that was wearing her down.

Since working animal control, she had developed an even greater appreciation for the men and women who toiled in shelters around the country. No wonder the rate of burnout was so high. She wondered if they binged on ice cream and french fries, or indulged in crying jags as she had done lately.

The dogs were stirring. She would take them for a walk—that always cheered her up. She needed to get control of her emotions. Doc Christy was coming today to look at Madeleine, the twelve-week-old beagle mix pup she had found tied to the fender of a junk car.

As she changed into comfortable walking boots, Faith comforted herself that they *were* making a difference. Michael kept telling her of all the good things that were happening, the progress they were making. More people were coming for their spay and neuter clinic, and some in town were actually wanting to adopt animals.

The cloud cover had dissipated by the time Faith stepped from the trailer. It was going to be another beautiful, crisp, blanket-of-blue-sky day. Doc Christy and his ready smile would be here soon. And she had promised Diana to look in on the "Maggot Kids."

Faith smiled. What an unfortunate name! But the tiny white kittens that had turned up at the dump were riddled with the wriggling white larvae. What else could they call them? Faith hadn't seen Diana in a week. Catland being two miles away was no excuse. She wondered how her friend was doing.

Diana Asher wanted to talk. "I was coming to find you," she said to Michael, falling in beside him as he left the bunkhouse.

"Good timing. I'm thinking of stopping by Catland."

Diana slid him a sideways glance. "Let me guess. Tomato."

"I thought I'd see how he's doing."

"You like that kitty, don't you?"

Michael answered carefully. "He's interesting."

Diana laughed, a deep throaty sound that disconcerted him somewhat. Michael knew it hadn't escaped Diana's notice that he had visited Tomato almost every day since the orange-and-white kitten had been discovered, barely alive, stuffed in a garbage can. Just yesterday morning she had come upon him in serious discourse with the lilliputian tabby cradled in the crook of his arm.

"What's up, Tomato? Are they still giving you your disgusting, yucky medicine?" The little one kept up his end of the conversation with a series of surprisingly loud kitten squeaks.

"I see, I see," Michael cooed. "A bit rough yesterday, was it? Let me look, then." His sensitive fingers lifted the infant to eye level. Tomato immediately sneezed in his handler's face. Michael quickly turned his head.

"Time for his disgusting, yucky medicine. Shall I show you?" Diana said sweetly, holding out a small bottle.

"I know how to do it. I had Judah show me."

With those few words Diana knew. Michael rarely revealed the sentimental side of himself. The discarded kitten had touched the quirky Englishman's heart.

They walked the last hundred yards to the quarantine trailer in companionable silence. From Diana's worried frown, Michael guessed she had something on her mind. He was equally certain she'd tell him in her own good time. From intimate habit Diana always confided in Michael. The two of them had remained close over the years. "We have tenure," she often joked.

Now she paused in front of the trailer. "Be prepared for some changes since yesterday, Michael. And we need to move fast."

"Fast?"

"You'll see."

Diana opened the door a couple of inches, then quickly stuck her leg against the jamb. A round Tuxedo head immediately butted her boots.

"Blackjack," Michael exclaimed with sudden understanding. The three-legged kitty was the most notorious escape artist in Catland, able to slither through an opening faster than water through fingers.

Diana nodded. "Back, back, Blackjack," she urged, sidling sideways into the room. Michael followed her lead and squeezed through the inadequate space.

The twelve-by-fourteen-foot rectangle was crowded with cats, but Michael immediately spotted Tomato. "Has he had his medicine?" he asked, picking up the tabby.

"Right before his breakfast," Diana promised.

Michael held Tomato against his chest, nuzzling the tiny head as his eyes swept the small area. "Aren't there an awful lot of cats in here?"

"That's what I want to discuss with you," Diana said, pointing to the room's one sofa. "Let's sit down a minute."

They nudged aside some of the snoozing bodies that had appropriated every available cushioned area and made themselves comfortable. A dozen cats immediately cozied onto their laps while more rubbed against their ankles, purring for attention. Michael couldn't help but notice that they were all special-needs felines.

"We're getting more cats from farther away because, somehow, people are hearing that we don't kill our animals," Diana began. "Can you believe, a couple from Salt Lake called yesterday?" She shook her head and worry deepened the furrows between her brows. "Anyway, a lot of them have problems. I'm particularly seeing more upper respiratory sickness." Diana eased the furry mass from her lap and stood. Michael waited as she paced the small space carefully avoiding any little body in her way.

"As you know, I've been keeping as many as I can manage in the bunkhouse with me. . . ." Diana winced as from nowhere a silver-gray kitty landed on her shoulder and dug his claws deep into her denim jacket. "And then there're the Blackjacks and Tongs of the world. Okay, Tong. Okay, baby," she soothed, stroking the cat's head.

"What's the problem?" Michael prodded gently.

It was as if he had touched a hidden trigger. Diana lifted a pale face to his and let the tears waterfall over her cheeks. "I've got the feline leukemia cats in the next room. I've put all our upper respiratory and special-needs little ones in here together because I haven't anywhere else, and they really need to be kept more separate from each other, and . . ." Her words coursed out jagged, erratic.

Michael quickly transferred Tomato to his warmed spot on the sofa, and went to Diana. He took her into his arms and let her sob out the frustration against his chest. Little Tong teetered on her shoulder like the last drunk out of a bar, but Michael knew that trying to remove the Velcro'd-on rider would only cause the cat to dig his talons in deeper. He cupped the pint-sized body in his palm to keep it from falling and held Diana close. "Easy kid, easy. You just need more space."

"I want more than just space. I want to build a nice, warm house for them. With individual condos, and cubbyholes, and climbing stairs, and a little foyer so there's a little kitty lock between them and the outside so . . ."

"So Blackjack can't skip," Michael finished for her.

Diana pulled away carefully so as not to disturb Tong's balance. "Not only him. What if someone accidently leaves the door ajar and doesn't see Timmie wander out? Look at that poor baby. It would be a disaster if he got out."

Michael couldn't find the little black male at first. Then he spied him behind the scratching post by the window. As always, Timmie plied his endless circumambulation, swaying uncertainly as if buffeted by a strong wind. Round and round, the undersized feline carefully placed one paw ahead of the other, milky eyes concentrating on every step of his chosen perimeter.

Timmie had a neurological disorder that stemmed from his mother having feline distemper when he was born. The brain-damaged Timmie would never walk like his peers, but he was the most affectionate cat and he always found his litter box.

As Michael watched, an enormous one-eyed gray-and-white with the longest whiskers stiff-legged over to hunker beside the diminutive Timmie. Michael had to smile. Benton could have been an actor in another life the way he played his walking-stick leg.

The portly male had been given away by a family who were leaving the area. Benton couldn't comprehend that they didn't want him anymore. He had wandered abroad to find his people and got hit by a car. The veterinarian thought he would have to remove the paralyzed limb, but Benton didn't seem hindered by the impediment.

On the contrary, he used his game leg with great charm, often waving it around like a conductor's baton. Benton got a lot of sympathy with that little display. Now he gently nudged the circling cat to the floor and proceeded to groom behind his ears. Timmie closed his eyes in quiet contentment.

Blackjack hadn't been so lucky. He had been struck by a van, but nobody thought to call a vet, or Best Friends, for two weeks. By that time gangrene had so rotted the thigh bone that Dr. Christy had no choice but to remove the leg.

Like Timmie and Benton, Blackjack was sweet, but he did have one minuscule flaw. He was an "affection biter." The tuxedo cat would hook an unsuspecting person by the hand and calmly bring the fingers to his mouth and chomp down. Michael had painfully experienced Blackjack's loving feelings more than once.

"You see what I mean, Michael?" Diana dried her eyes with the back of her sleeve. "I can't bear making do for them any longer. . . ." Her voice trailed off as Tong shuddered abruptly on her shoulder. "Oh no, he's having an epileptic fit—but we're giving him his Dilantin. Michael, don't you see what I mean?" she cried distract-edly, catching the cat as he fell.

With the utmost tenderness, Diana laid the puny body on the floor and crouched beside Tong. "How could anyone throw a per-fectly healthy kitten into a freezing stream? For something like this to happen . . ."

Tong's spasms lessened as Diana took him on her lap. Michael thought she looked as forlorn as the depleted creature she cud-dled like a baby. As if she were a magnet, two albino cats, the lame and half-blind Benton, crippled Blackjack, five sniffling kittens, and a cat with no ears converged on the compassionate woman in their midst.

Michael eased down beside her, struggling with the outpour-ing of emotion within himself. More clearly than ever in his life, he "got" the bond Diana created with her damaged creatures. The affectionate nickname Best Friends had bestowed on her was more true than any of them realized: Chief Cat was emotionally united with her beloved charges: their pain was her pain, their happiness her happiness. It was from this deep, subconscious identification that Diana understood everything feline.

A sensation of yielding softness, the lightest tickle of whisker against his hand, and the music of "meows" attached themselves to the river of Michael's mind. Yes, they were always scrambling to take care of the never-ending flow of animals that needed them—that was Best Friends' commitment. And yes, maybe they were overextended at the moment, but that would change in time. These crippled, one-eyed, no-tail, injured felines were more than special-needs cats. They were special in their own right, deserving of the best tender, loving care Best Friends could manage. Michael hugged his knees. "I've just thought of a name for the new housing."

Diana's blue eyes met his. "That is a yes, isn't it?"

"It won't be fancy, but I'll get it started today. Is that soon enough?"

The smile that suffused Diana's strong face made her look clear and young again. She slipped a soft hand from under Timmie and laid it over Michael's clasped fingers. "Thank you."

"Don't you want to know what I think we should call it?"

"Pray tell, oh wise one," she teased happily.

"The TLC Club. You know, Tender, Loving Care."

Diana's shoulders started to shake. She rocked back and forth, pressing her lips together in a vain effort to control her giggles.

"What's so funny?" Michael said, a tad offended.

"Nothing. Aren't laughing and crying the same release? Besides, I don't think you realize."

"Realize?"

"Michael, don't you get it?" Diana was positively radiant. "TLC is the name *they* told me we should name their new home."

Her delight was contagious. Michael smiled, then chuckled. The man and the woman who loved cats sat on the linoleum floor, hemmed in by the ones who needed them most, and laughed, and laughed, and laughed some more.

CHAPTER NINETEEN

Puppy Mills . . . and the Wall of Triumph

Faith couldn't understand where the winter had gone. People always said time flew as one got older, but she was barely in her forties. The theory didn't compute.

The past few months had been quiet, but then that came with the season. When it dropped below freezing, people liked to hunker down, eat hot soup, and generally, as they say, let sleeping dogs lie.

Now that Faith came to think about it, she hadn't had a call from dispatch all week. She expected that would change now that the first buds of spring were tentatively dressing the landscape.

The phone sounded particularly loud in the untroubled afternoon. She took another bite of her banana-and-mayonnaise sandwich and stared at the emotionless instrument. Even before she picked up the receiver she knew who was on the other end. "Hello?"

"Hi, Faith. Sure nice to feel a bit of warmth, isn't it? Got one for you. Neighbors lodged a complaint about the smell." The cheery female voice paused, then continued in a more serious vein. "It's allegedly a breeding kennel for Chesapeake Bay retrievers."

Faith was already unhappy. Chesapeakes were bred as hunting dogs. It was not only that Faith was averse to the sport; she resented that the retrievers were rarely being treated as part of the family.

Dispatch was still talking. "But from the description sounds more like one of those puppy mills, if you know what I mean."

Faith grimaced. Puppy mills were breeding factories where bitches were forced to produce litter after litter only to have their pups taken away for quick sale, often before they were properly weaned. "Can you give me the details?"

"Can't tell you much. We don't have a file on the guy. He's married with four children, and as I said, we have no rap sheet on him. Do you want to take it?"

"Is Officer Crosby around?" Ever since she had experienced a frightening altercation with a drunk one night, Faith requested an officer if she had any concerns. She had come to rely on the clean-shaven, boyish Doug Crosby, and on the official authority of his snappy tan pants and crisp blue uniform shirt.

"He's out on a call."

Faith pondered. A married man with four children was no guarantee that she wouldn't have a problem. But after three years on animal control duty she figured she had a handle on most of the troublemakers in the area, and this man's name was not on her mental "beware" list.

"I'll take it," Faith said.

The address was a few miles inside Kanab's city limits. Faith drove slowly, considering her options. She had no illusions about what she would find. She had seen these places in Pennsylvania, Illinois, New York. They were invariably the same. If she could report truly horrendous conditions in violation of the health and safety code, the operation could be shut down and the dogs rescued. On the other hand, she hated to think of the suffering the animals were enduring if that were the case.

Faith could have predicted the trashed garden overgrown with waist-high weeds that fronted the man's box-like house. She rang the doorbell and waited.

The bearded man who answered looked like he ate a lot of meat and washed it down with a case of beer. He was amiable enough until Faith explained her errand.

"Who the hell you think you are?" He hitched up his pants over his spongy paunch with his butcher's hands, squinting at her past the broken veins in his bulbous nose. "You get the hell off my property or you'll know what for."

Faith wished she had waited for Doug Crosby. She enunciated

carefully. "The police department has requested I make a report on your operation."

"Who is it?" a female voice interrupted, and Faith was relieved to see a questioning face peer over the man's shoulder.

"I've been sent to check on conditions in your kennels," Faith explained. "If you or your husband have a problem with this, I suggest calling the police. They will verify my authority."

The big man stepped toward Faith. "If you don't get off my step, so help me . . ."

He stopped in mid-sentence as red-chipped nails tugged on his T-shirt. "We don't want any trouble, dear. If the police sent her . . ."

Her husband shook his thick arm like a dog trying to dislodge a flea. Rage flared in the wife's face before she let go.

"It won't take long," Faith said soothingly, holding her ground. She mustn't show fear. "And I'm sure you don't want me to say I couldn't do my job."

There was an unfathomable expression in the woman's veiled eyes. Faith could almost imagine she was pleased that animal control was on her porch step. "Just let her look, dear," she urged tightly. "Then she'll leave."

The man glared at Faith and his wife in turn. "You got five minutes," he said and stomped back into the house, slamming the door on both of them.

The woman cocked an ear to make sure her husband was out of earshot, then smiled carefully. "Follow me. It's around back."

It didn't matter how many puppy mills she'd seen, it was always a shock. This time the yard was even smaller than the front garden, with not a tree or shrub protecting the bare earth.

Faith had some experience with Chesapeakes and knew their normal weight was between sixty and seventy pounds. The pathetic specimens chained with barely room to move averaged forty pounds at most. Still, there was a plywood shelter, which Faith knew had to leak, and in which the dogs had probably spent a numbing winter. There were water and food bowls, though empty at the moment. The stench of excrement was disgusting but no law was being broken here.

She counted twenty-five before seeing the last bitch. Faith couldn't believe what her eyes were showing her. A massive mammary tumor hung to the cold earth on which the female stood. Worse, she was obviously pregnant. Faith unlocked the pen and slipped inside.

"What are you doing? Don't let her out," the woman screeched.

Faith ignored the worried whine and crouched beside the dog. She ran her hand over coarse, curly fur and winced as her fingers found the bare spots. The bitch growled and raised her upper lip as Faith felt the hardness protruding from her belly. "It's all right; I'm going to get you some help," she whispered.

Faith straightened. "What's her name?" she demanded.

The woman looked blank. "Don't know."

"How long has she been like this? And when is she due?"

The wife crossed her arms. "I don't bother myself with stuff like that. Let him worry about it." She jerked her head in the direction of the house. "Thinks he's gonna make a fortune off these dogs. I say he should get a proper job and get me and the kids some money."

Faith had heard the tale before. Behind every abuse or abandonment of an animal there were people who weren't doing well in one way or another. She would like to gather up all of these Chesapeakes and take them to Best Friends. But as horrific as the conditions were, the man was providing the bare necessities. The dogs were within the legal limits of being fed and sheltered, and there was no law against continuous forced breeding. But there was something she could do.

"A Dr. Christy will be by to remove that tumor."

"The old man won't pay for it."

"I will," Faith snapped.

Sly greed shone in the woman's eyes. "She'll still have her pups, won't she? He won't let the vet operate otherwise."

"Unfortunately, yes."

Faith sneaked into IGA Foods on the way home. She left with a quart of strawberry ice cream and a giant bag of frozen fries.

The Chesapeakes seemed to obsess her. Faith told anyone who would listen of the mean conditions in which the dogs were bred. "And there was nothing I could tell the police to cite him for. Nothing I could do," she repeated.

Francis called a week later. "You busy?"

"Always."

"If you've got a minute, come down to The Village. There's something I'd like you to see."

"I've not finished feeding yet."

"I think you should come down. See you in the meeting area."

The meeting room had been the first section of The Village to be finished. Linked in everyone's mind with the fond recollection of its first support beams tumbling down the cliff, the meeting area had emerged as the airy, picture-window core of the low, sun-dappled building shaded by trees nobody wanted cut down, and surrounded by beds of flowers lovingly planted over the years.

With corridors of rooms for people to live, and offices where records of the animals would be kept and prospective adopters could be interviewed, it was the most ambitious structure on the property, and the men were rightly proud of it.

There was nobody around when Faith walked through the door. She walked outside and waited. After ten minutes she figured Francis had gotten sidetracked, and listlessly she went back inside.

Something was different. Faith stopped in the middle of the room and stared at the long back wall. There had been an empty bulletin board up there last week. Now the space was covered with newspaper and magazine clippings.

Faith stood before the collage of pictures and stories and repeated the banner headline out loud: *Wall of Triumph. Wall of Triumph.* For half an hour Faith devoured every word, absorbed each accompanying photograph.

The *Wall of Triumph* was a collection of all the good things that were happening with animals: the paramedic who crawled down a storm drain to rescue a puppy; the mama cat that braved a fire to rescue her kittens; the German shepherd that saved his elderly owner from being mugged; the pregnant squirrel that adopted orphan kittens; the firemen who rigged up a sling to rescue a foal swept away in a flood.

The stories came from all over the world, as far away as Calcutta. Faith felt herself wanting to bawl. Someone had taken a lot of time and trouble to put this wonderful reminder together. She felt ashamed at having gotten so caught up in the trials and tribulations of her small neighborhood. With this display somebody was shouting to all who took the time to look that the glass was indeed half full, not half empty.

"Do you like it?"

Faith hadn't heard Francis walking up behind her. "Oh yes," she said. "Oh yes. Thank you, Francis. I needed this."

"It wasn't me. Michael did it."

"Michael?"

"He said Tomato gave him the idea."

Faith nodded. The notion that Michael communed with Tomato the cat was not a surprise to either her or Francis. They had been caring for animals long enough to have experienced their own psychic connections. Francis believed that animals communicated with their persons on every level. "Don't you know when your pet is trying to tell you something?" he would sometimes say.

Nor was she surprised at what Michael had created. The Englishman had his own unique way of caring. Faith thought of Sun, and talky Tomato, and McMuffin, the white German shepherd he had mourned for months in stoic silence.

She understood in that moment how all in the community of Best Friends had their own special gifts. How different they all were, and yet how they all meshed together for the same goal. The people of the canyon did not live in each other's pockets, yet they interacted for the common good of the earth and the animals.

Faith felt renewed. Whatever happened in the years to come, as long as they held to their truths, they could go on.

CHAPTER TWENTY

Summertime

Jana de Peyer was on the phone from Las Vegas. "Faith, you'll never guess what I'm getting." Jana's distinctive laugh sang down the phone line.

Faith wouldn't even try to imagine. Just a couple of months earlier Jana had trucked in an A-Frame kit: an honest-to-goodness house packed in boxes. It really was the cutest thing when they put it all together next to the bunkhouse. By popular vote it was decided that Francis should move in, seeing as he had twelve dogs and six cats living with him in one room. "Let me see now. The Governor's mansion?"

"Maybe even better." Jana paused for effect. "Sunrise Humana hospital is renovating their pediatric wards and giving away all sorts of stuff. I'll be driving up this weekend with a U-Haul full of surgical lights, windows—oh, wait til you see what I've got!"

Faith knew this hospital had only top-of-the-line equipment. She could hardly believe their good luck. They had desperately needed Dr. Christy's Silver Bullet, but already the quarters were cramped and overcrowded. She dreamed of one day having a real clinic. No, dreamed wasn't the word. Faith had visualized every operating and recovery room, every detail of what they would need.

"And listen to this," Jana trilled. "I got an end piece of linoleum from a company that's giving half to us and half to Mother Theresa's group. Not bad company, eh?" Again her laughter made Faith smile. "See you then." Jana rang off.

Faith placed the receiver back in its cradle. Knowing Jana, she would arrive with a U-Haul van crammed with everything they could possibly need, bless her heart. All that would be required of Best Friends was some extra money for the building materials, and John should be able to juggle that somehow. Faith wandered out of Octagon Three, deep in thought.

A whimpering that sounded like a lost child distracted her. Faith looked down at the white beagle mix whining around her ankles. "Aren't you the neediest little thing, Maddie," she exclaimed. Faith had quickly decided that Madeleine was too formal a name for the anxiety-ridden mutt she had found tied to a fender last fall. Maddie was a better tag, and there were days when "pest" suited her best of all.

"Oh, all right then." Faith stooped to pick up the dog. In one second she was flat on her face in the red dirt. She didn't have to look around. "Amra!" she shouted. Faith had forgotten the new rule around Dogtown: keep your eyes peeled for the Sheriff.

"Amra," Faith sighed as she sat up. The malamute trotted around to look at her, tail wagging like a metronome. Rhonda, as always, was at his heels. Faith met the mischievous amber eyes and swore the animal was grinning.

Amra had discovered that he could sneak up behind an unsuspecting person, thrust his haunches between their legs and, with a toss of his head, upend them. The saucy trick was the best fun, and Amra's new goal was to tumble as many persons as possible.

"Need a help up?" Tyson strolled over and extended a hand.

"Thanks," Faith groaned.

"The Sheriff's having a good time today. I found twenty-two bowls under his favorite bush."

That was another habit Amra had adopted, confiscating feeding bowls and hiding them while Tyson and Faith did their rounds.

The two of them walked Amra across Victor's line and watched him bound on down the lane. Little Rhonda straggled too far behind her mate to be among the privileged, and so was obliged to stop on a dime at the invisible barrier.

It took the malamute a few seconds to realize that "Deputy Number One" wasn't with him. He stopped, stared down an enclosure of German shepherds, then yelped at Faith to escort him back out of the Dogfather's domain. Amra lay down beside his mate and covered her small head with wet, sloppy kisses. Rhonda finally agreed to being placated, and the two canines ambled happily away to play.

"I wish I never had to leave the property," Faith said wistfully. She looked at Tyson. "I don't suppose you could go to town and pick up a prescription for me? I need to see John."

Tyson nodded. "Do you need anything at IGA?"

She picked up the forlorn Maddie. "I've got a list in the trailer. Thanks, Tyson."

Jana arrived with everything, including the kitchen sinks. As Francis said, "How can we not build the clinic?"

Every morning now Faith greeted Paul, Steven, Virgil, Gregory, and Francis, watching with mounting excitement as the clinic's foundation went down and the framing rose up like magic. Even her mood swings seemed somewhat muted, and she was making a real effort to stay away from Denny's Wigwam cafe and curio shop and that addictive strawberry ice cream.

Faith found herself enjoying the camaraderie of the old "upper body brigade." She realized she had been spending too much time alone in her trailer, and she promised herself to hang out with her friends more.

August brought the relief of extra hands to help groom, medicate, scoop the poop, socialize with the animals, repair fences, paint—all the little jobs that needed to be taken care of on a regular basis.

There was a sense of happy anticipation in the air. The men and women who had committed to Best Friends seven years before— Faith couldn't believe how quickly the time passed—were visiting more frequently, making plans to wrap up their businesses and bring all their collective energy to Angel Canyon. Some had even begun poking around Kanab, looking for possible places to stay while they figured where they would build on the property.

The animals never stopped coming, and rabbits and a one-winged owl were added to the mix. When a ragged troop of white geese were unexpectedly dumped at The Village, Michael hunted down a secondhand wading pool and the orange-beaked gaggle made themselves right at home.

Nathania Gartman loved it all.

The Alabama woman's first love was children. Nathania liked nothing better than to dress up as "Daffydil" the clown and visit the terminally ill in the hospital.

By nature shy and serious, as "Daffydil" Nathania metamorphosed into a colorful, playful character in a costume of multi-colored iridescent pants, red-and-yellow shoes, and a beribboned, oversized forest green jacket that swamped a scarlet polka-dot shirt.

The eyes of the frail boys and girls who would never leave their beds would grow big when Nathania produced her enchanted lightbulb and wizard's coloring book. A youngster had only to blow lightly on the pages for pictures to appear and rainbow into color.

The visit always ended with the magical appearance of stuffed animals, toys, games, and books from Daffydil's voluminous pockets. It was no wonder that when Nathania moved to Las Vegas to work with Jana and Raphael she quickly became the most beloved visitor to that city's children's wards.

Nathania had hiked the canyon with Michael the summer before anyone had moved onto the land. "I'm so happy. I'm so happy," she cried, tears tracking her high cheekbones.

The spirited woman had seen the possibilities of Best Friends from the beginning. To her, their animal Eden meant not only a place where all manner of furred and feathered creatures could find refuge in beautiful, safe surroundings, but a place to bring children. "We can hold seminars—educate. And I can teach, and truly be able to say that not one animal will be put to sleep," she declared to Faith on her first visit to Dogtown. "Unless, of course, they're in desperate pain and dying," she added quickly.

Faith used her sleeve to wipe the sweat from her forehead. She thrust a dozen feeding bowls into Nathania's arms and led the way out of Octagon Three to the waiting Nissan truck whose bed was already packed with the dogs' dinners. "All in good time, Nathania. All in good time. Right now we've got five hundred dogs to feed."

Nathania cruised the vehicle expertly along the narrow lanes, but Faith noticed that she did not rush to join her when they stopped at the enclosures. "It will go quicker if you come inside and help me," she called, not unkindly.

Nathania hesitated. Slowly she extricated herself from the driver's seat and watched Faith enter a compound of lively black Labrador mutts. Still she hung back, seemingly hypnotized by the fifteen dogs that jumped, barked and whipped around like crazy beasts as Big Mama put down dinner in their preferred eating spots. Faith felt Nathania's reluctance. "What's the matter?"

Nathania's face flushed beet red, and Faith knew it wasn't from the sun. "I'm frightened of dogs," the Southerner finally managed. "I was attacked by a cocker spaniel when I was five."

Faith placed the last bowls and shut the gate behind her. She took Nathania by the shoulders. "Why didn't you tell me?"

"I wanted to be part of whatever y'all were doing. I'm not scared of cats or geese. I figured I'd get over being terrified of dogs, but . . ." Nathania's whole body was a picture of distress.

"Oh, dear. Oh, dear," Faith repeated. "How about little dogs?"

"I'm not sure."

"Well, stay with me while I finish this lot, and then we'll let David and Tyson take over." Faith smiled at the miserable Nathania. "Hang in, girl. You don't have to like dogs, you know. There's lots of other animals around here."

Nathania presented herself at Dogtown the very next weekend. "I've decided I want to do this," she announced, her small face solemn with determination. "If you can do it, Faith, I can do it."

"Good girl. Let's start with the basics. Food."

Faith walked her new student into Octagon Three. She knew from long experience that the concentration required to mix the kibble and moist, to count the pills, to measure the morning's medicine, could be as calming as any meditation—especially in the beginning. In preparing their separate dishes Nathania would also start to see the dogs as individuals, instead of as an amorphous mass of four-legged creatures to fear.

The teacher didn't push. She let Nathania doggedly lag her rounds all day Saturday and Sunday. She noticed when the woman forgot herself one time and leaned into an enclosure to hand Faith a bowl. Nathania almost smiled when a Rottweiler's head bumped against her hand . . . almost.

On Labor Day weekend Faith was called to pick up a pup that was hanging around the town's transportation yard, and had to leave Nathania with Tyson.

The dog was a juvenile Chesapeake. Faith was immediately reminded of the derelict conditions of the puppy mill she had tried so hard to forget all summer. She told herself she must be getting overwrought. This young dog with his poor conformation so resembled the clutch of pups she'd seen a few months earlier. But that couldn't be. The bitter-faced man she had confronted last spring chained his breeding stock too tight; he would never let one free to wander into Kanab.

The dog was all bones, and it didn't hesitate to jump into her truck when coaxed. "You look like a Bailey," she told the bedraggled animal. "We'll put you with the little dogs to wet your feet. You'll feel much better in a few days." Faith's soothing tones continued on the eight-mile trip back to the sanctuary.

To Faith's surprise, Nathania was actually inside the far enclosure John had just fenced for a new pack of small canines. The Southern woman's smile could have lit up an auditorium. "They like me," she marveled. "There's a westhighland-something in here, and he rubbed up against my leg. Watch, Faith." Nathania cautiously approached a sleeping, white-furred mutt. "Hello. Hello," she said. The westie opened one eye and promptly went back to sleep. Nathania looked so disappointed, Faith felt like hugging the courageous woman.

"Maybe you can help me with the one I've got in my truck," she said. Nathania related her hour's adventure while they made their way back to Faith's vehicle. "Tyson was busy," she started. "And these little dogs just kept barking and barking."

"They do that," Faith said.

"Well, I figured it was now or never. I got bowls and walked into this pen. Faith, I was scared to death. And then this westie came over and rubbed against me. It felt like I was being loved all over."

Faith smiled at Nathania's awakening. She made no attempt to restrain the Chesapeake that jumped from her truck as soon as she opened the door, and glanced around in trepidation of these new surroundings. Nathania froze as he snuck around her legs, sniffing. Faith knew what would come next. Nathania had been around dogs all afternoon. She smelled of dog. The Chesapeake would react accordingly.

The animal didn't disappoint. He sniffed and sniffed and circled the paralyzed female. Finally he rubbed his filthy head against her thigh and leaned his whole skinny body on hers.

"His name is Bailey," Faith said briskly. "Would you mind escorting him to the enclosure we just left? And stay with him. He may need reassurance. Oh, and make sure the others don't get on his case. I'll get some treats for him. You okay with that?"

Nathania nodded as if in a dream. She picked up the Chesapeake's leash and, in imitation of Chief Dog, talked the new arrival back to the far enclosure.

"You got it, girl," Faith murmured, watching. "You got it."

By Halloween, Nathania Gartman had not only conquered her fear of dogs (although she still kept a wary distance from Tyson when he walked the "biters"), but had fallen in love with Coyote, the shepherd-husky mix that the Grand Canyon rangers had brought to Best Friends in the early days. "Coyote's so sweet he should be our greeter," she declared. "The children will love him."

"All in good time," Faith reminded her. "All in good time."

CHAPTER TWENTY-ONE

Chesapeake Bay

Faith pretended not to hear the obstinate jangling on her bed-side table. She rolled over and pushed her face into the pillow. The Ides of March were already living up to their name. It was a cold wind that blew outside. She was tired and her bed was warm. But whoever was calling wasn't giving up. Faith stretched an arm from under the blanket and picked up the phone.

"Sorry it's so late," Officer Crosby's voice apologized.

Faith squinted at her watch in the darkness. "It's after eleven, Doug. What's up?"

"We've got an emergency here. You remember the breeding kennel you inspected last May?"

"How could I forget."

"The guy pulled a gun on his wife and she called it in."

"What?"

"We're on our way to pick him up. She's pressing charges. Can you get the dogs?"

"What do you think?"

Doug Crosby chuckled. "Atta girl."

It took Faith less than five minutes to dress, pull on her boots, and knock on Tyson's trailer. "I need you to chum up some of the dogs and free up a run," she said to the sleepyhead. "We've got a kennel full of Chesapeakes coming in." She hesitated. "See if you can rouse Francis. I have a hunch we might need his help."

A chaos of police cars and sheriff's vans awaited Faith when she arrived at the frame house. Blue lights inscribed flashing circles into the dark. Radios crackled incessantly.

Six officers tromped down the starved weeds in the frost-killed garden, and Faith was just in time to see the sullen breeder, his arms handcuffed behind him, being escorted down the steps of his porch by three deputies. The police looked most serious. Kanab didn't get much violent crime. A man brandishing a gun with possible intent to harm was a grave matter in these parts.

"How many can you take?" Doug Crosby asked as he walked her around to the backyard.

"I have nine kennels with me. I'll take the ones in worst shape and get the others tomorrow."

"Gotcha."

The Chesapeakes were frantic. They rushed their tiny pens to the limited length of their chains, shattering the night with their terrified howling. This didn't disturb Faith in the least, but something else bothered her.

"Where are the rest of them? I only count fifteen. There were twenty-five when I was here last. I know there have to have been some litters, and he couldn't have sold that many."

"You sure?"

"I'd like to talk to the wife."

"No problem. Come on."

The wife cowered on a shabby sofa, flanked by police officers taking down the details of the assault. She was a different woman than the one Faith had encountered months earlier: abject, shrunken into herself like a dying flower, oblivious to the four sniffling children scrunched beside her.

"Oh," she said in pathetic answer to Faith's question. "He couldn't sell a bunch and didn't want to keep feeding them, so he took 'em up some canyon and shot them. He does that sometimes. One escaped last year, and was he in a fury." She turned poor-me eyes on Police Chief Bladesdale. "I tell you, he's bad. It's better for me and the kids that you're locking him up."

The smallest child was bawling. "Take the youngsters out of here," Chief Bladesdale wearily ordered a female officer. Faith was disgusted. So Bailey *had* come from this place. But his mates hadn't been so fortunate. She wanted to get away from this house of abuse. "Can you help me load up?" she asked Doug Crosby.

The choice of dogs to go to Best Friends this night was not easy. All of them were in poor shape. Faith walked the line, assessing each in turn.

There was one the woman had called Ginger, who appeared positively malnourished. The little female was the most under-weight breeding Chesapeake that Faith had ever encountered. Her ribs showed through her curly golden fur and she was filthy. Ginger absolutely must be taken. Then Faith recalled a comment the pitiable woman had made on her first visit.

"Ginger's his best breeding bitch. Lucky she's alive, though. The old man put her in with that one over there." The woman pointed to the scrawny hunting dog standing in two inches of mud three pens away. "She almost killed Ginger." The woman giggled inanely as if it were a big joke.

But, as usual, there was "no room at the inn" at Best Friends for dogs who would kill each other on sight. However, both breeding bitches looked so poor that Faith, in all good conscience, had to take both. She wasted no more time making her selections.

Faith stood silent and still, allowing each growling dog to get her smell before removing their chains and slipping a simple col-lar and leash around their necks. She still had one kennel free when she came to Ginger's cramped quarters.

The Chesapeake dam set her front legs, standing her ground as if daring this stranger to estrange her from the two grown pups who slunk behind their mother's haunches. Faith didn't have the heart to separate the little family. "We'll put them in together," she told Doug Crosby.

Not only Francis, but insomniac Michael, too, was waiting with Tyson when Faith drove into Dogtown amid a cacophony of bark-ing loud enough to ensure that all four-legged residents were awake and ready to play.

Willing hands unloaded Faith's precious cargo from the back of her truck, and kennel by kennel, the frightened Chesapeakes were freed into a spacious compound. Even the older dogs roused themselves from their warm dreams and hobbled out from Octa-gon Three to investigate this unusual nighttime activity. Sheriff

Amra gave his seal of approval to the proceedings by sniffing each cage as it was unloaded and wagging his tail in greeting.

Ginger's was the last. "We can't put her in with the rest," Faith said. "We'll have a dogfight from hell on our hands with the other breeding female."

Michael opened the mother Chesapeake's kennel and lifted the frail bitch into his arms. "First thing we need to do is give this lady some dinner."

"Give them all some dinner," Tyson echoed and quietly padded away to fetch some food.

Michael carefully placed Ginger at his feet. The dog didn't seem to know what was expected of her. She toddled a few cautious steps, piddled a long, steady stream, then slunk back to the truck to cower under the tailgate.

Amra wasn't having any of this behavior. The Sheriff bounded under the Nissan's wheels and nudged the Chesapeake's backside out into the open. The stunted female offered little resistance as, covering her little face with his signature sloppy licks, Amra tried to assure her that she'd arrived in a canine Camelot.

Ginger was in no way threatened, but Michael scooped the bewildered dog away. This animal had no social experience and wouldn't know how to relate to others of her kind. Meanwhile Amra, having done his job, trotted back to his waiting Rhonda.

Michael held the bitch at arm's length, studying the squirming dog who cocked her head at her tall rescuer as if taking his measure. "You know what?" he said, folding the dog against his chest. "In spite of all she's been through there's an inner happiness here—something that won't let her give up."

Faith watched his protectiveness of the Chesapeake. "What are you thinking?"

Michael looked up at a sky bright with stars. "All she's ever known is being chained, continually force-bred, and her pups taken away. I say we let her have the run of the place with the older dogs. Let her taste what freedom's like for once. Our way of saying F.U. to puppy mills everywhere."

"What if she runs away?" the practical Francis asked.

"She won't run away," Faith said quietly. She scanned their moonlit surroundings and pointed under the shielding branches of a young juniper two trees away from the Dogfather's invisible line. "Let's put her over there. She'll be away from the other dogs, but close to Victor, and that could be a comfort. Oh, thank you, Tyson," Faith smiled and took the heaping bowl of food.

Michael put the Chesapeake down, and all of them watched the dog tentatively pick at the food while cautiously watching the people's reactions. Then she wolfed it down as if she had never eaten in her life. Tyson placed more food and water nearby and brought her pups to eat alongside their mother.

"Well, let's get to it," Francis said. "I don't know about you lot, but I need some sleep tonight."

Within an hour they had knocked together a great doghouse for three and placed it out of the wind under the juniper. Michael drove to get blankets from his own bed to make sure Ginger would be cozy. He was delighted when she pawed a place for herself inside her new home and stared back at him from the dim interior. "She's not sure yet," he pronounced with authority.

"Yes, Michael," Faith smiled.

"Well, you get some rest now," he addressed the unmoving Ginger. "I'll come and see you in the morning. You'll need a nice bath, and how about treats? You don't know what treats are, do you? You will."

As Faith had foreseen, Victor took Ginger under his wing and they became close doggie pals. Even so, in all the years to come, the Chesapeake never violated the Dogfather's protection by crossing his boundary unaccompanied. While Best Friends was to find safe homes for most of the other Chesapeakes, Ginger was no youngster, and her offspring, Cheshire and Mace, both had health problems.

Still, nobody could tell Ginger that life might be any better. Before long cowering was a foreign behavior to the dog whose sun-burnished coat grew in so thick and curly and who, Michael declared, "simply grinned" every time a person walked by.

Soon her corner of Dogtown was dubbed Chesapeake Bay in her honor. The juniper tree was called the "Federal Reserve" to acknowledge her undying devotion to the retrieval and deposit of tennis balls. Ginger and her pups, like their canine colleagues Victor and Amra, definitely had their job: to keep the economy of Dogtown humming by keeping tennis balls in circulation.

Every afternoon they could be seen trotting side-by-side down the lanes, scrabbling under bushes, pawing behind trees, gathering up every mutt's lost and stolen favorite toy. The other dogs paid homage to the importance of Ginger's role by visiting the "Federal Reserve" tree every day to withdraw from the tennis ball bank.

It was the beginning of another of the many legends of Best Friends.

CHAPTER TWENTY-TWO

Burnout!

Faith was behind this morning, dragging herself out of bed too late to enjoy her early morning walk with the dogs. It didn't help her mood any to find Michael, impeccable as ever in his pressed chinos and cotton shirt, personally bribing Ginger with treats while he sneaked tennis balls to hide for her to find later. Faith hadn't had the energy to wash her overalls last night, let alone iron them.

"What do you think, Faith?" Michael was apparently without a care in the world this morning. "Shall I stash them at the Great Temple of Food or under Amra's favorite bush?"

The Great Temple of Food was a silver-blue corrugated-tin structure that Raphael de Peyer had brought to Dogtown. Jana and Raphael's July yard sale had become an annual event to raise money for Best Friends. Last year it had attracted Joby and Judy Swanson. Joby was in the steel frame business, supplying the big Las Vegas casinos. "My wife and I are very supportive of animal causes," he said. "Is there anything you need?"

Two weeks later the tall, good-looking contractor appeared at 6:30 A.M. on a Friday morning with six of his crew. Thinking it was feeding time, the dogs went crazy, barking, whirling, and raising a cloud of red dust that drifted over everything. Joby smiled knowingly. "Just as I thought. You need a clean place to keep food," he said to Faith. "I have the materials with me. But you work with us," he insisted to Raphael. Four weekends later, the

Great Temple of Food stood on the outskirts of Dogtown in all its gleaming glory.

"Tennis balls behind the Great Temple of Food or Amra's favorite bush?" Michael repeated.

Faith only half heard the question. She felt tired and blowzy after a restless night's non-sleep. "How do you do it?" she demanded truculently, ignoring Michael's chattering question.

"Do what?"

"Always look like a damn country squire surveying your estate in England somewhere?"

Michael's smile faded and Faith immediately wished she could have bitten her tongue. What was wrong with her lately? Every little thing bothered her.

"Not exactly a great way to start the day, Faith, would you say? I came to give you a hand. Thought Tyson and I could feed the dogs and give you a break."

"I never miss feedings," Faith snapped.

Michael took his hands out of his pockets, his body language reflecting Faith's tension. "That's your problem. You've got to do everything. Has anyone told you you're getting singularly unpleasant to be around lately?"

Faith was shocked. She couldn't ever remember Michael raising his voice before. "I'm sorry. I didn't mean . . ."

"Forget it, Faith. You think you're the only one who's tired? We're all overwhelmed, in case you haven't noticed. But then you're not noticing much of anything outside yourself, are you?"

The sweet, familiar dull thud of hammers hitting nails suddenly registered on Faith's consciousness. She followed the pounding and was surprised to see Steven, Paul, and Virgil back at work on the clinic.

John Christopher Fripp had judiciously called a halt to construction several times over the winter. The buyer of the old Arizona ranch had been late more than once with the mortgage payments, and the accountant had rightly ensured the care and feeding of the animals before allowing more building.

Faith had understanding but increasingly little patience. "Doesn't the man realize we need a real infirmary?" she fretted when by August the clinic was still only a skeleton structure. "Can't you tell him how many animals we have now?"

John had made a tally and was disturbed to find that the numbers topped 500 in Dogtown alone. He had driven back to Arizona that same day to meet with the developer. Faith wasn't aware he'd returned yet.

"John came back a couple of days ago," Michael said, reading her mind.

"So we'll be getting regular payments again?"

"John said they worked it out. You try to have a better day, Faith."

"Look, I'm sorry I . . ." Faith began when Tyson popped his head out of Octagon Three.

"There's somebody from town wants to talk to you, Faith," he called.

"Be right there."

"If that's animal control, why don't you let me or Francis take it?"

Faith was instantly on the defensive. "I can still do my job, you know. Besides, I know the routine. You don't."

Michael shrugged. "Suit yourself."

The call was not from dispatch.

"I don't like to bother you, but I know how you feel about these things." Faith vaguely recognized the woman's voice. "My boy hangs out at school with this kid I don't like, but what can you do?"

"Excuse me, but please understand, I'm already late this morning."

"Oh, of course. Anyway, this kid confided that he'd gotten sick of taking care of their pet rabbit. His mother won't skin it, so his dad's gonna let it loose. Thought you'd like to know."

Faith felt the weariness descend again. A domestic bunny stood about as much chance in the wild as a fish on land.

"Did I say something wrong?"

"No. No, it's fine. Thank you. Have you got the address?"

The woman's directions led to a shambles of a dwelling at the end of a potholed road. Faith didn't have to knock on any door when she arrived. A mound of putrid rubbish, overdue for the dump, lay rotting in the sun outside a falling-down fence. Perched on top of the spilled heap was a plywood rabbit hutch.

Faith stared at the silky gray lop-ear, grown too big to turn around in his tiny feces-filled coop. She held her breath to avoid the nauseating odor as she carefully lifted the doe-eyed creature out of its prison.

"I gotta dog you can take while you're at it," a man's voice said at her back.

Faith turned to confront the reedy twang. The man was singularly ugly, she thought, with his ratty beard, black nose hair, and bloated belly hanging over his pants. "Why don't you want the animal?"

"The bitch keeps dropping pups, and I'm tired of getting rid of them. The kids have lost interest, like they do everything else, so I'm waiting until she finishes the bag of food, then it's her turn." The father mimicked a gun to his head.

Faith couldn't look at the man. Was he just saying this to get a reaction out of her? Or was this the way he lived his life? She nodded numbly. "I'll take them both."

The drive home was a blur of tears. Faith almost didn't see the glassy-eyed black-and-tan shepherd mix shivering on the verge of the county road. The dog was so terrified it took her almost an hour to coax it into the truck. By the time she eased the emaciated body onto the comfort of her lap, the volcano that had been seething inside forever was ready to erupt.

Faith recognized this mutt. Less than a month ago, he and his brother had been adopted out to two local families. When she drove back to Dogtown, she didn't even call "hello" to the men toiling on the clinic, just gave the three orphans to Tyson and stormed into her trailer.

The acknowledgment in the *Southern Utah News* read exactly as she remembered from the day before. "Employee of the month," it blared. "Valued member of the church; loving family man," the description continued. Faith didn't need to be psychic to guess it was this same wonderful man who had callously dumped the helpless puppy. But she needed to be sure. Once again she roared back to town.

Her first stop was to check on the other adopted dog, whom she was sure was in a fine home. But she questioned her instincts lately. "Hello," she smiled at the pleasingly plump young wife who answered her knock on the door. "Thought I'd stop by to see how the pup was doing."

"Oh, Faith, we just love him to death. He's such a comfort to us. He's changed my husband's life. He has him in the shop with him right now. We're taking him to Lake Powell with us this weekend, he so loves to swim." The woman laughed. "Dearie me. Where are my manners? Won't you come in?"

Faith could have stayed on this lady's porch forever, but she shook her head. "I was passing, so I thought I'd see if everything was going all right. I can't thank you enough for loving him."

"Oh, no, thank *you*. Thank *you*."

Ten minutes later, Faith made her second visit. The look on the face of the woman who answered this time could have curdled milk. "Yes?" she said wearily when she saw who was on her doorstep.

"Do you remember me? Faith Maloney? You adopted a pup from us recently. I'd like to have a look at him. See how's he doing."

The woman ignored Faith to glare at the sulky child clinging to her rose-printed cotton frock. The three-year-old's nose was running, and she was wiping it on the sleeve of her frog pajamas. "Will you stop that?" her mother shouted, smacking away the girl's hand. She returned her attention to Faith. "My husband brought him back to your place yesterday."

"He did not return him to Best Friends. He didn't have that decency." Faith could hear her voice rising. "He dumped him. Abandoned him for coyote bait. Do you hear?"

"I'm terribly sorry, but I can't help you." The door closed in Faith's face.

"Damn you. *Damn* you!" Faith slammed the steering wheel as she broke all speed limits through town. She skidded astride two parking spaces outside the store and stomped inside. The "employee of the month" was smiling insipidly at a pretty female customer. Faith was beyond courtesy. "What the hell did you think you were doing dumping that dog?" she screamed in his face.

The man stepped back as if he had been slapped. He glanced fearfully around at the gathering knot of curious shoppers. "You can't talk to me that way. You don't care that—"

"You're damn right I don't care about your so-called reputation, if that's what you're worried about. I hope these people hear me because you could have called anytime, day or night, and I would have come and picked that pup up! You just couldn't be bothered. You just dumped him out of your car and drove off, you, you bastard!"

The man whitened. Faith saw matching fury pulse the purple vein in his neck. "Yes, I tossed him, and I had to drive off really fast, too, because the stupid thing kept chasing the car!"

An awful silence lay over the store. Customers turned away as Faith lifted her chin and stared down each in turn. "I have no more to say to you," she said, quietly now, her anger spent. She gathered her dignity and walked out of the store. Strangely, she felt no sense of victory, no vindication. Just a numbing sadness that made her wish she could sleep and never wake again.

Francis was waiting when she got home. "Somebody called, didn't they?" Faith asked. She sat bent over the steering wheel, suddenly too weary to move.

Francis opened her door.

"I lost it, didn't I? I don't know what came over me."

"Let's go to your trailer, Faith."

Neither spoke while he put on the kettle for tea. Faith idly stirred the spoon around her cup, making no attempt to drink the steaming, sweet liquid he poured.

Francis broke the impasse. "You can't go on like this."

"I know. I'm sorry. I've been under a lot of stress lately."

"We all have, Faith. Not that I don't understand. I'm not exactly known for my sweet temperament. But this is no way to present Best Friends."

"I know, I know." She stirred faster.

"Why don't you take a sip. It'll do you good."

"I know."

"Stop saying 'I know,' Faith. You're better than that. Don't you think we've all seen what's been going on? Don't you think we know the pressure you're under? But you won't let us help."

"I will now."

"We can't go on like this—any of us. John says we're marching toward bankruptcy and we're all too exhausted to eat half the time."

"I know. Oh—I'm sorry, I didn't mean to say that."

Francis studied the woman who had worked alongside him for so many years. Misery exuded out of every pore. "I think you should just take yourself to bed for the rest of the day, Faith. The sanctuary will still be here when you get up."

Faith nodded.

Francis stayed controlled. "We're going to make some changes," he said evenly. "We can't wait for the ranch to pay off."

"What are we going to do?"

"I don't think you're ready for this right now."

"Please, Francis."

"All right. No more animal control."

Faith looked stricken. "But. . . ."

"Hear me out. We'll offer to rebuild something decent at the airport. And we'll monitor what goes on. We'll still take in strays and the abused. That won't change. But we can't be the dumping ground for the world. Not right now anyway."

"I think I know a guy who might like to take over," Faith said with sudden energy. "There's a nice elderly gentleman who told me he thought what I was doing was real cool."

Francis looked across the table at the director of Best Friends. She was a true warrior. Sometimes down, but never out. "Sounds good. Let's work on it. Meantime I'll write an apology from the mad Englishwoman."

Faith managed a smile. "I think I should do that, Francis." A flash of fear crimped her features. "I don't know what's going on lately. It's going to be all right, isn't it? We're going make it, aren't we?"

Francis rose to leave. "What do you think? Now get some rest."

DECEMBER 29, 1990

A happy life, a fulfilling existence, the complacency of certainty—all shattered in a nanosecond.

A doctor's diagnosis, and the day is suddenly dark; a random act of violence steals a loved one; an earthquake in the night kills family and friends; raging floodwaters sweep away a life's treasures.

For the men and women of Angel Canyon, it was the phone call on December 29, 1990. The mortgage holder on the Arizona ranch had filed for Chapter 11 protection from bankruptcy. With one penstroke their future was gone.

BEST FRIENDS WAS BROKE.

PART THREE

Reaching Out
1991–1997

CHAPTER TWENTY-THREE

New Directions

The blue truck died on April Fools' Day. Michael wasn't surprised. He fully expected Paul's green pickup to follow in short order. Sweet serendipity had deserted Best Friends. Murphy's Law had not only come but had taken up permanent residence in Angel Canyon. Building had come to an abrupt halt. Activities had dribbled down to eating (lightly), sleeping (fitfully), keeping warm (sometimes), and taking care of the animals (always).

It was as if a collective inertia had settled over the group—an unspoken decision to hunker down until the full reality of the situation could be absorbed or, as John said, "the dust settles."

Perhaps they should have seen it coming when the developer began missing payments. Perhaps they should have convinced Faith to step back from animal control months before. Perhaps they should have realized they were taking on too much too soon. Perhaps. Perhaps. Michael sighed and eased out of the dying warmth of Blue's interior. Everything was obvious in hindsight.

It was snowing again, as it had been doing intermittently for the past three months. A most unusual winter, the locals declared. That figured. Thank the gods John had persuaded the power company to keep the electricity flowing. It had been a pleasant relief to find that their word was indeed good in the community. The power company had allowed that Best Friends would honor their debts—albeit a little later than usual.

The sound of his boots crunched loudly as Michael trudged

toward the bunkhouse. Funny how they all gravitated to the comfort of the small and familiar. The Village, their pride and joy, was finished, but still it was the old kitchen with its chipped Formica table where everyone congregated.

Michael sensed the situation was coming to a head. He and John had waited until the new year to break the depressing news of their financial heart attack to the founders who hadn't yet moved to the canyon. After the initial dismay, everyone agreed to carry on as before. Surely among them all they could ante up the minimum needed to keep the sanctuary functioning until they figured out what to do next.

Michael knew what had to be done next. If Best Friends was to survive, the days of being a private endeavor—paying out of pocket, working out of their bedrooms, kitchens, and whatever— were over. Consciously they all knew it. Subconsciously they fought the shifts they recognized would change forever the sheltered informality of their daily routines.

John and Francis had gotten to the bunkhouse ahead of him. They sat around the comfort of the Formica table like two morose bears awakened prematurely from their winter's sleep. Neither spoke as Michael added boiling water to the pot that was always on the stove and poured himself a cup of tea with lots of sugar. A very civilized habit, he thought, the afternoon "cuppa," as they said in the old country. He pulled up a chair, ready to begin.

John Christopher Fripp didn't mince words. "It appears the Keating Five and the resultant savings and loan debacle is the reason our developer went belly-up. Worse, Arizona was the hardest hit in the real estate crash. Bottom line? Trying to sell the ranch now is a lost cause. People aren't touching land with a ten-foot pole."

"So forget being bailed out by another buyer," Francis translated.

"Has anyone considered that what's happened might be a blessing in disguise?" Michael ventured.

John's eyebrows knitted in concentration. "I wouldn't exactly call it a blessing, but I've got a hunch where you're going with this. We've been thinking along the same lines."

Francis's face hardened into that familiar intensity they knew so well. "Let's face it, the sanctuary's grown like Topsy. We've all been so busy taking in every needy creature that crossed our path, we haven't had time to plan. We've been running this operation like a private hobby. Talk about indulging ourselves."

"I wouldn't exactly call taking care of fifteen hundred animals an indulgence," John protested.

"I know what Francis is saying," Michael soothed. "Best Friends has already grown far bigger than we ever dreamed. And there's no way we can walk away from what we've built here. Besides, where would we go?"

John grimaced. "We hear you, Michael. We're all in this together, for better or for worse." He laughed without humor. "Sounds like a marriage. So, tell us your plan."

Michael sipped his tea, composing his words. A deep calm had taken over: a certainty that what he was about to propose was right. He spoke slowly, as the concept unfolded in all its surety. "Let's be clear on one point. Best Friends is not just for those of us living in Angel Canyon anymore. We've been entrusted with this incredibly beautiful place, and the only way we can protect it is to share it with the world. We need to create an organization—let others be part of what we're building."

A fleeting sadness crossed the faces of his friends. Francis sighed. "Board of directors. Job descriptions. Hierarchy. Fund-raising. Mailing lists." He sounded as if the end of the world was staring them in the face.

"For the animals," Michael said quietly.

"I'm just talking," Francis said.

Michael continued. "We can't scatter our energies anymore. All of those who originally committed to this dream need to come to Angel Canyon. We can't expect Maia, Charity, Anne, and the others to bleed themselves dry keeping us alive. We've all got to pull together and raise funds."

John's face registered the resignation they all felt. "We need to go to the cities."

Michael's was the face of a stoic. "Yes. We start over, sit in front of supermarkets, and tell our story."

"Tabling," Francis muttered.

Michael nodded. "But it's got to be done right. If somebody cares enough to give us a donation, we ask for a telephone number and address."

"So we can follow up with a thank-you call . . ." John was coming alive.

"Then a letter asking if they'd like to become a member of Best Friends." Francis, on the same page as Michael, smiled for the first time.

"And that is how we build an organization," Michael finished.

John, ever one to probe the problems they might face, played devil's advocate. "Why would anyone in, say, Los Angeles or San Francisco, want to support us?"

"We're already taking in animals from California. But you're right; maybe nobody will be interested. I don't know," Michael confessed. "It's worth a shot."

Silence.

"Okay," Francis said. "Enough talking. We know what we gotta do. Now who's going to tell Anne, Jana, and the rest of the gang they've got to shut up shop and come to Kanab?"

Michael sighed. "We can tell the Las Vegas contingent when they come up this weekend. I'm pretty sure they'll be with us. But I think I should go to Phoenix and Denver in person."

"I'll call everyone else," John offered.

"Well, now we're getting somewhere," Francis said. "At least we're not sitting around like a bunch of losers."

"I wish you wouldn't use that language," John sounded pained.

"Would a glass of wine be out of line?" Michael deadpanned.
Small smiles.

"I think we can afford half a glass each," John, the eternal treasurer, answered with his best poker face. "If only we had some."

Francis looked at Michael, who glanced at John's so-serious expression. The smiles were instantaneous, rolling from one to the other, until the relief of laughter echoed around the table.

"It isn't Sunday, is it?" Francis said. "Hell, let's go buy a bottle. Even we can afford the state of Utah's best red."

CHAPTER TWENTY-FOUR

All for One and One for All

Michael felt a familiar sense of *déjà vu* on seeing who, when faced with the actuality of leaving their own bailiwicks, would come to the beleaguered Angel Canyon. He likened the situation to people who have a second home: they love to visit, help support the place, but their primary focus is elsewhere.

Unlike seven years earlier, the commitment being asked for this time around was akin to jumping out of an airplane with a parachute that may not open. Best Friends could lose everything in the months to come. A massive balloon payment was due on the property next year. If they couldn't pay the bank, then everyone, and the animals, would be out on the street—literally.

And yet not one person in the canyon had elected to forsake the sanctuary. It was true Cyrus had gone back to Denver, but that was only to comfort his wife—Anne Mejia had been devastated at the turn of events. And Virgil had decamped to Arizona to caretake their white elephant of a ranch until further notice. The founders who still called the cities home, however, were a looming question mark. It remained to be seen which of them would truly be willing to join the first settlers in the rough times ahead.

John made the initial calls. As they suspected, there were a couple of people whose lives had taken them toward their own dreams, but John had good news when he tracked down Michael and Steven at The Village. "Silva Lorraine is with us," he announced, beaming. "I wasn't even halfway into my explanation before she interrupted. 'I came to the same conclusion, John,' she said. 'I'm already winding things down here. I'll be there in a few weeks.'"

"That's Silva," Steven said fondly. "Makes up her mind and just does it. That's how she came to Toronto, remember?"

Michael hadn't been in Canada when Steven, Anne, and Cyrus were there, but he knew the story. The slender, auburn-haired Englishwoman was an art major who had gotten a job as a gardener at Kensington Palace. Silva was a walking treasure trove of fascinating stories about Princess Margaret.

"Margaret had an abominable reputation with the English media," Silva told them. "But I found her very sweet, and she has a wicked sense of humor. I think she liked me because of the tortoises. She loved her pet tortoises; I don't think anybody knew that about her. She let them have the run of a whole acre behind the palace. Margaret insisted on letting the grass grow wild, but every time she went away the gardeners would manicure the place like it was Versailles.

"My special assignment was to protect the tortoises and make sure the grass wasn't mown. She said we had a secret conspiracy to foil the old men."

But working for royalty included being on call at all hours. Silva was thinking that this was no life for a twenty-year-old when a friend said she was going to Canada, and why didn't Silva come along? Two weeks later she was on a plane to Toronto.

"I used to tease Silva that she was the animals' Florence Nightingale," Steven remarked to Michael as they drove south the next day.

"You really like her?" Silva had been an infrequent visitor to the sanctuary, and Michael was still mulling the fact that she'd not hesitated when push came to shove.

"I've never heard her complain. Ever."

"That makes her very special," Michael agreed.

The two men broke their journey in Phoenix to see an old buddy of Steven's with whom he had been in the printing business.

"So, the grand experiment cleaned you out, huh?" the friend quipped as he showed them through his shop.

"It isn't exactly an experiment," Michael said mildly.

"Whatever. But you'd better think up a better way to get some dough than sitting in front of tables all day."

They had reached the very back of the building, an ill-lit room dusty with disuse. Steven's friend smiled as if at some private joke and marched over to the darkest corner. He whipped a dust-cloth aside to reveal a decrepit-looking piece of machinery. He grinned at Steven. "Remember this?"

"An AB Dick Three-sixty!" Steven exclaimed, running his hands over the ancient printing press. "We worked on one like this in Toronto."

"Back in the Dark Ages of the nineteen-sixties," his friend wise-cracked. "So, you want to do me a favor and haul this monster out of here? I warn you, the thing shakes, rattles, and rolls, and you'd better have a big supply of rubber bands to hold it together."

"You're kidding!" Steven said, thinking of the newsletter he and Michael had brainstormed on the way. "This would be a god-send."

"You might not say that when you fire it up. But if you talk nicely and genuflect every morning, it'll work well enough."

"We'll take it," Michael and Steven chorused in unison.

The two men were feeling pleased with themselves when, later that afternoon, they rang the doorbell of an Adobe-style house in the outlying suburb of Carefree.

A slight woman in a voluminous caftan flung open the door with all the drama of an Old Vic Repertory star making her grand entrance—which was nothing strange to her visitors. Charity Rennie had trained at London's Royal Theater and honed her skills as a BBC actress—a talent she never failed to employ at every opportunity.

"Are we Lady Macbeth or Queen Victoria today?" Michael inquired as she ushered them inside.

Charity's pout could have been the envy of any Hollywood diva. "*We* are not amused," she rebuked, as haughty as a dowager. "Actually, I'm in my Maggie Smith mode this afternoon," she informed him, gliding across the cool tile floor of the sun-splashed foyer and sliding open the glass doors to the living room.

The space was pure Charity. Out of an average white-walled subdivision house she had created a bright, color-filled, animal-friendly retreat to reflect her personality: throw rugs in hues of purple, saffron, and lime disguised the nondescript carpeting; long-fringed shawls streaked in rainbow blues, pinks, and oranges carelessly covered yesterday's divans and chairs; the tropical fragrance of vanilla lingered from last night's candles.

A dozen felines snoozed in wedges of sunlight that bored through uncurtained windows, and on a couch two more lay securely ensconced in Maia Astor's arms. A third woman, Sharon St. Joan, whom Michael had met in Paris where she was working as a librarian, sat with her legs curled under her on the sofa. He must remember to congratulate Sharon—she was gaining national recognition for her wildlife rehabilitation work in Arizona.

Michael and Steven made themselves comfortable as Charity poured iced tea for everyone. "Glad you're here, Sharon, and you Maia," Michael said.

An awkward pause settled among them as they sipped the mint-freshened cooler. Charity studied Michael's face. "So," she drawled in the silence, "what have the powers that be decided?"

Michael stretched his legs and steepled his long fingers. "First thing is, we're incorporating Best Friends under its own charter," he began.

He talked steadily for a half-hour. As she listened, Maia alternately stroked her cats and peeked in the numerology book she carried everywhere. Sharon fixed Michael with the unblinking stare of the owls she so loved. Charity was a picture of languid curiosity as she closed her eyes and rested wheat blond hair against the tasseled cushion behind her head. Michael finished and waited for the women's reactions.

"Let me see if I've got this right," Charity Rennie said with a smile that would disarm Attila the Hun. "You're suggesting we give up our comfortable abodes and our own rescue operations— which are going quite nicely, I might add—to live in a Spartan cell at The Village, in between sitting at a table outside a supermarket in some godforsaken, polluted city, asking people who, for the most part, don't want to be bothered, to support an endeavor they've never heard of, in a place of which they have only the vaguest notion, and let us not forget," Charity paused for breath, "all for which we don't get a brass nickel. Am I correct?"

"Spartan, yes," Michael said, thinking of the spare, clean rooms at The Village. "But then, Charity dear, you could make Alcatraz cozy, and you're absolutely correct on every point."

Charity sighed deeply. "Flattery will get you everywhere."

"August fifth is a very auspicious day to incorporate," Maia Astor interjected with mock seriousness. "You did say you thought John would do Best Friends' charter on August fifth, didn't you?"

"That's the date we're shooting for, why?"

Maia slid a thumb under a paragraph in her numerology book. "You add the numbers for August five, 1991, and they come out to five—a very good omen for this year."

Michael did the math in his head. "I make it six."

Maia frowned, then giggled. "Then you'll just have to incorporate a day earlier."

Sharon was thoughtful. "Would it be possible to have a bird sanctuary?"

"Would you come then?"

With the fluidity of a dancer, Charity rose out of her chair. She took center stage, wringing her hands with practiced remorse. "My dear, dear friends," she began with funereal solemnity, "I know you've traveled far. Still, I regret to tell you it was a wasted journey."

Michael closed his eyes, waiting for the verbal blow.

"Maia, Sharon, and I discussed the situation and decided that the idea of being heroines on a sinking ship was rather appealing."

Michael re-ran her last words. Slowly it dawned on him what the actress had said. "You mean . . . ?"

Charity lifted her chin and gazed out of the window. "It is a far, far better thing we do this day than we have ever done. . . ."

Steven snorted with laughter. Michael grinned. "You are too much, lady. By the way, you're mixing your characters."

"I am?" Charity murmured innocently.

"Shakespeare's Lady Macbeth wrings her hands; Dickens's Sidney Carton makes the speech from *A Tale of Two Cities*, and it's captains on a sinking ship."

Charity bestowed her famous Cheshire cat smile. "I rather prefer heroines myself. But you got the message? *We* didn't even *consider* bailing, Michael. Besides it's getting too damn hot down here. We'll hit Utah, with cats—ASAP."

"If you'd already made up your minds . . . ?" Michael asked.

"Why did we have you make the trip?" Charity pirouetted prettily. "Hadn't seen your nutty face for a while, silly. Why do you think?"

In a less dramatic fashion, Anne and Cyrus Mejia affirmed their commitment. "It's on the road again, I guess," was how Anne summed it up.

Steven and Michael had arrived at the red brick house in Denver, tired, yet heartened from their meetings in Phoenix. Michael was even more cheered when he saw Estelle Munro's sweet face. Michael always felt uplifted when he saw Estelle. She seemed to be surrounded by a pure light of goodness. He was not unaware that men, women, and children also seemed to recognize her clarity of spirit and responded in kind. For some reason Michael felt humbled before Estelle.

She eased awkwardly out of her armchair to greet him when he came into the room. "Don't get up, Estelle," Michael pleaded, closing the gap between them. A smile illuminated the angelic face as she sank back down and shifted her leg restraints into a more comfortable position.

Estelle had spent most of her youth in an iron lung since being stricken with polio at the age of two. How paradoxical that the young woman had the power to heal with her presence!

Michael hugged her close. "Are you with us?"

"I've been wanting to come to Angel Canyon for so long," she murmured. "But you needed people who were capable of hard, physical work. That wasn't me, Michael." She smiled. "But you're going to need someone to run an office, and that's what I'd like to do someday. Meanwhile I can table. I can tell our story. It will really make me feel part of everything."

"You've always been part of everything," Michael assured.

Over dinner, John Christopher's son, Matthias, couldn't stop talking about the secondhand IBM 386 computer he had gotten from a college mate. The dark-haired young man had the reasoned intelligence of his father, and the same piercing blue eyes that saw right through you.

Michael remembered John telling once how nine-year-old Matthias had scrambled up onto a stage in San Antonio and earnestly delivered a lecture on the future of technology. "And he's totally self-taught," John related in awe.

Michael and Steven listened to the student. Each knew what the other was thinking. Matthias Fripp would be absolutely invaluable in setting up a membership data base and organizing their records—and he was one of the family to boot. Steven nodded imperceptibly. Michael fired the first salvo. "Instead of spending a year in India, we could really use you at Best Friends."

Steven proffered the carrot of buddies the same age. "Judah Nasr and David Maloney are in the canyon helping with the animals."

"Cool," Matthias responded.

As simply as that the deal was done, and the next morning Michael and Steven were on their way back home.

One by one the wagons were closing the circle. Now all that was left was to make their forays into an indifferent world.

CHAPTER TWENTY-FIVE

Whatever It Takes

Summer's lazy heat brought the remaining faithful into the fold. Silva Lorraine was the last to make her way to the canyon, arriving on Independence Day in time for Nathania Gartman's Cajun beans and rice. Over dinner, the group filled her in on the new operation. A skeleton crew would stay at the sanctuary to take care of the animals. Everyone else would table for two or three weeks, return to the canyon for a few days' rest, then go out again.

Charity had taken it upon herself to call hotels in targeted areas. In a voice of milk and honey, she pled their case. "So if you have any rooms that are going vacant that you could donate for the animals, we would be oh so grateful."

The positive responses the actress received amazed everyone.

"We could never in a million years afford to stay in some of these places," Jana exclaimed in wonder as Charity rattled off the names of top hotels in a dozen cities.

"You've been keeping this incredible news to yourself?" Diana could hardly believe it.

Charity's Cheshire cat satisfaction was in full force as she basked in the glory of her triumphs. "I wanted to wait until we were all together," she said demurely. "I do so love a full house."

The smiles in the room almost matched her own.

Goldilocks, as always, had claimed pride of place next to Francis. Throughout the evening the golden-eyed dog fixated on the newcomer. Goldilocks stared from Francis to Silva, from Silva to Francis, getting increasingly agitated when neither understood her low whines. Finally the little terri-poo could stand it no longer. She bounded from the warmth of her person's thigh over to the new woman in town, snuffling her ankles, whimpering, until Silva, smiling, picked her up.

But Goldilocks wasn't satisfied. She squirmed out of Silva's arms and bounded back to Francis, then back to Silva, for all the world like a yo-yo on a string.

"Are we missing something here? Or do the rest of us have bad breath?" Charity inquired archly as the dog resisted all other efforts to pet her.

"She's making a nuisance of herself tonight," Francis said. "Ignore her, Silva."

"I wouldn't dream of it," Silva protested, nuzzling the soft, chubby body. "She's darling."

"She obviously reciprocates the feeling," Diana observed.

Francis looked from Goldilocks to the Englishwoman to whom his shadow had deserted. "Since that dog goes everywhere with me, maybe you and I should team up for L.A," he suggested to Silva.

It was near midnight before they had talked through all decisions and destinations. By week's end, the people of Best Friends would scatter to major metropolises west of the Rockies. Early mornings would find them ensconced in front of supermarkets or department stores. "Hello," they would smile at the shoppers. "Are you an animal lover?"

If a passerby showed interest they would offer a simple brochure Michael and Steven had put together showing the awesome beauty of the canyon, stories and pictures of animals at play—all the good news from the sanctuary.

Late evenings, the tired pilgrims would report back to John Christopher with the amount they might deposit the next day so he'd know what bills he could pay.

"It's important: get names, addresses, and telephone numbers," Michael reminded as everyone straggled to bed.

Charity Rennie clicked her heels and saluted smartly. "Yes, sir, Mr. Mountain, sir," she said as she marched out of the room.

CHAPTER TWENTY-SIX

Revelation

For the permanent staff of the sanctuary, sleep was a precious commodity. They dragged awake at dawn and fell into bed long after the moon had taken residence in the clear night sky.

Despite the long hours, as summer chilled to winter, Michael noted Faith was smiling again, happy to devote herself to the day's routines: prepare individual meals for 600 dogs; clean the areas of 600 hundred dogs; play, pet, walk, and talk to 600 dogs. Faith Maloney was taking back her life, reveling once more in being Big Mama to her beloved charges.

She still fretted over their constant scrambling to pay the bills. Like one of her dogs with a bone, she worried endlessly to Michael her fears for the animals if Best Friends didn't prevail. But this particular November morning, he detected a different tension in her voice. "I just heard from Frank Crowe," she announced as soon as he picked up the phone.

Michael couldn't make out right away whether Faith was elated or distraught. Frank Crowe was the animal control officer in charge of education for Salt Lake City. Faith and the officer had established a relationship after Best Friends had taken in a problem snapping turtle from Frank's petting zoo.

"Frank just got a call from Alpo," Faith elaborated.

"The dog food people?"

"Who else?" Faith laughed. "Michael, listen to this. There's sixty tons of dog food sitting in Salt Lake. It was en route to Japan from Alpo's distribution center in Nebraska but—Frank doesn't know why—the contract was canceled. Frank said Alpo needs to unload the whole shipment."

"Why don't they just resell here in the U.S.?"

"I asked the same question. You know what Frank told me? The Japanese allegedly love pink, so Alpo only manufactures *pink* dog food for that market."

"Did you say sixty tons?" Michael was still trying to get his mind around that much free food.

"Yes, and it's all in thirteen-ounce cans. Frank's given a lot away already, but there's still twenty-four tons left—about twenty thousand dollars' worth, he said."

Twenty thousand dollars' worth of pink dog food. What did American dogs care what the color was? What did Best Friends care? Twenty thousand dollars' worth of free food. Mixed with dry it would feed Dogtown for six months.

"There's one snag, Michael." Faith's euphoria faded. "We've got to get it in the next ten days."

"No problem, Faith. We can store it in the caves."

"You don't understand. We've got to pay the freight—two thousand dollars."

She didn't have to draw him a road map. The last time Michael spoke to John, they didn't have $200 to spare, never mind $2,000.

"Tell Frank we'll take it."

"Michael?"

"Tell him, *yes*, Faith."

Michael would say later that he didn't have time to think. The people who had asked to be put on their mailing list so far numbered exactly 420 stalwart souls. Yet when he hung up on Faith, Michael knew only one thing to do. He sat in front of his computer and let the words flow. . . .

Dear_____,

I just got a call from Faith over at Dogtown. The people at Alpo will donate 24 tons of food which will take care of our dogs for the next six months.

The only catch is that we've got to come up with $2,000 for

the shipping. Right now we don't have $2,000. But if only half of you can send just $10 we can load up the truck.

We could really use this free food right now, and it will really make the animals' Thanksgiving. It might make yours too!

Love from all of us,
Michael Mountain

Michael stared at the letter. What possessed him to write to people he had never met and ask for money? It was one thing to talk to someone face to face, quite another to solicit through the mail.

He was aware of a presence behind him and turned. Mommy the cat was in her usual place on top of the oven. It had been a natural name to give the feral black creature who had dropped six kittens under his trailer the year before.

Mommy, it appeared, had grown tired of fending for herself. She adopted Michael's stove as her permanent habitat and from that day forward was the silent chronicler of all his actions.

"What do you think?" Michael asked. "Is it okay?"

Copper eyes bored into his. Michael imagined he sensed a silent purr.

"I guess that's a yes, then?"

The letter went out that afternoon.

Exactly six days later the miracle happened—Faith always declared that "it was *so* a miracle." The mailbag for Best Friends was suddenly heavy with envelopes: brown envelopes, blue envelopes, creamy envelopes that wafted the sweet smell of money. Michael and Steven sat at The Village in stunned silence as they read each note.

Dear Best Friends: How nice you didn't tell me that all the animals would die a horrible death if I didn't send in my $10. Here's $25. I hope it helps.

Dear Best Friends: I remember telling Silva and Francis about the trouble I was having with my dog, Mac. They gave me better advice than my vet. Hope this $50 helps get that food.

Dear Best Friends: I told that nice woman, Anne, I'd like to visit this summer. I can only afford $5 right now, but God bless you for what you're doing. Could I help feed the dogs if I come?

Letter after letter along the same lines. It was a whole new experience for Michael and Steven. "We have the freight," Michael announced quietly as the afternoon shadows darkened the room.

"And a lot of goodwill," Steven observed.

"Especially that," Michael said and went to talk to Tomato.

The orange and white kitten had grown into a gregarious creature that shared dominant cat status in the TLC Club with portly Benton, he of the lame orchestra leg and one eye. Tomato immediately arched his back to be picked up when Michael entered the room.

"You all have a lot of guardian angels out there, little one," Michael said, making the cat comfortable in the crook of his arm. Tomato sneezed in Michael's face, lest he forget to whom he was talking, then proceeded to nuzzle his person's cheek in compensation.

Michael hardly noticed, so intent was he with sharing his thoughts. "I'm going to write each one of those beautiful people a personal letter and tell them not only did they help get our free food, but there's a little left in the kitty. What do you think?"

Tomato squealed his agreement.

Michael had to take a walk a week later when he opened the first letter in reply to his thank-you—it wouldn't do for anyone to see tears in his eyes.

Dear Best Friends: You are the first organization to whom I've donated that's ever sent me a thank-you without asking for more money at the same time. I am so glad you're getting the food for the dogs. Here's another $100. Make sure they never go hungry. P.S. Let me know what you're doing from time to time. You never know, I might be in your neck of the woods one day.

"The people out there are telling us what they want," Michael said to Steven over a lunch of brown rice and broccoli. "They like to be kept in touch, and more than anything to feel they're appreciated." He gazed through the window that afforded the view of their paradise. "We *will* survive, Steven. Then we'll show the world what a little kindness can do."

CHAPTER TWENTY-SEVEN

Tabling

The rain clouds that had threatened since noon finally delivered: a sudden mercurial deluge that within minutes turned the gutters of Los Angeles into rushing street rivers. It was only 4:00, much too early to pack up for the day; however, in the months he and Silva had made the city their territory, Francis had come to understand a lot about its citizens.

Los Angelenos had an almost fatalistic acceptance of the capricious fires, floods, mudslides, and earthquakes that nature visited upon them, but the slightest inconvenience would get them utterly bent out of shape—and rain was definitely not their favorite thing.

Francis watched them scurry to the sleek protection of Mercedes Benzes, Lexuses, and Jaguars in the Mrs. Gooch's parking lot. Other pretty people huddled inside the warmth of the upscale health food supermarket, waiting for a break in the downpour. Francis sat alone under an umbrella, watching the rain puddling around his table. There would be no more interest in anything animal today. He might as well go and pick up Silva.

It might be good for them to get an early night; Silva was nursing a miserable migraine, yet nothing he could say could dissuade her from going to Malibu. "It's the day before Thanksgiving, Francis," she said. "It could be our biggest so far."

He respected her common-sense assessment. But then Francis had come to admire a lot about the lady since he began working with her. Every morning at 7:00 A.M. he could count on finding

Silva in the lobby of the Holiday Inn ready to go, and she rarely quit before 7:00 P.M. He remembered how, that first month, they had laughed about how much the muscles in their cheeks ached from smiling all day.

Francis liked her caring and gentleness. From the very first week, people stopped to ask advice and help with their pets' problems. Silva always listened with patient empathy. Then, no matter what kind of day she had had, when they dragged back to the hotel, Silva would stand by his side at the public phones—it was far too expensive to dial from their rooms—returning calls left on their answering service, often until after 9:00 P.M.

Many a night, they didn't get to eat until 10:00. Sometimes they were just too tired to bother. When they did sit down, it didn't hurt that Silva was even more cost-conscious than himself. Francis remembered smiling the first time she suggested they never spend more than five dollars on a meal. They ate a lot of storefront Chinese. He smiled a lot around Silva, he had come to realize. And Goldilocks positively adored her.

Francis accelerated onto the Santa Monica Freeway, ignoring the angry blare of horns as he shot into the stream of rush-hour traffic. Making time along Pacific Coast Highway would be even more of a challenge than usual with the rain this afternoon. He hoped Silva would be ready to leave when he arrived. He would pick up some soup and insist she go right to her bed when they got to the hotel.

A watery sun struggled victoriously through a black shelf of clouds as Francis slid into a parking space at Hughes Market. He spotted Silva immediately. She had set up shop under the covered colonnade that fronted the giant food store. Goldilocks sat by her side, as adorable as only a slightly scruffy golden rug of a dog could be.

Francis strolled up behind them as a child pulled her mother toward the terri-poo. "Hello," he heard his teammate's cultured tones. "Do you like animals?"

The mother hesitated and averted her eyes while her daughter enfolded the stoic Goldilocks as if the dog were a stuffed teddy bear. "Are your pictures going to frighten my little girl?"

Smiling, Silva tendered a photo of Sparkles and Goatie trotting side by side in the meadow under Angels Landing. "We'd rather show you happiness than pain."

The child suddenly popped her head above the table and grabbed a picture of Ginger. "Mommy, can I have this one?"

"Now, dear," the mother chided. "You already have two dogs."

"I'll send you a letter from Ginger if you'd like, and that way it will be like you've adopted her."

The girl's mother studied the photo of the old mare and her goat friend. "I have horses," she said. "I know how much a bale of hay costs." She slipped a chic, miniature backpack with a discreet Prada insignia from her shoulders and rummaged inside. "This may help," she dropped a rolled note into Silva's donation jar

As if on cue, Goldilocks threw back her head. "Oww. Oww. Oww."

"She's saying, *thank you*," Silva beamed.

"She's saying she spotted me," Francis said, reaching her side as the mother and daughter pushed into the supermarket.

"Francis, what are you doing so early? Did you see? She left us a fifty-dollar bill! Oh, I've had such a good day! Wait till I tell you."

"Mine wasn't bad." Francis knelt to hug a frantic Goldilocks pawing his thigh for attention. "So let's call it quits. You were feeling rotten this morning, remember?"

"Not just yet. Do you see those two women to our right?"

Francis glanced down the colonnade. "There's quite a few."

"The beautiful one with the Latina woman."

Francis knew immediately to whom Silva was referring. An elegant woman, courtly in the European tradition, stood silhouetted by the light two columns away. "The blonde?"

"Yes, and the dark-haired woman is Ilma. She's from South America. She's stopped by the table, given a donation, and picked up our literature. Her friend's been with her at least two or three times, but she never comes over."

"I think she's gathered her courage," Francis said, standing back as the two women approached.

The graceful female silently surveyed the photographs on Silva's table. She raised her brown eyes to meet Silva's gray, and Francis had an uncanny sense of some kind of special communication passing between the two Europeans.

"You already know about Best Friends, don't you?" Silva asked.

The woman nodded. "Ilma gave me your material."

Francis detected an accent but couldn't quite place it.

"I have been hesitant to come over," the woman continued. "I am helpless for animals." Her shrug was more eloquent than words. "Ilma tells me you ask for names and telephones, but we haven't felt comfortable before." Again the slight lifting of her shoulders. Silva nodded understanding. "Ilma also informs me you have put out a bulletin to help adopt animals in Los Angeles. My name is Maria Petersen, if you need any assistance." She slipped a gold-lettered card into Silva's hand.

Petersen. Petersen. Francis repeated the name in his mind. One of his favorite movies, *Das Boot,* had been directed by Wolfgang Petersen, a German filmmaker. No, that would be too much of a coincidence, even in L.A.

"We will meet again," Maria Petersen said to Silva as she slid a check into the jar. "You have been here all day, have you not?" Maria turned to Francis. "You should take her home. She needs to rest."

"I just met a sister," Silva said, watching the sophisticated European walk away.

Francis was thoughtful. "I think she felt the same way. Now I'll get the car. You pack up. We've got a long drive to the canyon tomorrow. Come on, Goldilocks. You come with me."

Silva smiled. "Home. It will be nice to go home for a bit."

Outside a Whole Foods supermarket in Los Gatos, California, Anne Mejia watched a huge rig grind into the far end of the parking lot. A burly trucker with glowering eyes and legs like tree trunks climbed from his cab and strode toward the entrance of the store. *He looks like the price of gas just went up again.*

"Now there's a man with a heart," she called cheerily as the big man approached her table.

The trucker scowled. "I ain't got no heart, lady, so lay off."

Anne Mejia jumped up and impulsively put her small hand on his chest. "Oh, of course, you do. I can feel it." A curious knot of shoppers paused to watch the action. "He does too have a heart," she informed everybody.

Spontaneous smiles passed around the group. Someone started

clapping, and the rest of the crowd joined in. The trucker couldn't make up his mind whether to be embarrassed or angry. Good nature won out. He shook his head and pointed at Anne's display. "You have no idea how much I miss my dog," he shared with the men and women who had surrounded him. "It gets real lonely on the road."

His explanation was met with clucks of sympathy.

"You should bring your pet with you," a woman advised.

"Do you carry a picture?" another asked.

The trucker immediately pulled a wallet from his jacket and proudly showed a dog-eared photograph of a happily panting retriever with a bandana around its neck. Then he extracted a ten-dollar bill and handed it to Anne. "You're all right," he said and strolled on into the health food supermarket chuckling.

Others in the crowd followed suit. "Thank you. Thank you so much from the animals. Have a happy Thanksgiving. Thank you." Anne Mejia beamed as each bill was pushed into her donation can.

What nice people, she thought, as she seated herself behind her table once again.

Maia Astor wasn't having the same good day. She had conceived the idea of putting donation cans inside supermarkets, her first attempts being at the giant Smith's grocery chain with its forty stores in the greater Los Angeles area.

She had navigated the maze of paperwork and permissions needed for her operation through Smith's Anaheim office, and everything was going rather nicely, she thought. Maybe it was the adorable picture of the puppy that adorned the can. She didn't really know. All Maia saw was that people responded. Sometimes she collected $500 in a week.

Maia didn't know Los Angeles. Downtown, Watts, South Central were just neighborhoods to her. She would admit they looked a little more rundown than West Hollywood, and the people not as benevolent. But management had assured her she could place cans in every twenty-four-hour store in every neighborhood—and she did.

It was 1:30 A.M. when she stopped for gas after the last pickup in South Central. She stuck the nozzle of regular into the tank and leaned against the pump, trying to figure how much she might have collected by the weight of the cans. Maia was aware of shouting in the convenience mart behind her, but she was keeping too close an eye on the scrolling dollars to pay much attention.

She shut off the gas nine cents shy of her ten-dollar limit. Carefully, she extracted the correct bill from her purse and trudged wearily into the brightly lit market.

"You ain't getting no cigarettes unless I see the color of money." The bull-necked white man behind the counter defied the T-shirted African-American wrestler. At least he looked like a wrestler to Maia with his bulging biceps and shaved head.

The black man reached over and with one huge hand grabbed his antagonist around his thick throat. "You don't mess with me, m . . ."

Maia shut her ears to the profanity.

The men didn't seem to notice her. They snarled obscenities in each other's faces while Maia shrank back against the candy display. She thought of surreptitiously easing out of the store the same way she had come in—quietly. Somehow that didn't seem right. She had to pay for what she had taken. "Excuse me."

It was as if she were a ghost. The giant black man briefly raked her with stony eyes and turned back to his sullen adversary.

But it wasn't all going his way. In that split second the night manager reached under the counter, grabbed a rifle, and stuck it in his opponent's gut. The wrestler slowly released his grip.

"Not so bold now, are we?" The shotgun muzzle moved slowly over the muscled chest. Now it was the black man's turn to feel uneasy.

Maia thought the situation was getting quite out of hand. She coughed and stepped forward. "Nine ninety-one of regular," she murmured, pushing Alexander Hamilton's likeness toward the manager.

The two men froze. Maia didn't think it polite to repeat herself, but she really had no choice. "Ten dollars of regular at pump three, with nine cents change," she apologized.

The wrestler leaned cautiously away from the gun barrel, backed up three steps, turned, and ran out of the store. The night manager stared at Maia in disbelief. "Nine cents change, thank you," she repeated shyly.

Francis was beside himself when Maia told the story over Thanksgiving dinner. Only that past September the young woman had been tabling outside a K-Mart in Yuma, Arizona.

As fate would have it that sweltering 105-degree afternoon, a robbery was in progress inside the store. Outside, an uncomfortable Maia, with only five dollars to show for the day, figured it was a lost cause, dismantled her table, and returned to her car.

She turned the ignition. Nothing. She pumped the gas pedal. *Nada.* Maia sat sweating in the suffocating heat. Suddenly a skinny Hispanic kid sprinted across the parking lot toward the old jalopy parked in the adjoining space. Maia leaped out of her car. "Can you give me a jump start?" she asked in all innocence.

The teenager glanced back at K-Mart, but no one was following. "Okay, let's do it quick then."

Five Arizona Highway Patrol cars screamed across the tarmac as a grateful Maia waved good-bye to the hapless robber. "Muchas gracias, amigo."

"That's it," Francis declared. "I don't care how much we need the money. You're not tabling anymore, Maia. I think something's trying to tell you to stay here and help Judah with the cats."

"I'd like that," Maia said.

Everyone else, however, was reporting some success. Anne Mejia and Jana de Peyer, with the help of Rocky Raccoon the puppet, seemed destined to be stars. They regularly phoned in $300 a day to their ecstatic treasurer. Yes, tabling was hard, grueling work, but the bills were getting paid.

Still John repeated the mantra as if counting worry beads. "It's not enough. It's not enough."

CHAPTER TWENTY-EIGHT

Another Straw on the Camel's Back

The January blues dragged into February, with the monies from tabling falling off along with shoppers' Christmas generosity. John Christopher Fripp looked more grim every day at lunch at The Village. Lunch had become their daily time for discussion, and the communal ritual seemed to lift their collective spirits somewhat—except for John's. There was no sparkle in the sailor blue eyes these days. In spite of the fact that their situation was improving, the treasurer knew only too well by how thin a margin they held on. Even Faith couldn't cheer away his worry lines.

"I got another twenty-five-dollar check from Dolores and Homer Harris," she announced brightly. John slurped his last spoonful of soup without comment. "As soon as it gets warmer, Homer said he's coming to visit. He says the San Diego sunshine's spoiled his bones for anything less than seventy degrees. I can't wait to meet him. I wonder why Dolores isn't coming."

With all their troubles, Best Friends still responded to an animal in need. The year before, Diana had taken a cat from a local man, Jim Travers, who had found it in a ditch. A month later Faith received a check for twenty-five dollars from Dolores Harris with a brief note. "Use this for the animals."

Faith had no idea who Dolores Harris was. It was only later she discovered that Jim Travers and Dolores and Homer Harris were old friends. All Faith knew when she received the check was that she had never, ever gotten money in the mail from anyone before. She wrote an exuberant two pages back to the surprise benefactor.

Dolores took to mailing a donation from time to time, and the two women struck up a long-distance friendship.

"That's wonderful, Faith," John said. "I'm afraid I'm thinking about my meeting with Zions Bank next month. If they won't renegotiate our balloon nothing will help."

A sudden pall fell around the table. For the most part, they tried not to think about the $400,000 payment that was due on the canyon in less than six months. Their foundation's treasurer lived with the sword over his head every waking hour.

"Well, I had an idea," Jana said brightly. "I'm putting together a photo album of our unadoptables, you know, like Timmie, Tomato, and Maddie, and taking it tabling with me. We've all had people saying they wished they could have an animal, but they live in an apartment or something; maybe they could be a surrogate owner, like a sort of guardian angel."

Her suggestion was greeted with all the enthusiasm of an execution.

"Thanks, guys, I thought it might generate some extra money."

"Ssshh, I'm thinking," Charity announced, as if a brilliant revelation were about to unfold. "You know," she said thoughtfully, "I've got members who'd love something like that."

"I need to check with Dr. Christy what his vet bill might be. He's coming today, isn't he?"

"He should have been here already," Faith frowned.

"Anyway, if—" Jana paused as the familiar flap of rubber overboots signalled the arrival of the veterinarian. Everyone's smiles of greeting faded at his appearance. His eyes were red-veined and puffy, his skin the color of parchment. Bill Christy collapsed exhausted into the nearest chair.

"You don't look too well," Charity said, getting up from the table. "A nice bowl of hot soup will do you good."

"I'm sorry I'm late." The vet's voice was scratched and labored. "I've got laryngitis. I don't think I can swallow." He shook his head at the steaming broth Charity placed before him.

"You shouldn't be out," Faith exclaimed coming to his side.

"I promised Judah I'd test some cats for feline leukemia," Dr. Christy rasped.

"That can wait. They're perfectly safe in quarantine. I'm sending you home right now," Mama Faith ordered.

Bill Christy sighed. "I have appointments through tonight."

Faith cupped his elbow. "You don't need to be out in this cold. You need to get to bed."

The veterinarian didn't resist as she walked him out of the meeting room. "Maybe I will," he said. "I will."

Faith was exhausted herself by day's end and had gone to bed early. The call came around 9:00 P.M., and for a moment a sleep-dazed Faith imagined that she was back in animal control.

"Faith, there's been an awful accident. I picked it up on the police band. They had to do the Jaws of Life on the car. They think it's Dr. Christy. I thought you should know."

Faith was awake now. She knew it was common practice among the locals to monitor the emergency police band on the radio. She didn't recognize the woman caller's voice but her response was instinctive. "It couldn't be Bill Christy," she heard herself say. "We sent him home at lunchtime. He wasn't feeling well. It couldn't be him."

The bearer of bad news blabbered on. "He fell asleep at the wheel and wandered into the other lane. Did you know he was only thirty-nine? And everyone's so fond of him around here."

The words sounded unnaturally shrill in Faith's ear. "It wasn't Dr. Christy," she repeated and wondered whom she was trying to reassure. "We sent him home. He promised to go home."

"I hope you're right. I thought you should know, seeing how close you all are."

Faith sat spine-straight in bed and wrapped her arms around herself. "He went home. He went home," she repeated silently and wished for the dawn.

The police came next morning, arriving a few minutes before Francis and Silva drove in from Los Angeles. John quickly took Francis aside. In a wooden voice he said, "Dr. Christy's dead. He got broadsided by a van last night."

Shock, disbelief, denial—all had their turn on the face of the man who had been closer to the veterinarian than any of them. John didn't know how to react to the tears that squeezed from Francis's eyes. No matter how bad a situation, even with the animals he loved so dearly, no one had ever seen Francis cry. "I'm so sorry," was all John could manage.

"Do you remember how he used to fall asleep on the kitchen table—?" Francis couldn't finish. Silva, nonplussed, came to his side. Francis shook his head and continued his way into the winter stillness of the mesa.

"Leave him be right now, Silva. Leave him be," John counseled and went to talk to the police.

CHAPTER TWENTY-NINE

San Diego Angel

For the community in the canyon, the death of their beloved Dr. Christy was an even heavier blow than their financial heart attack of the year before. Being broke meant that they existed hand to mouth. But they were no strangers to empty pockets. Money was not at all their driving force.

But never again to hear the flap of galoshes preceded by the pungent fragrance of manure as the veterinarian clumped into the clinic. Never again to smile at the Charlie Chaplin charade of jack-in-the-box drawers. Never again to see that boyish, smiling face or hear that cheery "good morning." This was a loss with which they found it hard to come to grips. In this atmosphere of mourning no news was good news.

Best Friends appreciated Michael's insistence that they couldn't rely on tabling forever, and that they needed to do something more to keep in touch with the people who were responding to Best Friends.

For responding they were. Every night the men and women on the front lines of tabling would fax in names and information for Estelle and Matthias to feed into the data base. Daybreak would find a dedicated crew at the sanctuary, scrambling to compose a letter of appreciation to each donor to get in the mail before Kanab's 3:00 P.M. postal deadline. A personal call of thanks followed the next week. The resultant number of people asking to be put on Best Friends' mailing list was growing rapidly.

The response to the letters, the phone calls, and the Alpo appeal confirmed Michael's belief that people wanted to feel a part of the community of Best Friends, to know that there were others who felt as they did about animals. Their own magazine would be a way to connect with everybody and spread the good news about animals and the environment.

Right now his colleagues' enthusiasm for the twenty-four pages of stories, Steven's cartoons, and photos from their animal Camelot was muted by grief. Even John's news that Zions First National Bank would extend their loan barely raised their spirits.

And still there were the animals, the mortgage, electricity, gas, phone, food, and water—all the necessities of living that everyone faces when they get up in the morning. When you got right down to it, the Best Friends were no different from anybody else. Life went on; the months flew by, but Dr. Christy was always in their hearts.

As promised, Homer Harris came to Angel Canyon in the summer of 1992. He was a big man. At six feet five, with iron gray hair cut close to the scalp military-style, and a face scored by many years in the world of business or riding the range—John suspected a bit of both—he was an imposing gentleman. "Norm Cram said I'd find somebody here," he announced, striding into the treasurer's cramped office with a chap John knew in town.

"Hi, Jim," John greeted.

Jim Travers acknowledged the welcome with a quick bob of his head. "I was going to take Homer straight to Dogtown, but he wanted to see where the business was done." The local man, slight and wiry, looked to be about half the height and width of his friend, but John knew that Jim Travers had been a distinguished race car driver, winning the Indy 500 twice in his career. Homer was an avid racing car enthusiast, and the two men had been good buddies for years.

The man from California wasted no words. "My wife sends your Faith money now and then, and I've a mind to see where it goes."

John looked into the direct eyes of the man towering above him. *Shall I tell the gentleman that if the bank hadn't renegotiated our mortgage, there'd be nothing to see? Shall I ask him not to think too badly that there are fences demanding repair and everything needs a paint job, but we're pretty strapped at the moment? No, I think the man wants to meet Faith so he can tell his wife he was here.* "Why don't I show you around myself. There's quite a bit to see, and Faith's expecting you," John said, leading the way outside.

Homer Harris took in everything. "I notice you got goats to keep the horses company." He asked questions John didn't expect. "Are those wolf-shepherd hybrids?" referring to the long-legged, massive-bodied animals in an enclosure chummed up to the wildcat compound. "Not right of someone to crossbreed like that," Homer commented. Later, as the truck gratefully left the rutted tracks of the canyon and bumped onto the macadam road to Dogtown, he said, "Quite some space you've got here. Plenty of water I hope?"

"We've put in eight thousand gallons altogether."

"Looks like you could do with more. Lots more."

"We're working on it," John assured.

Homer frowned. "Hmmm."

Paul was kneeling on a two-by-four surrounded by a passel of curious mongrels when Jim Travers parked outside the clinic. John wasn't surprised to see a rack of boards stacked neatly beside a pile of used nails, but Homer was obviously puzzled by Paul's undertaking. He swung out of the truck and watched as the architect hooked the claw of a hammer under a bent nail, yanked it free, and tossed it on the heap.

"Someone forget to make a run to the hardware?" Homer asked.

Paul stood and wiped his hands on his jeans. He didn't know this man, and Paul wasn't about to tell a stranger they reused nails to save money. He smiled politely. "Something like that."

"Hmmm," Homer said again.

Faith came running out of Octagon Three when she heard the masculine voices. "Nice to see you, Jim," she exclaimed before turning her full attention to his companion. "You must be Homer Harris." Faith extended a wet hand and grinned up at the big man. "Sorry," she apologized as Homer slid a meaty paw around hers. "I'm fixing the dogs' dinners, but it can wait a bit."

Homer Harris said "hmmm" a lot as he toured Dogtown's dusty lanes. "Hmm," as he shook hands with Tyson and noted the pack of aggressive-looking mutts at his heels. "Hmm," when the dogs waited patiently for the Alpha Man before passing by an ancient Australian shepherd half asleep in the middle of a lane.

"He's the Dogfather," Faith said and told Victor's story.

"Hmm," at the mound of worn tennis balls jealously guarded by three feisty Chesapeakes under a juniper tree. Homer, however, said more than "hmm" when he bent to pet Ginger and found himself face-first in the dirt. "What the—?"

"Jesus Christ!" exclaimed Jim Travers, staring at the huge red malamute fanning his tail behind his buddy.

"That's our Sheriff," Faith said. She bestowed a dazzling smile and a hand up to Homer Harris. "I should have warned you about Amra. Are you alright?"

"I'm fine. I'm fine. Didn't expect it, that's all." To Faith's relief the big man's bemused grin matched her own. "Well, I'll tell Dolores the pictures in your magazine are for real. You don't keep the animals in a bunch of cages."

"Is that why she wouldn't come?" Faith asked.

Homer nodded. "She's got a soft heart, my wife. Can't bear to see the poor animals shut up like they are most places."

"She won't find that here!"

David Maloney's pickup belched behind them and they stepped aside to let him pass. Faith's son cruised down the lane, stopped his truck, left the engine running, grabbed a six-gallon plastic can from the bed, and staggered with it to the nearest enclosure. Ten excited dogs rushed the fence, a cloud of red dust billowing in their wake.

Homer Harris again watched, fascinated, as a sunburned David balanced the heavy water can against a fence with one knee while his free hand slipped the latch on the gate. "That takes some doing," he said in admiration as the young man pushed into a tumult of frantic caninity; managing somehow to keep all the escape artists where they belonged.

The big man smiled at the dogs' loud slurps of appreciation as David emptied the large buckets and refilled them with fresh water. He shook his head as a perspiring David repeated the oper-

ation in two more enclosures before moving the truck along.
"That boy makes me exhausted watching. How often does he do
that?"

"Twice a day," Faith said. "The water collects green algae in the
summer if we don't change it. In winter it freezes over, so we
break it up with a screwdriver."

"This is your water system?" Homer demanded.

"For the time being," John said.

Homer met Jim Travers's studied glance. "Hmmm."

Faith wasn't expecting to see Homer Harris again in the near
future. He had made it quite clear that he had only stopped by in
order to give a report to his wife, Dolores. And yet two weeks
later, when Faith walked out of her trailer, there he was with Jim
Travers, discussing their ancient trencher that hadn't run in two
years.

"Do you think we can fix this darn thing?" Faith heard Homer
ask as she walked up behind the two men.

Jim Travers regarded the green wreck of a machine dubiously.
"We might be able to do something with it."

"Good morning. What a nice surprise, Homer."

Homer Harris got right to the point. "There's plastic pipe being
delivered this afternoon, and we need a machine to dig the ditches."

Faith didn't understand.

"Dolores was upset when I told her how you watered your
mutts." The big man hefted a nonexistent belly. "You've got better
things to do than haul water to six hundred dogs. Most inefficient.
We're putting you in a water system." Homer turned to his smaller
pal. "What do you think, Jim?"

Jim Travers frowned, looking at the rusting trencher. "I think
we need to rent a ditcher, Homer. Take a week to get parts for this
thing."

"Let's do it. Excuse us, young lady. We've got work to do."

Faith thought of all the years Best Friends had broken their
backs worrying water to the dogs. Now this angel from San Diego
was laying pipe, putting faucets at the enclosures. She gazed into
the stern, no-nonsense face above her. A simple thank you wasn't
adequate, somehow. "We all get together for lunch around twelve,"
she blurted out.

Homer nodded. "Save us a plate. Tell John I need to speak with him, too." He turned his attention back to the trencher.

Faith regained her equilibrium. "Thank you. You don't know how much."

"Don't worry about it," Homer replied absently.

CHAPTER THIRTY

Illegal in July

Late in the afternoon, as was his habit, Michael walked his dogs. The summer heat induced a pleasant perspiration as he chaperoned Sun and the latest addition to the family, That Naughty Girl, she of the Heinz 57 variety.

He was thinking about how much he liked brainstorming with Tomato. Somehow the little cat enabled him to clear his head, to put things into perspective. Tomato was also taking on a most demanding personality, to the point of insisting that he have his own column. He had even chosen his title: investigative reporter. That way he could reveal to Best Friends members what *truly* went on at the sanctuary. Michael crossed the county road onto the sandy track to The Village. It was quite a trip having the saucy, cynical pussycat as his stand-in.

His thought process was disturbed by the accelerating roar of a six-cylinder engine. He stepped aside quickly as a smart new Jeep flew past, trailing a cloud of red dust in its wake. *Did they have to drive quite so furiously?* Suddenly the off-roader reversed and jammed back to his side. Two young, anxious faces craned toward him from the driver's window. "We were told there's a place that takes care of cats around here?" The boy's German accent rushed the question.

"Anything wrong?" was Michael's instinctive reaction.

It was the girl—tanned, fair-haired, blue-eyed—who answered. "We find a mother and kittens near the Grand Canyon."

Michael didn't let her finish. He knew it had to be bad. He scanned the vehicle's interior. An unmoving calico mass huddled inside a man's shirt laid on the backseat. "Excuse me," he said and yanked open the rear door. Gently he slipped long fingers under the shirt and lifted the matted, furry bundle over the front seat. "Hold them. It's not far. I'll direct you," he said, urging his dogs ahead of him into the backseat.

The girl look startled for an instant, then muttered something to her companion. The German boy nodded and the car bucked forward toward Catland.

Michael knew Diana was tabling in Arizona, but Judah should be on duty. *Let Judah be at cats*, Michael prayed. His glimpse of the feline family had confirmed his fears. Mother and babies were dreadfully dehydrated, and who knew what else. *Please let Judah be at Catland*. "Take the right fork," he instructed urgently.

Sure enough, Judah Nasr was at the TLC Club. Francis's son didn't say much as the trio trooped in. He had only to read Michael's face to know he had an emergency on his hands. Wordlessly, he led the way to the back quarantine room. The girl followed, cradling the felines to her breast.

Judah had been taught well by his father and Dr. Christy. With the efficiency of one for whom a veterinarian on call was no longer a privilege, Judah Nasr hooked up fluiding bags, filled a syringe, and eased the needles into the three inert bodies.

"What about the other kitten?" the girl asked. "Why do you not help him?"

"He's dead," Judah answered as gently as he could.

The girl hid her head in her boyfriend's shoulder.

Michael saw that Judah could manage without them. "You've done a wonderful deed," he said with feeling to the young couple. "We'll take it from here. Is there anywhere we can reach you, to tell you how they're doing?"

The boy answered. "Eva and I, we'd like to stay around."

Michael looked at the two drawn faces. They were so young, couldn't be more than twenty. If this was the future generation, there was hope after all. "Would you like to see our place? Perhaps a cup of tea at The Village?"

The two tourists gazed in wonder at everything Michael showed them. "It is a paradise," the girl Michael now knew as Eva said. She turned questioning eyes to him. "But what are you doing with all these cats and dogs?"

"Most of them are ugly, rambunctious, three-legged, or special-needs in some way. Nobody wants them. They'd be put down, you know, killed in a shelter. So we take in as many as we can."

Michael wasn't prepared for the immediate reaction. Two mouths dropped open as if he had told them the earth was flat. The couple conversed rapidly in German. "You don't mean . . . ?" the girl seemed unsure of how to phrase her concern. "They kill homeless animals in America?"

Michael nodded.

The boy was most solemn. "In our country, it is illegal to kill animals that don't have a home."

It was Michael's turn to stare. "Illegal in Germany?"

The boy seemed in shock. "Nobody would dream of doing anything like that in our country."

For Michael, it was a long walk back to his trailer that afternoon. Sun and That Naughty Girl, sensing their person's mood, trotted, subdued, by his side. Michael kept asking himself the same questions. *We are a civilized nation. The greatest peacekeeper the world has ever seen. And yet we treat our unwanted animals no better than disposable tissue. Why?*

Once again he pondered the apparent accidents in life after which nothing was ever the same. What were the chances of two German tourists hiking the wilderness of southwest Utah hearing the mew of a dying cat? What were the long odds that the car they stopped to ask directions to the nearest veterinarian would send them to Best Friends? And what even greater happenstance had brought them together with Michael?

For as surely as the early evening light caught the canyon in magic time, Michael knew that these two people changed the way he saw the problem of homeless animals forever. The concept of simply housing and finding homes for the unwanted wasn't enough. One day there must be no more homeless pets. For this, nothing less than a sea change in the way most people related to animals was needed. And that would require a radically different approach.

As he wended his way home, Michael felt a growing excitement. He knew this was a new beginning. He had started on a journey that would take him through the rest of his life.

CHAPTER THIRTY-ONE

Mollie

Best Friends had much to be thankful for as the holidays approached. For one thing, they were still standing. For another, the special Christmas newsletter they had sent out was proving a huge success and generating a bonanza of donations.

Then again, the number of their supporters was growing bigger every month, which meant that many more copies of the magazine needed to be printed and mailed. The count had grown to the point where Michael and Steven began to hold "label parties" to handle the mailing: Whoever was in the canyon when that month's issue was ready to send was shanghaied to The Village to stick on address labels.

The gatherings gained in raucous inventiveness as membership increased. In the sedate beginning they had Coca-Colas to help them along. Soon the general consensus was that things did not only go better with Coke. Beer, potato chips, nuts, and pretzels, coupled with rowdy cheers as they ploughed through each state's mailing, became the new order of the night.

Michael likened the atmosphere to that of a bingo parlor with people shouting out zip codes as if they were winning numbers. He also noted that subscriptions were coming from all over the country, with heavier concentration from New York, Florida, and the Northwest—which surprised him somewhat. But then that was how Mollie, the pot-bellied pig, came to Best Friends.

* * *

"She's not really a pig. I mean Mollie's more like one of the family. She watches television with my wife and me, and sleeps on the bed." The voice sounded young and very distraught.

"I understand perfectly," Estelle Munro commiserated.

"One of my parishioners gets your magazine. That's why I called."

"Parishioners?" Estelle queried.

A nervous laugh. "I'm an assistant pastor in Pocatello, Idaho."

"Why don't you tell me about Mollie?" Estelle encouraged and settled in to listen.

The story the pastor told was of the transition of a farming community to a spreading township, and of the disruptions that inevitably follow. Mollie was the couple's dearly loved companion. She was house trained, "as clean as a whistle." Mollie came when called, never left their sides, was never any trouble.

But as always, growth forced change. The new ordinances decreed no farm animals within the town's limits. Mollie had to go. "It would kill us if we thought she'd end up as . . ." The pastor couldn't voice the horrible idea of Mollie being bacon. "We can tell you're good people. We'd have some peace if Mollie was with you."

To Estelle had fallen the job of deciding which critters Best Friends would continue to take in. If an animal was healthy, young, and eminently adoptable, Estelle would gently direct the caller to a local adoption organization.

If, on the other hand, the animal was old, infirm, had special needs, or held little chance of living out its life in safety and comfort, then Estelle would likely welcome the innocent into their fold. Still, nobody had tried to give them a pig before. But it was the week before Christmas, and it was Estelle, not Good King Wenceslaus, who looked out onto the pristine whiteness of their wonderland and gave silent thanks. "It's a long drive," she cautioned the boyish-sounding minister.

The joy that flowed through the telephone wires made it all worthwhile. "We'll leave tomorrow. God bless you. God bless you."

None of the Best Friends made any salary yet, so it was a little hard to go on a shopping spree. And yet nobody felt deprived. A big old stove crackled and filled The Village with the nostalgic fragrance of burning sage and piñon. The Christmas tree sparkled with homemade ornaments. Heaped under its greenery were who-knew-what inventive goodies. And everyone was coming home for the holidays.

Michael and Faith, hanging the last of the decorations this late afternoon, thought it was one of their own when they heard a car stop outside the meeting room. They didn't pay any attention as the front door pushed open. "Hello?" a tentative voice called. "Have we got the right place?"

Their visitor had the gangling skinniness of youth. His eyes were solemn behind their wire-framed glasses, the sandy brown hair primly short. Although casual in jeans and parka, the man had a definite . . . Faith searched for the word . . . pious look. From what Estelle had reported this could only be one person. "You've brought Mollie?" she said smiling.

The tension drained from the pastor's face. He almost managed a smile, but worry won out. "She's outside with my wife," he said and ducked back into the cold.

A small, pale girl with straight bobbed hair stepped hesitantly into the room, led by a black potbellied pig on a silver-blue leash. Her husband struggled in behind them with a carved wooden bed that appeared custom-made.

"Do you need any help?" Michael offered. The pastor shook his head and placed the bed next to the pig and left once more.

Michael stared at the sleek, confident swine, who gave him the eye in return. Mollie had to be the cutest potbelly he had ever laid eyes on. Then Michael reminded himself he had never met an animal he didn't like. Still, Mollie had to be the epitome of adorable. Michael knew that pigs were among the most intelligent creatures on earth, but wondered how many more city ordinances would be changed before the current craze petered out.

The pastor returned with a soft, brown blanket and a wicker basket. Twice more he whisked outside to bring in shopping bags of toys and treats. His wife stroked the pig's rump continuously, the hurt plain on her face.

Finally, all Mollie's possessions lay beside the door. "You have a nice, clean place here," the girl ventured, "but excuse us, we'd like to know where Mollie might be living. She's used to being inside with us, you see."

"I'll show you the sanctuary, if you like," Faith said.

The pastor flushed scarlet. "We already took a drive around. I hope you don't mind."

Mollie had stood like a statue during the whole proceeding. Now she raised her head and Michael saw the soft, pink nostrils twitch. The little potbelly backed against her mistress's ankle and oinked once. The girl dropped the silver-blue leash and bent to her pet. "What is it, sweetheart?"

Big mistake. Michael had recognized Mollie's expression. Sun was the master at flaring his nostrils before the plunge for whatever food was in the vicinity. "Wait a minute. . . ."

Too late. Mollie plummeted forward with the velocity of a bullet, straight for the Christmas tree—and the presents. With unerring accuracy, the pig snuffled out a square box wrapped in shiny gold paper. Before they could stop her, Mollie had ripped open the gift and pushed her snout into the See's Candies.

"No! They'll make her sick," Faith yelled as she and Michael dove for the recalcitrant animal. Still Mollie managed to gobble two chocolates before they could wrestle the box away.

An ember caught in the fire and a log spat blue-green flames into the shocked silence. The wife sniffled, "Oh Mollie, how could you?"

Faith read the card on the lost present. "For me." She smiled. "Thank you, Mollie. I shouldn't eat chocolates anyway."

Michael had to laugh. With no more interest in anything else the tree might offer, Mollie ambled back to her persons and looked up at them like a naughty child.

"She's usually so well behaved," the pastor apologized.

Faith knelt and gently caressed Mollie's ears. Michael knew what she was thinking. What do we do with this "pig who is a person?" Faith spoke softly. "It's not like your home, but my place is warm and the doggy door's big enough. What do you think?"

Mollie looked from her persons to the woman who was whispering so sweetly in her ear. "It's all right, Mollie." The wife couldn't hold back her tears any longer. The pastor slowly lifted his foot and surreptitiously nudged his pet's backside forward. Mollie knew what was expected. She hesitated only fractionally, then trotted straight into Faith's arms.

Which was exactly where the newspaper reporter from Salt Lake City saw her three months later.

CHAPTER THIRTY-TWO

First Validation

Chris Smith wasn't in the best of moods. It wasn't enough that the story he had been pursuing had evaporated along with his source; he'd hardly gotten two winks of sleep in the rundown 1950s-era motel he had checked into across the Arizona state line.

The roving reporter for the *Salt Lake Tribune* was no stranger to lumpy beds salvaged from the Second World War—it was the loud lovemaking coming through the wafer-thin walls that had him looking at his watch at 3:00 A.M. It wasn't until he heard the thud of two pairs of knees hitting the carpet, followed by fervent prayers for forgiveness, that he wondered what deity he had offended this time. Still, he couldn't help smiling when he saw the prim, gray-haired couple emerge from the adjoining room the next morning.

On his way back to Salt Lake, Smith stopped to fill his tank in Fredonia. Sure enough, there they were again, the cute donation cans for Best Friends Animal Sanctuary. He had been noticing them for over a year now, every time he stopped for gas. The professional journalist in him appreciated the picture of the puppy wrapped around a kitten. Pretty smart idea. Somebody knew how to take a damn good photo.

Maybe it wasn't a wasted trip south. Animals were always good for a story on A1 or B1 of the paper, and there had to be an angle here. Who would put an animal sanctuary in the middle of nowhere—even if it was awesome country?

Chris Smith's first foray took him into Kanab. It was always a sound idea to hear what the local folks had to confide. He wasn't fazed to find that the objects of his inquiry were still viewed with deep suspicion by some of the older generation. After all, he was told, they were newcomers, been there less than a decade.

It got more serious when it was sworn by persons who should have known better that Best Friends practiced voodoo and routinely sacrificed animals in bloody rituals. "After all, what else would they be doing with all those worthless creatures? Not like they're breeding purebreds." That kind of outlandish fabrication didn't sit well with the reporter, but there might be a story.

After lunch he phoned the number on the donation can. "Would you mind holding a minute?" a woman asked pleasantly.

A beat later a male voice said, "Can I help you?"

"Chris Smith, *Salt Lake Tribune,*" he introduced himself. "I'd like to come see your place."

"I think we can arrange that. When would you be arriving?"

Chris Smith smiled at the proper English accent. No wonder these people were viewed askance by some of the locals. "How about twenty minutes? I'm in Kanab."

The smallest pause. "I'm Michael Mountain. Do you need directions?"

"I've had plenty of people tell me how to get there."

"I'll be happy to show you around," Michael said.

Michael put down the phone. From the reporter's tone he sensed this was not going to be your usual appreciative tour. He would bet his last dollar that Chris Smith had gotten an earful in town. The Salt Lake newsman would be looking for a scam. Michael sighed and walked out to his truck.

There was no doubt who was coming to visit when the silver Toyota 4Runner pulled into the canyon. The newspaper's logo emblazoned across the car's exterior was hard to miss. A tall, thin man with questioning eyes opened his passenger door as Michael approached. "Why don't we ride in my car," he said.

Chris Smith made no comment as Michael pointed out the ancient caves, the underground lake, Turtle Rock. He kept his counsel as they cruised past meadows still in winter's icy grip and his guide introduced the horses and goats by name.

Michael sensed the reporter's impatience as he showed him

Angels Landing. The man hadn't come to view scenery. "Why don't we go to The Village," he suggested.

Quite a few of the Best Friends had gathered for lunch in the meeting room: Francis, Paul, Steven, John, Estelle, Charity, and Faith—as fate would have it, with Mollie in her arms. Michael noted the reporter's quizzical expression at the pig's obvious contentment. He also observed how the man ran his keen gaze over the place, looking for . . . what?

"So tell me about your pig," Smith said after introductions all round. "What else have you got here?" was the next question after the story of Mollie and the pastor. Michael duly escorted the reporter from the *Salt Lake Tribune* back to his car for the drive to Dogtown.

Smith instinctively retreated before the cacophony of barking and rushing of fences that greeted his arrival. He stopped at each and every enclosure, eyes missing nothing. "You don't go in for fancy, do you?" he said, indicating the simple horse fencing. "But your animals seem to have it pretty good"—this last in the tone of a grudging compliment.

Even the professional trained to see beyond the obvious couldn't keep the surprise out of his voice when Michael pointed out Faith's home in passing. "The director of your sanctuary lives in a *trailer?*"

Smith was quiet as his tour guide finished Victor's story and offered to demonstrate how the bigger, more aggressive dogs simply would not cross the Dogfather's invisible line. He looked at Michael speculatively, as if he were measuring him for a suit. "I've been told some things," he began.

"Interesting, I hope," Michael said. "Did you hear the one about how we trained attack dogs for the CIA?"

He had to give it to the man. Smith didn't blink. "No, why don't you fill me in?"

Michael obliged. He told the newsman how they came to Angel Canyon during President Reagan's era. "It was during the time of the war in Nicaragua. The rumor was we were secretly training dogs to fight with the Contras."

"Interesting," Chris Smith said, mimicking his host's poker face. Both men smiled.

Catland was last. Michael could still feel the questing tension in the reporter, the nose sniffing for the story. Finally, only one shaded wooden building remained to be explored. Michael opened the door into the tiny foyer and let the reporter precede him into the main cat area. He didn't feel the need to talk anymore. The little felines would vocalize for themselves the beauty of their beings.

Smith walked in purposefully. He stopped and gazed upon the ones with no ears, with three legs, the snow-white-furred ones whose genetics had bred them to cancer, the incontinent, blind, circling Timmie, burned Sinjin, sneezing Tomato, three-legged Blackjack, and—leading the curious parade to the man's ankles— Sir Benton.

The silence stretched to five, ten minutes. The newsman squatted and allowed Tong to teeter on his shoulder. Tomato only had attention for Michael, but a crowd of purring cats clustered around their new visitor. Michael slipped outside to let the man be alone.

When he joined Michael twenty minutes later, Chris Smith didn't bombard his host with the usual tough questions. He didn't have much to say about anything. Michael was not to know that the *Salt Lake Tribune* reporter had looked in vain for the trappings of excess, the clues that the money they might persuade people to donate was going to something other than the well-being of the animals.

As he drove back to the city that night, Smith was glad his original lead had turned out to be a dead end. He was the first in the newsroom the next morning. For once he didn't participate in the usual camaradie that went with the coffee and doughnuts. He sat, intense, serious, writing the story that would take A1 space in his paper.

Chris Smith wasn't to know that Best Friends had been ambivalent about allowing a reporter into their midst: a local story would surely inundate them with so many more needy animals.

Despite their concerns, however, his article was to be their first validation, the first printed acknowledgment that Best Friends was truly a haven of healing and love. A place where a less-than-perfect animal could find refuge in a world all too ready—as it was with its people, as well—to reject and consign them to the garbage heap.

The article appeared on March 9. For Best Friends, Chris Smith was the first outsider to give credence to the right to life of all creatures. He was not to be the last.

CHAPTER THIRTY-THREE

Confluence of Events

Gregory Castle had gravitated toward Salt Lake City for his tabling efforts. It didn't take long for the quiet philosopher of Best Friends to learn the power of the press. "I read about you in the *Tribune*," was the oft-repeated announcement after Chris Smith's article appeared, and with it came a willingness to listen with open curiosity instead of cautious skepticism.

Judy Jensen's attention was caught by the photos of Bucky and Sparkles. She, too, had seen the newspaper piece and was thrilled to chat with Gregory. The correctional officer at the Utah State Prison took her love of the big equines a step further. Judy Jensen went to the sanctuary to see for herself.

A week later she was in veterinarian Rich Allen's clinic with her mother's sick cat. The door of the waiting room was ajar, and she heard the doctor waxing enthusiastic about a recent visit to Kanab where he went horseback riding.

"I couldn't help overhearing," Judy Jensen said to the veterinarian when it was her turn. "When you were in Kanab did you hear anything about Best Friends?"

"Can't say that I did."

"They're the most wonderful people, and they could really use some help. Their vet died last year."

The rich Dixie drawl made Faith smile when she answered the phone that afternoon. "I like to ride a bit. Thought I'd come see you all," Rich Allen stated.

Faith laughed. "We're an animal sanctuary. We don't *rent* horses. You must have misunderstood."

"Judy Jensen was telling me you didn't have a vet, either. Did I get that confused too?"

"No, you got that right."

Dr. Allen's Southern accent became more pronounced. "How primitive. How do you manage?"

"Basic," Faith corrected. "Not primitive."

Dr. Allen had already made up his mind. "Sounds like you could really use my help. I have just *got* to get out of this city for a few days. I'll be there this weekend. Don't worry, I'll bring plenty of everything."

Faith had the distinct impression that Dr. Allen had visions of himself as Albert Schweitzer, venturing into the wilds of Utah to help the animals. When she called Judy Jensen to inquire about the veterinarian, the horse lover gave him a five-star rating. "He's different, though," she conceded. "I think you'll like him."

As far as Faith was concerned Rich Allen could ride into Angel Canyon on a unicorn. She would blow a trumpet to herald his arrival. But would he come?

The Alabama man actually came bouncing into Best Friends in a Dodge Ram diesel groaning with veterinary supplies, as he'd promised. At a solid six feet, he was a good deal taller than Faith. He looked to be about forty, sporting a handlebar moustache worthy of any brigadier general.

As his Dodge jolted along the rutted roads of the canyon, Dr. Allen oohed and aahed at the glaze of afternoon light that painted the mesa in Monet pinks and mauves. He inhaled deeply of the sage-fragrant air. "Ah, the true wilderness." The veterinarian hummed happily as he was given the tour of Catland and shown the bunkhouse. "Very rustic," he pronounced with satisfaction.

His demeanor lost some of its ebullience when Faith took him to The Village. "This is very nice." Dr. Allen sounded as if they had done him a disservice.

The veterinarian appeared positively dismayed when they stopped beside Dogtown's clinic. He twirled his moustache in agitation. "Is something wrong?" Faith asked as she led him inside.

Rich Allen darted through the clinic like the Energizer bunny on new batteries. "Not quite what I expected, although you're a little short on equipment."

Faith didn't feel like explaining their financial straits. "I told you it was basic. But it's not a card table under a tent."

The veterinarian blushed bright as a traffic light. Faith suddenly realized that he had *hoped* for just such primitive conditions. She had actually disappointed him by having decent living quarters, and their clinic in a building.

Faith walked the good doctor down the lanes of Dogtown. She hid a smile as she watched Rich Allen perk up at their utilization of horse fencing for the enclosures. "Did I tell you about our first operating table? You saw it in the bunkhouse kitchen. That speckled Formica . . ."

By the time he joined everyone for dinner, the veterinarian had gotten the history of Best Friends. They in turn liked this jolly man with his off-the-wall humor.

"Okay," Rich Allen patted a satisfied belly. "I'll come down once a month and spend a couple of days—whatever's necessary to reinstate your spay and neuter program. But only if the young man here assists." The veterinarian grinned at David Maloney who nodded vigorously.

"Are you saying you'll help us out?" Faith asked.

Dr. Allen twirled the ends of his moustache until they thought he'd twist them off. "That's what I was thinking. If you could use my services, that is."

Michael scratched his beard and looked very solemn. "Well, I think we'll have to take a vote on it. I personally can't see how we can use a veterinarian when we have barely fifteen hundred animals, and it's only a three-hour round trip to St. George every . . ."

"Take no notice of him," Faith broke in. "We'd love to have you."

Dr. Allen's cherubic face beamed as if he'd won the lottery. "That's settled, then. We'll start in the morning."

When the kitty in the driveway of the Grand Canyon Lodge didn't bolt at her approach, the ranger knew something was wrong. She picked up the mewling black bundle. The tourists weren't even here yet, she thought in disgust, and already it was open season on dumping animals. Well, at least she knew whom to call.

Diana Asher was at the sanctuary that day. She took the kitten no bigger than the head of a wild canyon rose and examined it closely. "He's blind," she explained to the ranger. "He didn't run away because he couldn't see you."

"That's probably why he was dumped." The fair-haired woman stroked the tiny head with one finger. "I named him Ivan. Is that all right?"

"Suits him perfectly," Diana assured her.

As soon as the kitten was in Judah Nasr's competent hands, the woman who loved cats called Michael. The familiar voice answered on the first ring. "Hello."

"Hi, Michael. Got a minute? A ranger just brought in a kitty that can't be more than a few weeks old. It's been playing blind-man's buff in the Grand Canyon. We don't know how long."

"Will he make it?"

"As far as we can see. I thought you might like to write a story on him. Ivan's sort of special. He's the hundreth kitty to come to the TLC Club."

"I'll be right over."

Ivan's arrival cemented an idea that had been percolating in Michael's brain. Chris Smith's reaction to their handicapped kitties confirmed what he was reading in the letters Best Friends received every time the magazine featured the tale of a "less-than-perfect" animal: people were sympathetic to the plight of the abandoned and abused, but for the hopelessly unadoptable, their compassion knew no bounds.

In the middle of writing up Ivan's story, Michael pushed back his chair and grabbed his jacket. Within fifteen minutes he had invaded Steven Hirano's office.

He found his partner arranging the layout for the next issue. "We just got the hundreth kitty for the TLC Club, Steven, except that Diana can't keep them all together anymore in their old house."

Steven nodded absently, concentrating on the templates for the center pages.

Michael plowed on. "Don't you think it's time we built a big, cozy place for them? I think people would like to contribute toward a lovely home for the special-needs cats." Michael realized he was thinking out loud, only this time it was to Steven, not Tomato. He stopped talking.

Michael waited while Steven frowned and fussed with the page in front of him. The imperturbable mask of his friend's face yielded no hint of what he was thinking. Finally Steven looked up briefly. "Anything that makes life better for the animals is okay with me," he said and bent back to his work.

Michael studied his partner's profile. He hadn't expected any less of an answer, when he thought about it. Steven always agreed if it was good for the animals. When it came to ideas, stories, and pictures for the magazine they had battles royal—but who wanted a "yes" cohort, anyway? "I'll be off, then."

"Ummm," Steven murmured, squinting to get a better idea of his layout. Michael made to leave, but Steven wasn't quite finished. "I need another five paragraphs to make this page work. And I need them by four-thirty."

The Englishman smiled and went out into the noonday sun.

Michael couldn't wait for the start of Memorial Day Weekend. The people of Angel Canyon would be back from "tabling" for the holiday, the perfect time to gauge the group's interest in his idea. He knew that everybody was still aware of the constant need for operating funds, but, as Steven argued, their situation was definitely improving, and worry was giving way to cautious optimism for the future. Or, as a much cheerier John put it, "Not to be cliche, my friends, but I see a light at the end of our financial tunnel."

So it was, as the last weekend of May approached, the Best Friends migrated like homing pigeons to the canyon. Everyone was in a good mood, looking forward to a few days at home. Michael waited until everyone gathered for the Saturday night dinner to present his proposal. To his delight, the idea of a new TLC Club for the 100 special-needs kitties was greeted with unabashed excitement.

Paul Eckhoff spread out his paper napkin and drew quick, bold strokes over the crumpled tissue. "I should design a state-of-the-art structure," he declared. "I'll keep the costs down, but if we're going to build again we should be thinking about how the sanctuary's going to look ten years from now."

"If we last that long," John said, unable to keep the grin off his face.

Diana could hardly contain herself. "Let's really do it right," she enthused. "The new TLC quarters should have its own Chairpurrrson, and I've got the perfect candidate: Benton. He was absolutely born for the role."

Smiles wreathed the faces of the Best Friends as they saw in their mind's eye the portly gray-and-white who stole everybody's heart with the theatrical waving of his lame leg.

"And what do you all say to naming the building in his honor?" Diana threw out.

"She's got it. By George, I think she's got it," John pronounced approvingly in his best Professor Higgins imitation.

It was a happy crew that night who unanimously approved the building of Benton's House for their special-needs kitties.

Michael and Steven worked days and nights on the appeal for the new TLC building. Paul immediately set to drawing plans and mocked up a table model, above which Mariko Hirano could pose for a photo, holding blind Ivan in her arms. The floor plans occupied an entire page of the newsletter. And Benton, looking appropriately superior, was introduced as "Chairpurrrson" on the front cover.

Again, the response was overwhelming. Not only did their members send money, but they offered toys, blankets, and climbing kitty trees. Many made suggestions. One that Michael particularly liked was that a wall be inscribed with the names of all those who contributed.

Once again, it was the touching letters he most treasured—especially the one from a man who described the uncomfortable nightly routine he had to put his cat through for her kidney problem. "I know what's involved in taking care of those little ones," he wrote. "This check is in honor of my dearest companion who has kept me sane for over twelve years."

For all the donations, best wishes and encouragement, Best Friends' base of support was too small to raise all the money they needed. "We can make a start, pour the foundation, and begin framing," Michael declared. "We'll do a little at a time and keep our members informed of our progress. We *will* build it."

Nobody looking at the stubborn jaw on their editor was about to argue. Michael envisioned their future. He dared to see Best Friends as a force for change. "This is about far more than cats and dogs," he had once said. Just as Faith had understood a few years earlier that they had not been brought to this place for themselves alone, so Michael now saw the first glimmerings of what might lie ahead.

Benton's House was a step in the journey. It would be built.

CHAPTER THIRTY-FOUR

The Lady and the Water Snake

Dolores Harris loved three things: Homer and the kids, animals, and "a bit of fun," as she described her trips to Las Vegas. After her husband's initial visit, Dolores happily made her own way to the sanctuary. Faith took her around. She got a good feeling from the California woman the moment they met.

Homer's wife was in her early sixties, a few years younger than her husband, and at five feet four a petite, soft woman beside his height and solid frame. Mrs. Harris struck Faith as a female of simple tastes and needs, not afraid to show her emotions—a gentle balance to the take-charge demeanor of her husband.

Dolores had had an accident that necessitated her neck being fused and, Faith suspected, caused her some pain. Even so, she refused to let the injury dampen her enthusiasm for the sanctuary.

In Dogtown, Dolores was delighted with the barking, licking, and wagging greetings of Sheriff Amra, hyper Maddie, three-legged Shamus, and chubby Coyote. She got moist-eyed when Faith told the story of Goatie and Sparkles as they watched them grazing side by side under Angels Landing. She was captivated by Mollie the pig snuffling her pockets. At Catland she plain cried at seeing big, old Bruiser grooming each of the kittens in his latest orphan brood.

After that first introduction, Dolores took to dropping by on a regular basis. One of her biggest kicks was to call Faith from the road. "I'll be in Vegas in an hour," she'd laugh. "I told Lady Luck that if she smiled on me I'd give the winnings to the animals."

"May the slots be with you," Faith said fervently.

The director of the sanctuary always looked forward to seeing Dolores Harris.

But not on the night after Norm Cram's news.

After the arrival of Best Friends, Norm Cram had built a bigger house for him and his wife closer to the road. Many a morning John drove by and gazed wistfully at the Crams' old dwelling and four cabins, looking forlorn and empty against the backdrop of their red-rock cliffs. Best Friends were increasingly short of office and living quarters, and all that extra space was just sitting vacant! It was almost more than John could stand. Finally, a few months ago, he had approached their neighbor about renting the empty buildings.

Norm Cram was delighted to let them lease the structures, and Estelle and John had immediately converted the old house into the offices they dubbed "the Hamlet." "It's so strange," Mary Cram told them when the deal was struck. "After thirty years of living here, Norm's developed allergies. His throat keeps swelling up. We can't figure it out. So it's nice somebody will be close by."

From the moment they moved in they were aware that their new landlord was miserable. His new stone home was less than 200 feet from the Hamlet, and John heard him coughing and sneezing every day. Nevertheless, Best Friends were totally unprepared for Mary Cram's news one early summer afternoon. "My husband wants to move to town," she said. "I'm sorry, but we've put our place up for sale."

Almost as big a shock was Norm Cram's $650,000 asking price.

"Well, I can't blame anybody for wanting to get the most for their property, but that is a little rich. Nobody's going to pay that kind of money," Michael said.

John didn't look convinced. "I only hope you're right."

Both men knew only too well the potential ramifications of the sale of Norm Cram's thirty acres. Not only would they lose their new precious space, but if a commercial enterprise bought the land it might close the entrance to Best Friends. Then every week new people would be swarming over the sanctuary unsupervised—and who knew what else!

Their fears were realized all too soon. A month later Norm

Cram tromped over to the Hamlet. He perched on his chair in front of the treasurer's desk, his weathered face a mirror of concern, though John sensed a suppressed elation about the man and guessed what was coming even before Norm Cram opened his mouth.

"Nice day again," their landlord wheezed, and John saw his Adam's apple bob in distress. "I'll get straight to it. I have a buyer. Wants the place for a dude ranch or something."

John could only stare at him.

"I thought I'd tell you right away because all the dealing's done and they'll be here shortly to sign the papers." Norm Cram shook his head and excitement won out. An eager smile of expectation erased the creases of concern. "I can't say I'm sorry to go, what with these allergies from out of nowhere. But I know it'll be hard on you. So I thought I'd let you know right away."

Their landlord suddenly fixated on the jar of pens by John's elbow. "I don't suppose you could spare one of those. My Bic's leaking ink," he laughed, embarrassed. "Just my luck we get to signing and nobody's got a pen that works."

John automatically handed him a black ballpoint.

Norm Cram heaved to his feet. "A man's got to do what he's got to do. But you'll be all right. Fortune seems to shine on you folks." Norm Cram whistled his way out of the Hamlet.

John immediately called Michael. An hour later the two friends stood staring across their landlord's unkempt pasture of tumbleweeds, unable to tear their eyes away from the spit-clean Landcruiser parked outside his stone house.

The morning was unnaturally still, as if the canyon was holding its breath. A light breeze caught the trill of a woman's laugh through the open window of Norm Cram's stone dwelling. Michael imagined he could hear the scratch of a pen on closing papers. "I've got to take a walk," he mumbled.

Michael stopped and stared at the little pond in its handkerchief of grass as he passed the Crams' house. The koi could do with some shade. The summer's heat would bake the shallow pond to bathwater soon. A woman stepped out onto the porch and lit a cigarette. "Beautiful day, isn't it?" She waved cheerily.

"Beautiful," Michael agreed and trudged on.

He hadn't taken two dozen steps when a shriek to wake the

dead shattered the eerie silence. Michael swung around. The woman stood frozen by the pond, screaming. He started toward her, but Norm Cram and a heavyset man were already out of the house.

"Snake! Snake!" the woman screamed to her husband. "You haven't signed! Don't sign! The children—there's snakes here!"

Norm Cram's face went white. "No, no! We've never seen a snake here. You must be mistaken."

The woman turned on him. "I know what I saw. It ran right over my foot. You didn't tell us about the snakes." She started down the steps and made a dash for the safety of the Landcruiser. "Get me out of here!" she yelled to her stupefied husband.

Norm Cram was right. There was too much people and animal activity for there to be snakes on his property. At that moment Michael detected a slither through the grass. The tiniest, most innocuous water snake he had ever seen was sliding with all haste back to the tranquil surface of the water. Michael watched, fascinated, inching closer, unnoticed as their landlord puffed after his lost buyers. "There must be some mistake. Wait!" But the SUV was already in gear and jerking down the road.

Seconds later a dejected Norm Cram turned and noticed Michael standing by the pond. "What happened? Where did that snake come from? Where'd it go?" he asked, more puzzled than angry.

Michael had no answer. Norm Cram looked suddenly wary, then shook his head as if dismissing the suspicion. "They'll be other buyers. This can't happen again." He turned and hobbled back into his house.

Faith was far from her usual happy self as John drove them into Kanab the following evening. If it had been anyone but Dolores Harris she would have begged off the dinner engagement.

"Try and cheer up a bit, luv," John encouraged as they approached the Four Seasons motel, where Dolores and her daughter Arlene were staying.

Faith managed a tired smile. She knew she was hopeless at hiding her feelings. A facade was as impossible for her as staying in bed all morning. But for Dolores she would try. John was putting

a much better face on the latest disaster du jour than she, although
Faith noticed that anxiety had etched permanent lines of worry
across his forehead lately.

"Come in. Come in. I thought we'd have a glass of wine before
dinner," Dolores Harris ushered them into her standard-issue
motel accommodations.

"Ah, pinot noir, my favorite," John noted with appreciation.

"I figured we'd have beer with Chinese, but I brought some
good California red with me," Dolores chuckled.

Faith thought she was doing a fair job of filling her friend in on
the latest happenings at the sanctuary until Dolores bluntly asked
if something was bothering her. "Oh, not really," Faith said
brightly. "Just a funny thing with Norm Cram, that's all. What
time did you say you wanted to eat?"

"We have a few minutes," Dolores said.

Faith glanced at John. She couldn't read his expression, and
Dolores was waiting expectantly.

"You'll never guess what happened yesterday," she started and
told her friend about the Crams selling their property.

Dolores was very quiet when Faith finished her story. "This
must be very upsetting," she sympathized. Carefully she adjusted
the collar of her rayon blouse and looked at her daughter. "What
time is it, dear? I think we'd better get going. I'm sure Faith wants
an early night."

Dolores Harris never came to Kanab without stopping by the
sanctuary. Faith knew that she and her daughter were only in
town overnight this trip, but Dolores had said she would see her
the next morning. When Faith didn't hear from her friend by late
afternoon, she got concerned. "D'you think I upset her yesterday?"

"I can't see how, Faith," Michael comforted her.

Seven of them ate an early dinner at The Village and then John
said he had some work to finish. Michael drove with him to the
Hamlet; both men needed to talk.

The phone was ringing when John opened the door to his office. He quickly grabbed the receiver before the caller could hang
up. Instantly Dolores Harris was talking in his ear, apologizing for
not being in touch earlier. John listened for ten minutes, unmov-

ing. Michael watched impatiently. "What?" he mouthed. John shook his head for him to wait.

The treasurer finally put down the phone.

"What is it?" Michael asked worriedly. "What?"

John opened his mouth, closed it, opened it again. This time words came out. "Dolores bought Norm Cram's place. She's been with lawyers all day. That's why she didn't call or come by."

Michael stared at him. "Would you mind repeating that?"

"You heard right. Dolores Harris just bought this place."

"What about Homer?"

"Homer's up the Amazon somewhere. She couldn't reach him. So she called Cram this morning and had him meet her in town."

A thousand thoughts jumbled in Michael's head. The Harrises were wonderful, decent people, salt of the earth, and Faith adored Dolores—but who could possibly guess she would do something like this?

John read Michael's mind. "You never know, do you? Dolores said she's sure Homer's going to be miffed that she didn't negotiate with Cram for a better price, but she felt it was the right thing to do. She assured me the papers have been signed and we're not to think another thing about it."

Michael didn't answer.

"Did you hear what I said?"

Michael nodded. "I was thinking Dolores Harris captured the dragon's lair."

"What are you talking about?"

Michael smiled. "Nothing. Let's call Faith."

Homer Harris did have something to say, but only Dolores heard most of it. She told Faith that her husband's being upset didn't faze her for a moment. "It was mostly because I didn't negotiate," she said with a knowing smile. "Homer always likes to negotiate." Her expression was that of a woman who knew her strength. "Now we can both feel part of everything—although he won't admit it yet."

Escrow took four months to close because Mr. Harris was at least going to make Mr. Cram bring the septic and water systems up to par—at Mr. Cram's cost.

October saw Anne and Cyrus Mejia move into the back two

rooms of the Crams' stone house, with the rest of the floor space being renovated for Best Friends' first proper welcome center.

Anne immediately planted shade for the koi. She and Cyrus painted, put up shelves, hauled in a desk, displayed Jana and Raphael's photographs, and stacked T-shirts imprinted with Cyrus's impressions of the canyon. "Now we've got somewhere to greet people," she announced proudly.

To Best Friends' astonishment, Homer returned their first rental check for Norm Cram's property with a note. "Consider this a donation."

On their next visit, it was the Harrises' turn to get a surprise when everyone gathered to personally escort them to Dogtown. Best Friends had christened the path that ran by the clinic Dolores Lane, and the area behind the Great Temple of Food, Homer Hill. "It's the only way we have of saying 'thank you' right now," John said.

Dolores started crying. Homer stood straight as a military man and put on his sternest face. "This is very nice. Now, you do know that I'll be keeping an eye on your progress. So no slacking off."

As Faith was wont to say, "Who would have thought it?"

CHAPTER THIRTY-EIGHT

Volunteer Extraordinaire

Michael often wondered if the animals weren't in control of Best Friends. He wasn't entirely joking when he talked about a psychic pet network that communicated through time and space over which, when the moment was right, the word was passed to orchestrate events. Tomato just meowed and implied that that was for the animals to know and for persons to wonder.

The summer of 1993 brought another visitor to the canyon. Michael had no way of knowing the role Tom Kirshbaum would play in their lives. First, he saw the sanctuary as never before through the eyes of the one-time conductor of the Flagstaff Symphony.

Then he watched the man attack the bone-wearying task of scooping the poop in Dogtown, never seeming to tire. He watched the exhilaration with which Tom Kirshbaum petted and played with every mongrel, large and small. Where others saw only dogs, this gentle man discerned personalities, interactions, a society of animals. It took no time at all for Tom to become one of the dogs' favorite visitors, and for him and Tyson Horn to become fast friends.

Michael was touched by Tom Kirshbaum's humility and joyful understanding of how much he was needed. Whenever he could, the man would drive 210 miles on a two-lane highway to spend a few days at Best Friends. And nobody ever again thought of the cacophony of noise that could erupt from the throats of hundreds of mutts in unison in quite the same way after he described his experience.

Tom liked to camp out in Dogtown when he came to Best Friends. After dinner one evening, he recounted lying in his tent, squashed between Bubbles, his basset, and Amra and Rhonda—who insisted on sleeping with them—and listening to the excited 2:00 A.M. barking of dogs disturbed by the thump of a jackrabbit down the lane.

"It starts with a few muted yips and yaps," he began to an enthralled audience as he wove the music of the night. "Then, from a hundred surrounding enclosures, the vocalization picks up: a harmonic progression of low growls punctuated by staccato bursts from deep-chested bodies.

"Soon the accompanying melody joins in: a siren-like rise and fall too subtle to be called 'baying.' Now the concert explodes in wave after wave of textured sound, like some colossal oratorio."

"I think maybe I'll take out my earplugs tonight," Faith murmured into the awed silence.

The director of the sanctuary had come upon Tom Kirshbaum one summer morning, arms to the sky, dancing in the sand around a puzzled Dogfather. "There was nobody about," he said to a blue-aproned Faith wielding a can opener. "It felt so free."

His wife, Anah, Tom Kirshbaum explained, had met this blond Englishwoman tabling in front of Wal-Mart and gave her what she thought was a ten-dollar bill for a copy of their magazine. "Oh no, I think you've made a mistake," the Englishwoman said, handing back the $100. "Anah was most impressed," Tom recounted.

"That must have been Diana," Faith exclaimed.

The conductor had checked out of a boring tennis camp in nearby St. George. He remembered his wife's experience with Diana Asher and, seeing that he was so close, thought he would come see what Best Friends was all about. The worst that could happen was that he would have a story to take back to Bubbles the basset.

"It's funny," he confessed on his third visit. "I was never particularly crazy about animals. Never paid dogs much mind until Anah suddenly got obsessed with basset hounds."

As he told the story, Anah began stopping every time she saw a basset on the sidewalk. Anah would get a winsome look on her face at every wizened, drooling hound and call Tom to come to the baseball field "to see the most adorable little creature."

"As you know," Tom Kirshbaum rolled his eyes. "Eighty-pound bassets are hardly little things. But I knew what was coming. We knew a couple who had two bassets they dearly loved and were breeding for just one litter. A few weeks later we were sitting in their front yard watching the rambling antics of seven fat puppies on three-inch legs. One little sausage left her mama, trotted straight to me, scrambled in my lap, and fell asleep. That was Bubbles."

What was so significant about being chosen by a dog? Nothing, really. Happened all the time, Tom Kirshbaum realized. Except that after Bubbles entered their lives, the interests and values he and Anah had held so important somehow faded into the past. Life was so much richer with Bubbles as part of the family. They also found that the basset had spondylosis, a spinal condition that if not treated, could severely hamper her movements. It made their time with her even more precious.

"You see, if we'd not gotten Bubbles, Anah would never have stopped and chatted with Diana. I wouldn't have bothered to read your magazine. And the last thing I'd be doing is standing on a sand dune, scooping dog poop—and enjoying it."

Tom Kirshbaum was suddenly serious. "You know I'm not remotely the same person I was before that pudgy little girl with the surplus skin, paws like boxing gloves, and those ridiculous ears went to sleep in my lap. Now I keep coming back here. What's that all about?"

Michael smiled at Best Friends' quintessential volunteer. "Beats me, Tom. But I can promise you we'll find out soon enough."

CHAPTER THIRTY-SIX

Chateau Marmont

The year 1993 had one more pleasant surprise for Best Friends. Silva Lorraine's sense of a life-changing connection when she met Maria Petersen had been prescient. Since their first encounter on Thanksgiving eve almost two years earlier, the women had formed a bond of friendship that normally took decades to build into trust. And Maria proved a good friend indeed.

When, as seemed the habit of Best Friends vehicles lately, the transmission of Francis and Silva's minivan expired, leaving them stranded, Maria insisted they use one of her cars while theirs got fixed.

Maria had quickly discerned that her new friends did not sit for interminable hours in front of supermarkets for the sole purpose of raising money. She watched how they responded to people who asked advice for problems with their pets, were looking to adopt, or sought to place an animal. She was not surprised that, as the months passed, a small band of volunteers formed around the team.

Francis was able to create adoption bulletins describing animals in the area that needed loving homes. Their volunteers distributed the lists in their local stores, yoga studios, and health clubs. For Francis and Silva it was the start of a Best Friends outreach program, their way of giving back to the city that was helping them survive.

Maria, for her part, knew that in a city like L.A. it never hurt to have celebrity support. She saw to it that the couple— "You are a couple, you know"—were invited onto her director husband's sets to meet their Hollywood circle. Laura Dern became a supporter. The singer J.D. Souther sent Best Friends $1,500 for subscriptions to the magazine for his buddies Jack Nicholson, Isabella Rossellini, Don Henley of the Eagles, and others in his orbit.

And celebrity support definitely helped Best Friends stage their first-ever benefit.

They saw the dogs first, a dozen of the sleekest purebreds ever to strut at the end of $100 leashes. The five-foot-ten redhead who controlled them was equally striking. Silva couldn't help but notice the sassy beauty did a rather theatrical double-take as she passed their table.

Five minutes later the dog walker was back. She stopped and picked up a photo, all the while staring at Francis. "You must know you're a dead ringer for Steven Spielberg in that hat."

Francis grinned and adjusted the brim to a more jaunty angle. "Who's Steven Spielberg?"

The redhead grimaced. "Very funny." She stuck out her hand. "I'm Caroline Marcus, dog walker to the stars in case you didn't guess. What you got going here?"

Silva gave Caroline their brochure and adoption lists. The redhead stuffed them into her fanny pack, pulled her pooches to attention, and strolled off.

Two days later it was the same parade. "Liked your stuff," the lady called as she sashayed past. An hour later she stopped back. "I have an idea for you. Any chance we could meet at Mezzaluna's around seven?"

Her idea was a benefit. "You know the Chateau Marmont, of course?" she asked, then continued before they could answer. "Well, Philip, the manager, is a friend of mine. I'm sure he'll let us use the hotel for this kind of a benefit. You *do* know Chateau Marmont?" Caroline demanded at their blank stares. She shook her head. "I'm gonna have to educate you some. But what do you think?"

"We've never done a benefit," Francis said.

Caroline Marcus's creamy smile was positively beatific. "Neither have I."

She sipped her cappuccino and studied them over the rim of her cup. "I looked at your brochure. Your canyon is awesome. I figure you must really need the money to haul your asses to L.A. and smell gas fumes all day." She paused and smiled. "And I happen to like animals, in case you haven't guessed."

The dog walker to the stars stood up and casually scanned the room. "Nobody I know here tonight. Ah, well, gotta go, kids. Leave everything to me, okay? Love that hat, Francis." With a perfect air kiss good-bye, Caroline Marcus sauntered away into the Los Angeles evening.

Francis and Silva weren't sure what they had agreed to. They finished their coffee and signaled for the check. The waitress simpered and glanced toward the door leading to the kitchen. A stylish woman, all smiles, was immediately at their table. "My chef would like to cook you something special."

Francis didn't understand why she would want to do this, but he had noted the menu prices. "Thank you, we have to go."

"Oh." The manager was obviously disappointed, but recovered quickly. "I couldn't possibly allow you to pay. It's on us. But please come back. You must try our food next time."

Francis started to protest, but the woman would have none of it. "I love your films," she said, as she escorted them out.

The Chateau Marmont was a legend in the 1930s, host to some of the most famous and infamous Hollywood movers and shakers. Overlooking the Sunset Strip in West Hollywood, it was still a very trendy, hip kind of place, imbued with the faded romance of another era. On any given night, an eclectic assortment of names checked in at the Chateau Marmont. They liked the anonymity that came with the reservation.

Caroline Marcus's friends ranged over the Los Angeles society spectrum. Corinne Lorraine, the beautiful French owner of the upscale Cafe Luna on Melrose, and hopeless animal lover, insisted on catering the event. The vintner Domaine Chandon graciously donated champagne. A decent number of Caroline's actor and director clients promised to put in an appearance.

By late October, the Malibu fires that had kept CNN viewers spellbound for days had cast gloom and ash all over the city, and the fires were still smoldering. Indeed, some of the expected guests had been literally burned out of their homes. Ticket sales for the benefit were not great. Francis had every reason to expect a disaster, and did.

Maria Petersen watched the unfolding of events with interest. "Don't worry," she assured the nervous Silva and Francis, "Wolfgang and I will bring lots of friends. You will be a success."

Silva and Francis walked into a clamor of glamor that first Saturday night in November. A trio mimicking the Blues Brothers, complete with shades, added smooth bass, guitar, and drums to the buzz of conversations of pretty people.

Silva thought everything was going fine, but Caroline was disappointed. "I was hoping for a better turnout," she said.

Francis noticed his palms were sweaty. "Don't move," Silva said and fetched them both a glass of champagne.

Suddenly, Francis would later say, "It all flamed over." What nobody had anticipated was the attraction the benefit would hold for the hotel's guests. The party began indoors but spilled out into a courtyard. The outside area was an open-door invitation and everyone came to play.

Timothy Leary dazed onto the lawn. Claudia Schiffer, on heels to the sky, showed in a tartan micro skirt that drew the photographers like worker bees to a queen. Rene Russo arrived with Maria and Wolfgang followed by Jason Priestly, Bill Gerber, Dan Hallstead, Sally Kirkland . . . Francis couldn't keep all the names in his head.

In no time the place was packed. The band rocked into high gear. The buzz escalated. The press were frantic. "We felt like the Muppets taking L.A.," Francis told Michael afterward.

They didn't make much money, and the press frenzy faded with the morning. The affair did get some coverage in the *Los Angeles Times*, and, of course, Claudia's tartan appeared in tabloids around the world. More important, throughout the evening people wanted to know about Best Friends. Francis and Silva realized this could be a wonderful venue for increasing awareness of the sanctuary. The first Chateau Marmont affair would not be the last.

The man and woman whom Maria Petersen had called a couple recognized something else. In the intense months she and Francis had done their part to keep Best Friends afloat, Silva had discovered an extraordinary rapport and safety in being genuinely known for herself. She could be irritable, or terribly serious—a mood which Francis would find hysterical and jolly her out of. It didn't matter; he was always there for her.

Before Francis, Silva said, she felt that all her life she had been balancing on stones in a stream, trying not to get her feet wet. With this man of such infinite patience and gentleness, she was finally able to let go. It was such a comfort, such a joy.

They got married on Angels Landing. Maria shared a tradition from her homeland. "In Germany, if you have a good marriage you give a ring that has special meaning for you to someone you really care about as a blessing on their union." Maria Petersen removed a slender gold band set with two diamonds from her finger and slipped it onto Silva Battista's.

Silva wears Maria's ring to this day.

CHAPTER THIRTY-SEVEN

Earthquake

In her Toluca Lake hotel room Silva Battista fell out of bed—hard. At first she was disoriented, and her backside hurt where she hit the floor. She heard a low rumble as from the throat of a lion before it roars, and the room swayed, sliding her into the wall. "Francis, what is it?" she screamed.

Her husband rolled over. "Come back to bed. It's only an earthquake."

Silva struggled to her feet, staggered to the bathroom, and wedged herself between the doorjambs. "Francis, wake up. This is serious. The building could collapse."

Francis sat up reluctantly and stared at his white-faced wife. Silva looked as if she were about to throw up. He threw back the covers, padded to her side, and wrapped her in his arms.

"It's okay, darling. If the building were going to collapse it would have done so already. But you're right, we need to get up. I think—" The shrill jangle of the hotel telephone made Silva jump. Francis grinned. "Operation Earthquake is about to begin."

It was January 17, 1994, Martin Luther King, Jr.'s birthday. Silva and Francis were living through what Angelenos ruefully dubbed disaster #10,987,436—the Northridge Earthquake.

Francis called Best Friends as soon as he got a chance.
"Are you okay?" Michael asked.
"We're fine."

"Of course; the real question is how many animals are you bringing back?"

"Gotta go," Francis said.

The Battistas had come a long way from the man and woman who didn't know about voice mail when they arrived in the City of the Angels three years earlier. Now they carried a laptop loaded with a sophisticated data system that connected them to all the parts and pieces of their L.A. outreach program.

They were as ready as anyone for this emergency. They had become adept at organizing volunteers; they were in touch with the shelters; their lost-and-found pet hotline had been in place for over two years. Through their Hollywood connections the Battistas were media-savvy. As soon as was feasible, Francis intended to contact the television networks to scroll their hotline number to match lost animals and their persons.

But at 6:00 A.M. all was quiet. The dawn was just fingering the sky. It was time to go outside and see what nature had wrought.

Francis and Silva walked into a Salvador Dalí world of the surreal. There were no lights, yet the streets were filled with people afraid to stay in their homes because of aftershocks.

Police cars crawled along the road, blue lights flashing, bullhorns urging everyone to stay calm. Fire hydrants spouted water ten feet into the air, flooding the gutters. Couples pushed baby strollers along the sidewalk, ignoring the crash of glass from a store being looted.

Like gamblers to a casino, people gravitated to the nearest Von's Supermarket parking lot, where they congregated in knots and talked animatedly with neighbors whose names they'd never known.

For Best Friends, the disaster would be a test of the fledgling outreach programs they were putting in place. For Los Angeles, the Northridge Earthquake was a turning point in the often acrimonious relationships between animal organizations and the city's shelters.

With the media spotlight upon them, the shelters and the volunteers called a truce and worked side by side. Television coverage generated interest in how the city's pounds operated, forcing long-range innovations for the benefit of both animals and their persons.

Francis likened the earthquake to Best Friends' financial heart attack. It was a disaster, but it forced nothing less than a tidal wave of change.

CHAPTER THIRTY-EIGHT

Feathered Friends

Nathania Gartman missed her friend Sharon St. Joan, the only one of the Best Friends who hadn't yet made her home in Angel Canyon. When their financial crisis mandated that not even another doghouse should be built, Sharon had graciously offered to caretake the Arizona ranch. By her taking on this responsibility from Virgil Barstad, the ranch was not abandoned to fall into disrepair, and Sharon's feathered friends would be with her until adequate accommodations could be built for them in the canyon.

By the spring of 1994, with Best Friends already a haven for dogs, cats, rabbits, horses, goats, ducks, geese, sheep, and a pot-bellied pig, the time was right for the woman who had made a name for herself as one of the finest wildlife rehabilitators in the Southwest to come home to Angel Canyon.

Paul and Virgil built a temporary aviary in the meadow by the Welcome Center. Sharon found a couple she could trust to keep an eye on the Arizona ranch. And on the first Monday in May, the woman who loved birds loaded an old Suburban with her precious cargo and set forth for Kanab.

King Ming the peacock was the first to be made comfortable. He had been found as a dehydrated brown chick struggling to stand on a sidewalk in Phoenix. Under Sharon's expert care, he matured into the most gorgeous, swaggering bird with a fantail of glossy cobalt-blue-and-emerald feathers. Peaches and Fairy Dance, his consorts, were snugged in next to their mate.

One by one Sharon made room for the disabled geese, three

great horned owls, the brilliant-hued Conure parrot who liked to affectionately nibble her ear, a dozen finches, and thirty common pigeons, one of whom was cursed with a crossed beak and couldn't eat properly. Sharon's friends always marveled at the hours she spent patiently feeding the crippled creature.

The last cage she placed on the passenger seat next to her. It held a one-winged yellow-headed blackbird named Troubador. The sweet bird had been so badly abused by its owner that he could never be rehabilitated into the wild, which was always Sharon's goal. So she built him his own house with a bird-size swing. Every morning the little singer thanked her with his beautiful song.

Oftentimes, listening to Troubador's spring trilling, Sharon was reminded of the time she lived in the Colorado Rockies. She'd walk for hours entranced by nature and the long, sweet melodies of the meadowlarks. She could understand why some thought the birds were a spiritual link between heaven and earth.

Sixty feathered friends in all found their place in Sharon's van. The slender, elegant woman who knew birds as Faith and Diana knew dogs and cats, anticipated no problems on the journey to Best Friends. A weather front was moving in, but not until tomorrow. She would arrive in the canyon before sunset chilled the air for her charges.

But the snow started as she passed through Flagstaff: fluttery wisps of flakes that turned the Coconino Forest into an unforeseen winter wonderland. Sharon turned up the heat and soldiered on. Half an hour later the van was inching through a blizzard. It was 11:00 P.M. before Sharon crawled into the canyon. The Welcome Center was dark. She maneuvered the van through a foot of powder toward a dim glow in a cabin next to the Hamlet.

Nathania was dozing on the couch. "You got here," she yawned happily, stretching the cricks out of her neck. "I figured you might be late. Need some help unloading?"

"Thank you," Sharon said gratefully. "We've got to move fast or the birds will catch cold."

Nathania pulled on a fleece jacket and bounced out of the cabin. "Let's do it."

Paul and Virgil had built the temporary aviary at the lower end of the meadow, not 50 yards from Sharon's new home. The two women worked quickly, nesting the protesting birds in the warmth of their respective quarters. Nathania's happy chatter bubbled into the night, bringing a smile to her tired friend's face—which was exactly what she intended. Nathania's laugh echoed around them. "I'm so glad you're here, Sharon. We've got so much to catch up on."

The snow stopped as they nestled the last bird. Nathania made them a cup of chamomile tea, then she and Sharon stood side by side on the porch, bundled in scarves and gloves, gazing over a carpet of white, heeding a silence so complete and unsullied by the unsubtle sounds of the city that it begged reverence.

Suddenly in the midnight air they heard a fierce Whoo, Whoo, Whoo. "It's three owls," Sharon whispered. "A family. Hear the little one squeak? The babies stay with their parents for six months after birth. That's what they sound like." She cocked her head listening, then turned to the dark mass of the cliffs. "They're on the ridge behind us."

Nathania squeezed her friend's hand. "They're welcoming you home, Sharon."

CHAPTER THIRTY-NINE

Medicine Man

With the June 1994 issue, the magazine's circulation topped 10,000 and finally outgrew the label parties. The get-togethers were fun when there were only a few thousand zip codes to slap on envelopes, but they became drudgery, and totally inefficient, when the number passed five figures—and growing every month. Steven now had to ship the magazine layout to his friend in Phoenix to print and mail, and at the same time he moved his office to The Village.

He needed a quiet place to work. The Hamlet was getting to resemble Grand Central Station. Mariko Hirano, Chandra Forsythe, who had worked with Cyrus and Anne in Denver, and Faith's daughter Carragh now helped Estelle and Charity full time with the letters and phone calls.

The activity was spilling over to the new Welcome Center. Anne Mejia was no longer surprised to have two or three families a day stop in and ask if they could tour the sanctuary. It was becoming evident that as Best Friends reached out to the world, so the world was finding its way to the sanctuary.

To Cyrus it was clear that another chapter was unfolding. He remembered how when he first arrived, old Grant Robinson mentioned a Paiute medicine man whose people had once inhabited the canyon.

Once again he thought of the looting of the sacred places, the litter, and the carelessness of those who had passed through in earlier years. Cyrus felt that if people were again to be welcomed to the canyon there should be a cleansing and apology to the land for all it had endured. Cyrus would ask a blessing on Angel Canyon from the spiritual leader of the Paiutes.

Clifford Jake was a very old man. His movements were slow and stiff and he leaned heavily on a stout, polished staff as Steven helped him from his car.

Michael felt the eerie chill of *déjà vu*. Once again he flashed back to the ancient prophet who had appeared on a beach in the Yucatán Peninsula to foretell their coming to this place.

Anne and Cyrus weren't sure what they expected, but they were somewhat disappointed to see the medicine man in Levis and cowboy boots. The old Indian smiled. "We don't go around in feathers and breechclouts anymore," he reminded gently.

Cyrus walked around the koi pond and took the old man's worn hands between his. "Forgive us. We are so honored to have you here." He turned to Anne, who passed him a pouch of tobacco and the sage smudge stick he had made. Cyrus had been told that it was proper protocol to give a gift when you asked for a ceremony to be performed by such a powerful leader. He'd taken great care wrapping the sage branches, tying them into a wandlike rod, and drying the stick in the sun before the Paiute's arrival. The old man took the offering and nodded. Respect had been paid.

As cirrus clouds scudded across an azure sky the spiritual leader explained that most every curve of the canyon had been defiled by those who knew no better. Yet there was one sacred place from which his benedictions could heal all. With stately dignity, Clifford Jake directed the little band to Angels Landing. There, on the grassy carpet beneath the vigilant watch of the red rock dome, he carefully arranged the paraphernalia of ceremony.

The medicine man stretched his arms to the vast spaces of the mesas and intoned for the benefit of his untutored listeners. "This is the place where the nations used to gather to seek guidance from Mother Nature for their future."

Clifford Jake closed his eyes. Silence swaddled them like a cloak. On the still, transparent air the distinct, true notes of the rarely seen canyon wren wafted sweetly in the afternoon. The Indian smiled. "Now we begin."

Cyrus and Anne held hands as, from a worn leather pouch, the Paiute sprinkled cornmeal and tobacco in four directions. Steven and Michael listened quietly as he chanted words they couldn't understand. Clifford Jake culled a small, smooth stone from his effects and offered it to the heavens, the earth, the rush of spring river and surrounding cliffs. "I am calling the spirits back to make right what wrong has been done here," he said.

Last to be chosen from the medicine man's belongings was a beaded drawstring bag. With utmost care, the old man opened the multi-colored purse and showed them an exquisite fan of beaten silver. "Now I invoke a blessing for all of you, and for what you're planning here."

Clifford Jake instructed Cyrus to gather some juniper sprigs. "Only pick those upon which the full sun shines." Cyrus brought the juniper and the old man lit the tips of the branches.

The twigs smoldered as he walked the perimeter of Angels Landing. The silver spines of the fan ruffled the smoke under the varnished rock of the cave, over clutches of scarlet-flowered globe mallow, purple mulberry, and gray-green mullein, finally enveloping the still forms of his hosts in the fragrant vapors.

After the spiritual leader had taken his leave, the little group repaired to the Welcome Center. The prayers of the medicine man had a powerful effect. Each felt the blessing to go forward, sensed the presence of the spirits of the canyon.

Cyrus put forth a suggestion. He and Anne should find another place to live nearby. Norm Cram's stone house should be dedicated to receiving the many thousands of visitors the old Paiute predicted would be coming.

Before the evening shadows descended it was agreed that the Welcome Center should be Anne Mejia's province. As the acknowledged master of the history, flora and fauna of the canyon, artist extraordinaire, and grand teller of tales, Cyrus would be their new ambassador and conduct the tours of the canyon.

Anne had a million plans. "I'll put in a lovely gift shop. We'll make a video of the sanctuary for people to watch in the living room." She glowed with excitement. "I love the pond. After all, it was because of that pond we have our Welcome Center. I want to plant a beautiful wishing garden, a place to thank everyone for helping the animals."

"Interesting," Michael said. "How would it work?"

"People would send in their wish. We would inscribe it on special biodegradable paper that we'll then wrap around a flower seed and plant. We will bless the flower and pray that as it grows their dream comes true."

Michael smiled at her enthusiasm. Anne Mejia would turn the stone house into one of the most inviting and welcoming places in the sanctuary. She and Cyrus would be the ideal gatekeepers for the canyon.

As Faith had realized years before, each of them had their own special gifts which contributed to the whole that was Best Friends, and Michael was soon to see even more clearly the truth of her prescience.

CHAPTER FORTY

Finding Their Gifts

Michael walked slowly. Up ahead, That Naughty Girl and three newcomers he was fostering for Faith romped and teased an increasingly irritated Sun. The Doberman didn't want to be bothered this afternoon. He still enjoyed his daily exercise, but Michael saw that the dog moved stiffly lately. The whirling, twirling bounciness of youth had given way to sedate, deliberate meanderings along familiar trails. Sun was showing his thirteen years.

The daily hikes with his dogs had become a pleasant ritual. Michael never tired of their frolicking, and in the solitude of the high desert he did some of his best thinking. At that moment he was pondering how each of the Best Friends were finding their own niche in the new scheme of the sanctuary.

Nobody had dreamed that Virgil Barstad, their soulful violinist, composer, and lover of John Deere tractors—the bigger the better—had a talent for math.

"I need help!" John Christopher groaned after one particularly grueling month of juggling income with outflow and still coming up short.

Virgil was home from tabling in Colorado. "I had a pretty good head for figures in college," he offered.

John opened his drawer and tossed over an accounting primer. "If you can make sense of that you're mine."

Virgil found bookkeeping pretty easy. John was delighted; he could possibly go to bed before midnight once in a while when

Virgil was in the canyon. Gradually the violinist spent more days easing John's work overload, much to everyone's relief. They all loved their gruff treasurer with his dry humor and big heart.

Then there was Gregory Castle's surprise.

When Francis was at the sanctuary, he and Michael liked to stay up and talk after the others had gone to bed. Gregory usually was among the first to leave the supper table. Tonight he stayed.

Michael was aware that their soft-spoken friend was fidgety, only half listening—most unlike him. Finally Gregory could stand it no longer. "I heard from Governor Leavitt today."

Michael stopped in mid sentence. "How was he feeling?" he deadpanned.

"I only spoke to his office, he's fine and—" Gregory paused as he realized Michael's bait.

"Ignore him," Francis said. "What's this with the governor?"

Gregory wasn't used to being put on the spot. He started slowly. "Of course, it's sort of a fund-raising thing, but Michael's always talking about a nationwide network of animal lovers. So why not start with a state? Maybe a Utah's Week for the Animals. It could be a fun, festival sort of thing with adoption fairs, spay and neuter marathons, doggie contests, pet block parties . . ." His words tumbled fast now around his ideas.

"Do you know what would be involved in pulling that together?" Michael asked.

Gregory was momentarily nonplussed.

Francis frowned. "Michael's got a point. We've been doing stuff along the same lines in L.A. but nothing on the scale you're talking about, Gregory."

"All I'm saying is that besides the organizing of all the events and volunteers, we'd have to enlist the support of city officials, humane societies, veterinarians, the media," Michael explained.

Gregory had a rare stubborn look about him. "I made a promise to myself. If Governor Leavitt would endorse the idea, whatever it took I'd make it happen."

Michael looked at the very serious face of the philosopher in their midst. He could just see their reticent Gregory sitting behind a table in a Salt Lake City mall on a slow Monday, dreaming of his great festival for the animals. He also understood the months of preparation for the presentation of such a plan.

Gregory Castle had been with them from the beginning, an unobtrusive force on which they could always depend. Suddenly he was taking center stage in the state they called home. In the Best Friends outreach to the world, Gregory Castle was claiming his place and would not be denied. Michael poured them all a glass of wine. "Why don't you tell us more, Gregory?"

One revelation followed another. The next morning Chandra Forsythe had something on *her* mind. The girl with the wheaten hair that framed Russian Blue cat eyes sat across from Michael in the meeting room, inhaling the steam from her breakfast mug of fresh-brewed coffee. "I can't live without my caffeine." She smiled.

Michael waited.

"You know I answer all the letters concerning rabbits?"

Now it was Michael's turn to smile. Chandra Forsythe had been brought up on a farm on the Canadian side of Niagara Falls. Her father had a fondness for rabbits, letting them breed indiscriminately in their barn. "Sometimes we'd have as many as five hundred of them," she had stated matter-of-factly.

As a child Chandra could never understand why the bunnies would disappear all the time, only for new ones to arrive and the whole cycle repeat itself. When she was ten her farmer father told her the facts of life. Chandra was shattered to hear that her gentle friends ended up on dinner plates. She never went into the barn again.

Chandra Forsythe had worked with Anne Mejia in Denver, often volunteering to drive supplies to the sanctuary, invariably staying an extra couple of days to help with anything she could. When the crisis of 1991 forced all the Best Friends into tabling, she was right with them. When Chandra made the canyon her base, Faith was happy to turn over the care of her rabbits to the competent young woman.

Now Chandra fished in the pocket of her cardigan and handed Michael a letter. "I really liked the article you did a couple of months ago about Tony the Tasmanian devil dwarf. The lady who wrote this really liked it too. She asks why you don't do more bunny stories."

Michael laughed. He'd rather liked Tony himself. A visiting member had found the palm-sized creature cowering beside the highway outside Kanab. For the first twenty-four hours, the tiny brown rabbit had squatted frozen in Chandra's living room.

Taking pity, Chandra tried stroking the terrified animal. The rabbit latched onto her finger with needle-sharp teeth and refused to let go. Since she didn't want to frighten the three-pound infant any more than it was already, she gritted her teeth and endured the surprising pain.

They found out later that Tony had escaped from a trailer where the only place a couple with eleven children could find to keep him was in a bucket. Tony showed his undying appreciation of Chandra's loving care by following her around and nuzzling his velvet nose against her ankles at every opportunity.

Michael could just see the circumspect Canadian tiptoeing around her room to be sure she didn't accidently step on the diminutive creature. "Your lady's right. All the animals should get equal coverage."

"Oh, no." Chandra said quickly. "I realize more people relate to cats and dogs. But I was wondering . . ." Michael noticed her hands were trembling. "You want to do something for the rabbits, don't you?" he said with a sudden rush of understanding.

"I have members who'd like a rabbit house. If I wrote to each one personally, I think they'd support building one."

Michael looked at the earnest face of the woman who had always helped her friends. Chandra adored her rabbits. She would raise the necessary money. "It's a great idea. I'll tell our members about it in the magazine."

Chandra laughed happily. "Do you think Rabbit Redford's House would be *too* cute?"

Michael retraced his steps to his trailer. He saw the journey clearly now: a winding highway down which they had come, stretching into the infinite future. One by one, at each bend in the road, the people in the canyon slipped into the roles they hadn't known were waiting for them. He couldn't wait to see what tomorrow would bring.

CHAPTER FORTY-ONE

Community of the World

Tom Kirshbaum knew when to get Michael Mountain's attention: that afternoon sliver of time the *Best Friends* editor would take time to be with his animals.

"Hello," the familiar British voice answered on the third ring.

"Michael, got a few minutes?"

"Hold on, I'm in the middle of feeding the cats." Tom Kirshbaum waited. "Okay, I'm all yours."

"Do you know anything about CompuServe?"

Michael did. "I'm a member."

"I have a contact in New York at Time Warner. They've set up a Dogs and Cats Forum on CompuServe to promote their animal books. Two of their authors are running it, but they're really too busy to give it their full attention. I suggested you guys might be interested in taking over."

Michael took a few seconds to reply. A million possibilities swirled through his mind. He knew the TW Dogs and Cats Forum, had visited its bulletin boards more than a few times. He had been amazed at the way this fledgling online global medium was able to link hundreds of thousands of people with a commonality of interest. The idea of Best Friends interacting with this international community of animal lovers was staggering. "What did they say?"

Tom Kirshbaum laughed. "They didn't know who Best Friends were, so I took the liberty of sending them a couple of your magazines and a brochure. They love the whole warm, good-news feeling you guys foster. They'd like you to go to New York. Are you interested?"

Michael didn't hesitate. "Oh, absolutely. When?"

"Next week too soon? We could meet in Phoenix and fly together from there."

"Sounds like a plan."

The U.S. Open Tennis Championships were playing at Flushing Meadows the Thursday Michael and Tom Kirshbaum touched down at JFK Airport. Michael remembered the last time he had been in New York. Had it really been over a decade since he had picked up Sun, that crazy, whirling Doberman that had become his heart's companion?

A long limousine glided silent as a cloud to a stop at the curb beside them. A peak-capped, skinny chauffeur exited and stepped smartly to open the rear door. Michael smiled. The Cadillac's windows were as dark as the sunglasses he had donned to get Sun on the United flight back to Las Vegas. He ducked into the unfamiliar luxury of the soft, cushioned interior. This was certainly a different time, a different trip.

As the limousine wended its way toward Manhattan Michael was quiet. Even in the sedan's hushed interior he could feel the pulsing energy of the city, yet he felt strangely discombobulated. He was no stranger to the great metropolises of the world; he had been perfectly comfortable living in them in years past. It was unlike him to feel at a loss. Maybe it was the stranger-in-a-strange-land syndrome. He dismissed the impression from his mind as the car deposited them in front of the Time-Life building. He didn't have time to think as he and Tom pushed their way through the hurrying afternoon throngs into the imposing lobby.

The elevator whisked them skyward at dizzying speed to Warner Books, home of TW Electronic Publishing. An attractive, thirtyish woman waited to escort them to a corner office. The first thing Michael noticed as the secretary showed them into the president's domain were books, books everywhere.

Books stacked on the thick-carpeted floor, scattered on the deep-cushioned couch, crammed onto bookshelves, piled on the highly polished conference table that could seat twelve people without crowding. Books dominated every niche of the expansive space except for the endless wall of glass that afforded a stupefying view over Radio City. A few feet away from the impressive windows, three executives talked quietly among themselves.

Tom stepped ahead confidently, shaking hands, making introductions. For a split second, Michael was overwhelmed with an unaccountable sensation of acrophobia: his feet refused to take him forward. He mentally shook himself. This sudden fear of heights was ridiculous. The mesas of the canyon soared much higher than this building. He hiked them every day. Tom turned toward him, questions in his eyes.

Michael had already discerned the person to whom the others deferred. He swallowed his fear and strode toward the man. "I really like your Dogs and Cats Forum. In my opinion, it's the most intelligent animal site online," he said extending his hand.

"We like your product," the president responded as everyone followed his lead and sat at the table. From that moment the meeting flowed. For the next hour they discussed what Best Friends might bring to the table: a library, a "saying good-bye" section to offer sympathy and support for grieving owners, an education board, and much more.

The president listened, only occasionally injecting an observation as the ideas volleyed back and forth. As the business day drew to a close, the conversations trailed off into an expectant pause. The man at the head of the table spoke into the void. "We can sort out the mechanics tomorrow," he said. "What I'd like you all to be thinking about is what Warner wants Best Friends to bring to the Forum. It's the upbeat, positive community spirit they project that will build an online following for us. I call it the Best Friends tone. That's what's important here. All the rest will come with experience."

Tom Kirshbaum was thoughtful on the way back to the hotel. "He really got it, didn't he?"

All day Friday, Michael, Tom, and the Warner executives battle-planned the takeover of the CompuServe site. The discussions were long and detailed, but as Tom had predicted, by 4:00 they shook hands on an agreement: Best Friends would be the online navigators for the Time Warner Dogs and Cats Forum.

From the first week messages were posted from Germany, Denmark, England, Japan, Canada, Mexico, all points east and west. Far up the Amazon River, Alberto Suarez was struggling to save a sick pink dolphin. A Sea World veterinarian responded, not only with conventional medicines Alberto might use, but also with the names of several plants native to the rain forest that might be more readily available.

The Greek Cat Welfare Society trumpeted that they'd reached their goal of spaying and neutering 1,000 of the multitudes of strays in their country. And by the way, if anyone was passing through Athens they could really use some extra hands to feed the homeless kittens that congregated in the National Gardens.

Ralph Donner wrote from the Netherlands that he was going to Zambia to study the dwindling elephant population with the hopes that his findings would spur more effective law enforcement against ivory hunting. He still needed accommodations if anyone could help. They could.

La Sociedad De Animales Felices in Argentina shared their success with a newly implemented spay and neuter program and the unique methods by which they had involved the local neighborhoods.

On and on the messages flashed around the globe. Still the biggest eye-openers to Michael were those routed from the contested zones of Eastern Europe, Israel, and Northern Ireland revealing how people on both sides of the conflicts were coming together to help the animals.

Not everything was serious. They actually got downright silly at times. After several months of postings concerning cats throwing up had degenerated into endless jokes, Tom declared wistfully that he would like to notify the senders to "clean it up" but was reluctant to upset their online community. Flame wars were the last thing anyone wanted.

Michael had no such compunction and posted the following. "The new rule regarding cat vomit is that no one is allowed to download a file while their cat is throwing up—or, moreover, evermore discuss same." To make sure nobody missed his point, he uploaded a sound clip of a cat throwing up.

The clincher that eternally cemented his curmudgeonly reputation was the missile concerning the bulletin board discussions of where to find the best ice cream in Europe.

"Please remember our principal subject is animal welfare.

From recent postings somebody could easily assume that Best Friends is in fact an ice-cream store! A fun topic should be obviously labeled as such, e.g., 'Today's Doggerel.' General conversations of no particular relevance should be posted in the lounge. So call me Grumpy! But if you do, put it under a relevant subject heading!"

To regular onliners' delight, from that day forward Michael would forever be known as "Grumpy!"

Then there was the long-haul truck driver who would plug in at rest stops, talk about his travels, and post the delightful cat fiction he wrote to pass the hours on the road. It wasn't long before Mike Blanche had his own following.

But perhaps the most touching connection within this international network was the candle ceremony brought by Marion Hale to the Pet Loss Support section of the Forum.

Under Marion's guidance, people wrote in for their sick pets. "My cat Sadie is very ill with cancer. Would you please add her name to your prayers." At a certain hour every Monday night, the community of the world would light a candle and silently send prayers and best wishes for the recovery or passing without pain of the beloved animals.

In essence, Marion Hale became a shepherd of an international online healing circle that brought comfort to thousands. The simple sharing of prayers was so healing and powerful that the ceremony continues on the Internet to this day.

The TW Dogs and Cats Forum consumed everyone who participated, often demanding twelve-hour days to maintain. The service reached more people than Best Friends could have ever dreamed, and the experience and lessons learned were invaluable. When Time Warner decided to phase out their CompuServe Forums, Michael and his friends were ready for their own site on the fledgling World Wide Web—www.bestfriends.org.

But that would be three years in the future. Meanwhile, life at the sanctuary went on.

CHAPTER FORTY-TWO

Hello and Good-bye

Harriet tried. She really did. But the undersized black-and-white cat was too sickly when she was brought to the clinic. Diana Asher watched Dr. Allen remove the stillborn kittens from the young cat's belly. "She didn't have enough nourishment for them," he said sadly, placing the sedated feline into a carrier.

"I guessed as much, poor little thing. You'd think I'd be used to sick, hurt, deformed kitties by now, wouldn't you? I've seen enough of them. But you never get used to it, do you, doc?" Diana lifted the carrier off the table. "I think this one could sorely use some of Bruiser's loving care right now."

Diane took the skinny little cat to the bunkhouse and made up a bed in her bathroom where the patient could recover in peace. Then she fetched Bruiser. "This is Harriet," she introduced.

Diana sat beside the tub watching the grand old pro sniff his new charge. Bruiser knew exactly what to do. He lay beside Harriet and cupped his bulk around her tiny frame like a spoon. Carefully, he began cleaning the matted fur.

The feline stirred. Her nurse continued to lick. Harriet twisted her head and Bruiser lapped around her eyes. Diana saw the female's claws extend. Bruiser paused, golden eyes meeting the female's green. She hissed. He waited, calmly matching his breathing to hers.

Slowly the black-and-white's talons sheathed. The cat seemed to disappear into the long fur of the protector she had never had. Diana caught a glimpse of Harriet's face pressed hard into Bruiser's neck. Once again she blessed this cat who loved all who came into his world. Diana eased to her feet and tiptoed out of the bathroom.

Bruiser nursed Harriet in the bunkhouse for three weeks. One afternoon, toward the end of their stay, Diana walked in to see the big cat stretched full length on the floor, purring, while Harriet crouched behind, grooming his ears. The little female looked at Diana. "Go away," she seemed to say. "It's his turn for some love."

Diana bought them a basket for two. Every night she peeked in the bathroom to smile at the sight of the orange and black-and-white bodies curled around each other as if they were one. When a new motherless litter was in need of Bruiser's ministrations, Diana moved Harriet back with him to the TLC Club.

Her king of cats now had a teammate. Harriet cleaned and played with the kittens along with Bruiser. Diana loved nothing more than to watch the surrogate father sit in a circle of kitties as if he were teaching the facts of life, his friend Harriet always at his side.

When their duties were done, the green-eyed feline would rasp her tiny tongue over her protector's long fur, grooming until he purred with contentment. Never a night passed without the two sleeping together, often with their latest brood piled on top of them. Diana was reminded of Rhonda's tending of Amra. "Thank you, Harriet, for making my old boy happy. Thank you."

Tomato, investigative reporter par excellence of *Best Friends* magazine, stalked around the TLC Club for all the world like he was Sam Spade on a case. Michael's personal feline think tank declared to his person that he had waited long enough for an assistant. How was he expected to properly conduct his investigations if confined to the TLC Club? It was imperative that he have an outside undercover agent to sniff out the gossip. After all, he was getting his own mail nowadays.

Members not only wrote to Tomato asking about his fellow kitties and the latest intrigues; they sent toys and treats for him and his friends. Tomato reveled in the limelight. Michael thought the little orange cat was getting to be quite the prima donna. But nothing compared to Benton!

Benton must had gotten wind that the new TLC Club was to be

named after hizzoner and in the not-too-distant future. He took wholeheartedly to the role of star of the show. He preened and pouted and insisted on being the first to greet any visitor, mainly by cowing the rest of the special-needs cats and waving his game leg. He would only give way to the rest of the crowd when he had gotten his required share of tickles and strokes. "What happened to that sweet feline?" Diana wondered out loud. "He's become a legend in his own mind."

Tomato, however, would have none of it. "*I* am the investigative reporter. Only *I* know what really goes on," his saucy, capricious little countenance seemed to communicate. "But I really need a sidekick to scout the scandal."

He got his sidekick, but from a most unexpected direction. Tammy was of a breed that made money for mankind—as long as they were fast enough. But the underfed greyhound was too small to go up against her bigger brethren on the Tijuana racetracks. Tammy failed miserably to win purses for her owners. Well, there were other ways to get money from a living possession. Tammy would be donated to an experimental laboratory for a tax write-off.

But the Psychic Pet Network had other plans for shy Tammy. California Greyhound Rescue stepped in and paid the ransom for the dog, but her years of abuse made her too skittish for a home and she would bolt in terror at the mere sniff of a man.

"No problem. She can race into the trees if she sees Tyson or David," Faith said when the rescue group called her in desperation. Tammy, however, was even afraid of her own kind—dogs, that is. Faith had a notion. Maybe Tammy should live with Diana for a bit. The dog couldn't be frightened of cats, surely. The investigative reporter smiled. He had a hunch about this hound.

Every day Tomato commandeered his favorite scratching post and watched Diana encouraging the jittery racer. Every week he would spy on the volunteers and visitors who parked at Catland, and woe betide them if they left a window down.

Like a homing pigeon, Tammy would be inside the car and out again with precious keys, clothing, or maps in her jaws. Other times Tammy would race past Tomato's lookout perch with coffee cups, purses, books, all sorts of stuff from who-knew-where. Only

Tomato knew of Tammy's secret stash hideout down the hill until Diana spoiled the fun by following the dog one day. Chief Cat discovered items that had been missing for months.

Watching Tammy's predilection for crime, Tomato made his decision. The greyhound was a skittish, shy, paranoid kleptomaniac—the perfect assistant snoop.

"Hello," Tomato conveyed to the bashful black and white hound. *"How would you like to team up with me? The pay's good. Plenty of love and treats. I'm the boss, of course. And you'll have to get used to Michael, who takes my orders. But all-in-all, you could do a lot worse. What do you say?"*

Tomato had engineered things very well when Michael thought about it. The feline journalist now had a reporter to do the work while he took all the credit. "You're bad, Tomato. Bad," was all he could say.

However, there was nothing Michael could say to Sun. The twirling, whirling, impossible bundle of energy was looking thin and tired. No matter what vitamins, supplements, or changes of diet Michael tried, Sun was weary. Dr. Allen delivered the bad news.

"He's old and has cancer, Michael. You can either put him through some miserable treatments or let him live out his last months in dignity."

By early fall, Sun was not up to their afternoon walks together. The Doberman that had rarely let Michael out of his sight since that hot, humid noon in Kennedy Airport only wanted to lie by his person's feet as he worked on the computer. Michael got to glancing from Mommy on the stove in her sphinxlike concentration on his every word, to Sun in his ever-drowsy somnambulence.

One cool morning, as the canyon signaled the winter to come, Michael noticed that his companion was not by his side. He felt a sudden foreboding. He ran from the trailer calling, "Sun, where are you? Sun, where are you, little one?" Sun did not run from behind a nearby juniper. Sun did not come trotting to Michael's voice. Sun was gone.

Michael called everyone in the canyon. "Sun is missing," he

said, and that was enough. Within minutes, John, Faith, Virgil, Sharon, Judah, David, and Tyson were at his trailer. In silence, they fanned out to search for the dog he loved.

Michael had the suspicion that Sun had made his way to the creek. Why, he didn't know. It was a long hike down the cliffs. At the bottom the river's curving banks lay swathed in cottonwoods and softened with the last cool grass of autumn.

It was only right that Michael should find his best friend. Sun lay asleep, hidden to all but the most insistent of searchers, in a thicket of sheltering willows. Michael knew why Sun had chosen to leave him. The Doberman had followed his animal instinct, knowing the time had come to go off by himself—to die.

Was it that he didn't want to bother me? Or is it just that as close as we are to our companions, there is a rhythm, a knowing in their genes of what must be done at the end of a life? Michael's own animal instinct told him to leave Sun where he was in the willows—to honor his choice.

Yet even the creatures with whom we credit a higher understanding of the seasons of life are not infallible. Michael had observed that too many times. What if his best friend woke up, was hungry, cold, and needed Michael's comfort?

Judah and Virgil fashioned a simple stretcher. Michael walked beside his dog to the trailer, apologizing for doing what he thought was right, apologizing for possibly interrupting the Doberman's passage beyond this life.

Yet Sun was not ready to say good-bye. In the warmth of Michael's home, on his favorite thick fleece bed the Doberman slept, ate, and licked the hand that fed him. For two days, Michael never left his dog's sight.

On the third morning Michael felt something compelling him to go into town. He needed some food and supplies, but they could wait. Still, he felt he ought leave. He lay on the floor beside Sun until the early autumn afternoon came to call. "I'll be back soon," he promised as he dragged himself away.

Michael closed the door of his trailer carefully behind him. Subconsciously he knew what to expect on his return, knew the silent agreement that had passed between him and his companion of nine years.

Sun died peacefully, in the place he loved best, in the privacy that all animals crave. He lay exactly as Michael had left him, curled on his favorite doggie bed.

Sun's friends, Mommy, That Naughty Girl, Snoozums, and Squeakypop, sniffed and paid their respects. Afterward, Michael hiked with his subdued dogs across the mesa, encouraged them to play, and gave them way too many treats. But humans and four-leggeds knew that this was Sun's wake. The dog that had loved and romped and lived in their circle of friends would not have wanted it any other way.

Michael buried the Doberman under a sandy mound near the trailer. "Good-bye, Sun," he murmured. "You died happy, I think. What more can any of us ask at the end of a life?"

CHAPTER FORTY-THREE

Benton's House

Steven Hirano had approached the construction of Benton's House as a general on a campaign. He had meticulously kept their members informed of each step of the building process, updated the appeals, and tracked every dollar with John. Finally, as the first snows dusted the mesa, he made the announcement. "We have the funds to finish Benton's House."

Diana and Judah slapped an ecstatic high five. Michael nodded sagely. The meeting room at The Village exploded in cheers. "What a wonderful Christmas present!" Jana exclaimed.

Benton's House would be finished the following April. If all went well, the grand opening would be May Day of 1995. Michael and Steven planned a very special newsletter inviting everyone to join them for the moving-in day party. Those who couldn't make the trip were encouraged to lift their glasses at 7:00 P.M. Mountain Time—after the cats had enjoyed their afternoon treats, and just before they got tucked in for the night—in a toast to themselves, the members, without whom there would be no Best Friends.

Michael added a footnote: "If you can't manage 7:00 P.M., the kitties have a way of transcending time, so they'll just rearrange the temporal continuum to your convenience."

Amazing things happen when you put something good in motion.

* * *

From the first of the year Estelle was getting letters of confirmation to attend Benton's party. Other members asked if they could come a few days early to help with any final chores.

Then there were the presents: toys, blankets, beds, kitty furniture, paint, drywall, fencing. One couple sent a package of Norwegian salmon with a note:

> This is a gift for Benton and his friends on opening day. It's our kitties' favorite birthday present. Tell the "special needs" cats we love them. They are an inspiration to us all. God Bless You.

The weeks leading up to the grand opening were a frenzy of building and last minute preparations. Diana fretted when the washer/dryer wasn't delivered. Judah obsessed over the arrangement of the kitty furnishings. Paul's concentration was on the "Great Wall of Contributors." He personally designed the golden plaques and lovingly set each one in its place. Virgil kept everyone laughing with his out-of-the-blue chants for help as in a ship going down—"Mayday! Mayday! Mayday!"

A few days before *the* day, everyone calmed as, with loving care, the 100 less-than-perfect kitties were moved to their new quarters. In Benton's House, hizzoner the Chairpurrson would hold court in a playroom fitted with carpeted nooks and hiding places in Benton blue. Bruiser and Harriet would comfort their broods in a cozy, sunny space furnished with toys, kitty condos, and extra large easy-access window ledges on which to snooze.

Tomato, of course, couldn't make up his mind where he should live. Finally, he settled on a north-facing room, which filtered the light. This was the special haven for white cats, who needed protection from the sun because of their genetic disposition toward tumors and cancer. By a series of insistent meows, Tomato declared it to be perfect for his new office—after all, it came complete with a white-collar staff. Michael accordingly provided an ancient typewriter and a small table for the exclusive use of the magazine's favorite columnist.

With Benton's House, Best Friends also incorporated an idea raised by Jana de Peyer. "More people are asking if they can adopt special-needs animals," she reported on more than one occasion after coming back from tabling.

Anne Mejia seconded her observation. "Me too."

Michael knew exactly what Jana was saying. "People are always talking about the unconditional love of animals, but what you're seeing is the unconditional love of *people* for animals."

"Exactly," Jana exclaimed. "These folks aren't looking for the perfect pet. They want one they feel really needs them."

Michael nodded. "I think this is just the beginning of something. And can anyone tell me why these little creatures shouldn't have a chance for a loving home of their own?"

Nobody could quarrel with that argument. So in Benton's House the less severely handicapped were given their own "adoptables" room.

From its opening, the response to the "adoptables" room astounded everyone. It pioneered a program that, in the years to come, would encourage thousands to offer homes to less-than-perfect members of many species.

For their willingness to try this radical new approach, Best Friends would receive widespread recognition as a refuge for the truly helpless. Their example would blaze a change of thinking throughout the whole animal movement: No creature should be lightly cast aside; all deserved a chance to live.

On May Day of 1995, it was time for celebration. Hundreds had written in to report that they were celebrating at home, and 150 people flew in from around the country for the festivities. Michael wasn't sure who had the better time: the members, who sensed they were part of something truly special, or the animals, who were outrageously spoiled and coddled all day long.

As dusk lengthened its shadows over Angel Canyon, the rush of the past weeks suddenly hit home, and a weary Michael felt the need to be alone for a while. Few noticed when he slipped away and steered his Jeep toward his own personal sanctuary.

The Englishman was in a reflective mood and almost dismissed the flash of color he caught out of the corner of his eye. He parked by the trailer and walked unbelieving toward the red dirt mound under which he had buried Sun.

The knoll was a profusion of multi-colored blossoms. How had he possibly missed them? Michael stared down at a carpet of golden aster, sego lily, mule's ears, Indian paintbrush, sweet clover, angel trumpet, and wild rose. He inhaled the sweet, heady fragrance of evening primrose. "Good grief," he murmured wonderingly, "Sun's turned into flowers."

Michael sat down beside the petaled grave, clasped his arms around his knees, and looked out over his kingdom. Sun was showing him that there was no finality to death. What was dog was now beautiful plants providing food for bees, hiding places for insects. What a splendid gift the Doberman was bestowing on his old playground.

He recalled Paul Eckhoff's suggestion only a few months earlier that they dedicate a memorial park near Angels Landing for themselves and their members. Cyrus Mejia had immediately designed a great domed gate eight feet high, wondrously adorned with rabbits, cats, dogs, birds, and lilies. The canyon's own red rocks would be laid one upon the other to fashion a wall to surround the sacred place.

They chose a flat, shaded plateau across from the horse field on the road to The Village to create their Angels Rest. Now, as he sat in the quiet of the fading afternoon, Michael imagined he could hear the faint cathedral music of its wind chimes echoing across the mesas.

Michael gently ruffled the delicate blossoms that honored Sun's place. The Doberman had been one of the first to come to Best Friends. It was only right that the canyon's most fragrant flowers should bloom on his grave. Slowly he eased to his feet.

"We'd better be careful when Benton passes over the Rainbow Bridge," he murmured. "That cat will demand an Amazon rain forest to sprout in his honor, complete with parrots."

CHAPTER FORTY-FOUR

Utah's Week for the Animals

Gregory Castle hurried along the corridor toward the Green Room, the holding area for guests booked on KSL television shows. He was slated to appear on the "Our Town" program in less than fifteen minutes. The anchor wanted to focus on the Festival of the Animals in Trolley Square, which was fine with Gregory. That's where the adoption fair was being held, and from all reports things were going well.

Actually, the soft-spoken man from Best Friends was quite enjoying himself. Gregory projected a natural ease and passion for his subject that was appealing to viewers. He was a popular guest, with hosts often asking for a return appearance.

Even more important for the success of Utah's Week for the Animals was his discovery of heretofore hidden diplomatic skills. The state was home to a dozen or so often-fractious animal welfare groups. With his bold new idea, Gregory managed to persuade them to reconcile their differences and work together for the common good. Then too, the response from the schools was more than they could have hoped for, thanks to Nathania's gift with children.

Above all, the weather was smiling on them, unlike last year, when the worst ice storm of the season all but scuttled the opening festivities. Only a few brave souls had turned out for the inaugural dinner last November. This year Best Friends had gotten smart and moved the event up to early October.

When he put it all together, Gregory was most pleased with the way things were progressing. He was so engrossed in his thoughts, he almost bumped into the gregarious young man who strolled out of a studio ahead of him. "Sorry, Nick." He smiled an apology to Salt Lake City's popular news anchor.

Nick Toma flashed his famous elastic grin. "Didn't I just see you on a "Pet-of-the-Week" segment this morning?"

"Yes," Gregory smiled. He had gotten to know many of the personalities around the NBC affiliate's studios in the past month. It was a big joke around the station that Gregory must have a secret camp in the basement. After all, how else could this man manage to pop up on television at least twice a day with such unruffled ease.

"Now let me guess." Nick Toma pretended great concentration. "You're on in fifteen minutes with Shelley Osterloh?"

Gregory nodded happily. Raphael de Peyer's persistence had paid off. "You leave the bookings to me," he had assured Gregory. "I'll have you doing three interviews a day before I'm finished."

Raphael outdid himself when he arranged for Questar, the local gas utility, to promote a reduced-rate spay and neuter program. For twenty-one days leading up to Utah's Week for the Animals, Questar donated a sixty-second spot on NBC's coveted "Ten O'clock News." Every night people were encouraged to call the Best Friends 800 number for a referral to a veterinarian in their area participating in the low-cost program.

"Tell your media guy he's all right. If he ever needs a job, I'm sure we could find a place for him," Nick Toma assured him as he passed out of sight.

Media guy? Raphael would get a kick out of that tag. "Thanks, I'll pass it on," Gregory called after the retreating newsman.

Forty-five minutes later the man from Best Friends was soothing two large dogs in the back of a taxi on its way to the KISN radio station. Three-legged Shamus wasn't much trouble. The shepherd mix had become comfortable with being fourth greeter in line after Amra's eagle-eyed approval and Rhonda and Cameron's trotting enforcement of the Sheriff's wishes.

The sweet dog had the most endearing habit of sitting with, as Faith described it, an "eyes 101" gaze that made visitors search frantically in their pockets or purses for any kind of treat to assuage the soulful plea.

Buster, on the other hand, was a rambunctious hound left behind by the Crams when they moved to town. Mary and Norm loved their pooch dearly, but Buster had lived all his life in the canyon, and he knew Best Friends. The galumphing creature would often disappear only to be found, long, pink tongue salivating, outside Octagon Three at feeding time. "I think he'd be happier with you all," Norm Cram groused when the dog refused to leave.

Shamus, Gregory knew, would steal the hearts of Todd, Erin, and Fisher, the drive-time talk show hosts. Buster would probably provoke havoc. On the other hand, a little lively interaction might be just the ticket.

The three radio personalities were waiting when Gregory and company arrived. Buster took an immediate liking to attractive, strawberry-blonde Erin. The great hound placed two hairy paws on her shoulders and proceeded to demolish all traces of her makeup with his affectionate tongue. Erin melted. "No, no, it's all right," she smiled when Gregory attempted to restrain the happy animal.

Host Todd was playing with Shamus. "Hey, boy. You don't know you've got only three legs, do you?" Shamus conferred his best "eyes 101" and lifted his front paw for a handshake. Todd broke up. "Did you train him to do this?"

"He's a natural born ham," Gregory affirmed.

Erin wiped her face with a tissue. "We don't really need you, Gregory." She grinned mischievously and winked at her co-hosts. "We planned to only interview the dogs. Of course, you can speak for them, but do you think they could sort of bark and growl or just drool on cue?"

Gregory was sure the dogs would articulate most any sound Erin asked. Buster, he could see, was totally in love. Shamus couldn't take his eyes off hip Todd with his dark hair to his waist and urban chic jeans and shirt. Gregory fished a liver cookie from his pocket. "Shamus will bay at the moon for you if you treat him right," he smiled, handing over Shamus's bribe.

Fisher shook his head laughing. "Five seconds to air time. Let's do it, guys."

* * *

A side bonus of Utah's Week for the Animals was the semi-load of dog bowls, blankets, pooper-scoopers, kitty toys, doggie gyms, and cat scratching furniture contributed from all over; and the soaps, disinfectants, cleaning products, and incredible forty tons of cat litter donated by Huish Detergents, Inc.

In every issue of the magazine, Michael and Steven found room to feature other animal organizations that needed assistance. When lady luck smiled on Best Friends with such an abundance of goodies, it was only natural they share the wealth.

Michael would always remember the devout Catholic couple who ran a lovely little sanctuary outside Santa Fe. They drove twelve hours in a pickup, trailer attached, to load up with supplies. "You have no idea how much this helps," they repeated again and again along with their novenas.

All in all, Gregory pronounced Utah's Week for the Animals the best thing he had ever initiated.

CHAPTER FORTY-FIVE

Kid Lady

Cyrus led the party to the grizzled veteran snoozing in the April sunshine. "This is Victor the Dogfather, capo among canines." The shepherd opened one eye and promptly slipped back to dreamland. Cyrus smiled. "Victor guards the heart of Dogtown. He's sleeping on an invisible line in the sand that no dog dare cross unless accompanied by a person."

A brown-haired young woman squatted to stroke the patchy fur on the shepherd's head. "He looks so old and feeble. Why don't the others just ignore him?"

"Ah," Cyrus said. "It's all in the image. You see, when Victor first arrived . . ."

Michael listened to their ambassador expound on the legend of the Dogfather. Cyrus had a big group this afternoon, but then Michael had never seen so many people as were coming this summer of 1996.

Cyrus conducted two tours a day now. This year, too, Best Friends was seeing volunteers trek in from every state in the nation, as well as from Canada and Europe, to spend a weekend, a month, an entire summer vacation. Others came for the week-long seminars on all things animal. And thanks to Nathania's programs, students could now earn college credit by spending hands-on time at the sanctuary.

The word around town was that the local merchants were most pleased. This sudden influx of visitors brought a whole new breed of customer to the shops and motels of Kanab. That place in the canyon might have merit after all.

Michael strolled toward the clinic. Behind him he heard the growl of a mini-van's engine halting in front of Octagon Three. He turned and watched Nathania Gartman open the doors for a group of high-school boys. Michael was happy for Nathania. The dream she had envisioned fourteen years earlier was at last taking shape: the children were coming.

Of all of them, Nathania was the one who invariably attracted the inquisitiveness of the youngsters when she went tabling. After Chris Smith's positive article, she began receiving invitations to speak at schools around the state. As always, when Nathania chose to surprise everyone as Daffydil the Clown, her reception was rapturous. It was inevitable that the children would clamor to visit the sanctuary.

It wasn't long before kids from kindergarten through high school trooped through Best Friends. They petted the cats, walked the dogs, played with the rabbits in Chandra's new Bunny House, fed the horses, and ogled the birds as Sharon explained their care and habits. Michael had gotten used to seeing the eager upturned young faces crowded around an ebullient Nathania.

However, that didn't look like the scenario unfolding this afternoon. The adolescents slouched out of the van sulky and defiant. Their teacher scrambled out behind them, distress pinching her face. Nathania just looked sad.

A big boy with bad acne, affecting the bored indifference of an indulged child, leaned against the hood. His buddies fanned a half circle around him. "This is stupid," the kid said loudly.

Michael walked quickly toward them. At that moment Faith came out of Octagon Three. She caught his eye and shook her head. *I can handle this.* Michael paused, waiting.

"Tyson," she called. Alpha Man, ominous dark shades and breeze hat hiding his eyes, was immediately at her side. Michael smiled. Faith and Tyson were well able to handle the situation. Still, he wondered what was going on with the youngsters.

Nathania filled them in that night. "I had quite a day with those children," she rolled her eyes. Nathania went on to tell that the same teacher had brought a class last spring and everybody had a great time. This year she had arranged for her fifteen-year-olds to camp out for three days at nearby Coral Pink Sands north of Kanab to study stream biology and archaeology, and to work with the animals at Best Friends.

"The boys right off copped an attitude," Nathania said. "The ringleader—you saw him, Michael—swaggering kid, made these belligerent remarks everywhere we went. First words out of his mouth as he got off the bus were, 'what a bunch of losers, taking care of animals.' "

Nathania refused to let the youth rile her. At Feathered Friends, Sharon similarly ignored the rude comments about her birds. "Pigeons!" the juvenile hooted. "We've come all this way to hear about pigeons."

Things didn't improve at the Bunny House. Chandra was relating the story of how Tony, the dwarf rabbit, used to live in a bucket. "When he came here, Tony only knew how to protect himself by biting all the other bunnies, so he had to live alone."

The ringleader kicked the nearest stall impatiently. "Stop that right now," the teacher warned. The boy made a rude face behind her back, to the smirking approval of his mates.

Chandra continued unperturbed. "Until Tiger Lily," she said, leading the way to the end of the building, where an enormous, twenty-pound orange-and-white rabbit nibbled cheek to jowl with her lilliputian friend. "Tiger Lily and Tony hit it off right away. We have a lot of creatures who've bonded for life in the sanctuary, so don't let anyone ever tell you animals don't have feelings."

"Oh look," a boy exclaimed excitedly. "She's cleaning him." He caught a scowl from his bigger buddy and stuffed his hands into the pockets of his low-slung jeans. "Big deal."

Judah Nasr would have none of it at Benton's House. The young man was giving Tomato his medicine when Nathania brought in the teenagers. The kid was smart enough to mutter, but Judah still heard the cruel remarks about the ugly white cats that should be put out of their misery. He put Tomato on his desk and, deadly calm, stood toe to toe with the adolescent. The boy quickly backed off. Judah didn't raise his voice. "Don't you ever denigrate an animal on this property again."

"What does denigrate mean?" the bully tried to brazen.

Nathania had never encountered such an insensitive group. Where was the usual happy enthusiasm? She wondered if it was a big joke to these kids to see how miserable they could make the trip. She was glad Dogtown was the last stop.

"Faith was great," Nathania giggled. "She sized up the scene without me saying a word." Faith, she said, disarmingly complained that she needed to go on a feeding-bowl hunt. Amra, the Sheriff, had developed a little quirk of stealing any container not picked up within the hour. "Would you help me search for Amra's stash?" she asked.

Stony silence. "Then we need to put you to work, don't we? Okay, you, you, you, and you," Faith separated half the group. "You'll walk dogs with Tyson. I suggest you pay attention because Tyson only likes the difficult ones. Don't you, Tyson?"

"I like them best if they're biters," Tyson snarled, getting into Faith's game. The teacher would escort another group, which left the ringleader sulking by himself.

Nathania knew exactly why Faith had separated the troublemaker from his buddies. With no one around to impress with his toughness, the boy might allow a kinder side of himself to show.

Faith gave the cocky adolescent a once-over. She winked at Nathania and led the boy to the sprawling mass of ancient canines snoozing in the sun. "I have just the dog for you."

Maddie immediately awoke as they came near and rushed to her Big Mama. "Not today, sweetheart," Faith soothed. She bent to scratch the ear of a big white Samoyed. "Sam will do nicely."

"He's old," the boy objected.

"So will you be one day," Nathania retorted.

Faith smiled. "Seems to me you need to chill, kid. You're walking Sam. And Nathania and I will be keeping an eye on you."

"Perfect," Nathania murmured as the kid shuffled off behind an arthritic Sam. The rheumy-eyed Samoyed might make his way with the speed of a giant turtle, but his courage and determination to enjoy his walks in spite of his ailments could give even the most belligerent delinquent pause to think.

The teacher and her charges returned within the hour, Tyson and his group soon after. But there was no sight of the bully. Tyson loped off to return with the report that the kid was merely taking his time. Nathania decreed that everyone should go to The Village, where cold drinks were waiting.

Another hour passed before the troublemaker and the Samoyed ambled back into Dogtown. "Can I feed Sam?" the boy surprised them.

His whole demeanor had changed. He stood respectfully straight, no slouching. Nathania could detect no derision in the eyes.

"Follow me," Faith said.

"Thank you," the youth said politely. "That dog's way cool."

The teacher called Nathania later that evening, first to apologize, then to relate how the kids had described their tour.

"The child who walked the white Samoyed," she said. "He's always given me trouble, and I was ready to wring his neck this time, but he surprised me. When I asked the boys how they felt about the day, as usual nobody wanted to say anything in front of their ringleader.

"Then he stood up and very thoughtfully, not in his usual bellicose manner, said he'd thought working with animals was stupid and unimportant . . . until he walked Sam this afternoon. Then he sat down and glared at everybody as if daring them to make fun of his confession. And that was it. He wasn't about to give any explanation."

The teacher laughed. "There was dead silence for a moment. You should seen the look of shock on those kids' faces. Then one of the other boys tentatively offered that he'd really liked the rabbits and birds." The woman paused. "They all asked how soon they could come back."

Nathania smiled. Neither she nor anyone listening needed to probe for reasons. They had seen the healing effects of the animals and the canyon many times before.

They would see it again.

CHAPTER FORTY-SIX

Oscar Heginbotham

Spring came early in 1997, with a warmer-than-usual March promising an endless summer. For Best Friends, the flow of visitors from home and abroad had already begun. Word of the sanctuary had spread far beyond the confines of the United States, and now they welcomed company from Norway to India, from Japan to Peru. So for someone to come from Saudi Arabia would not be out of the question. But for a couple to want to ship a cat from Dhahran to Best Friends was a little out of the ordinary.

Estelle took the call and immediately paged Diana at Catland. "A Bonnie Heginbotham is on the phone from Saudi Arabia to see if we can take her cat, Oscar. I gather it's an unusual situation."

"Put her through," Diana urged. She waited a second for the familiar click that told her the transatlantic caller was on her extension. "Hello, Bonnie. I'm Diana Asher, in charge of cats. What can I do for you?"

"I don't know quite where to start," Bonnie answered.

"From the beginning if you like," Diana said.

"It's rather a long story."

"I have time."

The relief in Bonnie's voice was palpable. "Thank you," she said. "It will be good to talk to somebody about this. Would you mind if I give you a little background? I'm a Delta Airlines flight attendant, but I took a five-year leave of absence to be with my husband in Dharhan—Ron is with Saudi-Aramco, Arabian American Oil Company." As Diana listened, Bonnie wove a tale about a cat named Oscar, as poignant as any told by Scheherezade.

Ron Heginbotham had gone on ahead of his wife to the Middle East. Bonnie would be bringing Walter, their beloved sheltie, and Ron wanted to find a house with a fenced yard on a quiet street for their pet.

Dhahran, the oil company's headquarters, was a beautiful gated compound, a world unto itself that enclosed an area about the size of a small resort town. Inside its ten-mile perimeter, Saudi-Aramco employees could enjoy restaurants, a commissary, library, movie theater, swimming pool, and children's play areas—all the comforts of home.

Within the compound, Saudi-Aramco also provided its people with accommodations of every style and size, from palatial sand-colored villas to apartments for the single staff.

Ron found a cozy two-bedroom duplex on Lemon Lane that had stood empty since its former tenants, an Englishwoman and her American husband, had moved out six months before. The minute he saw it, Ron knew Bonnie would love the place. His wife's passion was gardening, and the backyard was a riot of vegetation, redolent with the scents of frangipani, jasmine, and lilies, and bright with hibiscus and bougainvillea. He arranged to rent furniture until the Heginbothams' own household goods were shipped from America, and by December of 1994 everything was ready for Bonnie's arrival.

Bonnie Heginbotham's welcome, however, was not quite what she expected. "Oh, I love it, Ron. I just love it," she exclaimed as she wandered through the big, airy rooms, mentally deciding where their French country furniture would fit. "But a coat of paint would really make it homey. Something butterscotch I think."

Ron smiled, but before he could respond to his wife's enthusiasm the phone rang. "It's for you," he said, puzzled, and handed her the receiver.

"I know you only got here a few hours ago, but do you have a minute?" the frightfully British voice asked. "I'm Jackie, your next-door neighbor, and I noticed you brought your dog over."

"Yes," said Bonnie carefully.

"Oh, no problem. It's about Oscar, you see. Oh dear, I should explain myself." Jackie paused as if Bonnie should understand. "Oscar is Amanda's cat. She used to live in your house."

"Yes," Bonnie repeated.

"When they moved she took him with them, but he keeps running back here. Amanda and Jim, that's her husband, must have fetched him at least a dozen times, but Oscar won't stay in their new place.

"Jim has about had it. He says they have two babies to take care of, and he's not catching Oscar one more time. Amanda's to get the cat tonight and have him put down in the morning. I've been feeding him, but he won't come to me." Jackie rushed on. "I know it's a bit much, but I've gotten fond of the little devil. I wonder if you wouldn't mind dreadfully . . . keeping him?"

"I've never had a cat."

"Oh," Jackie's voice dropped in defeat.

"I didn't say I wouldn't." Bonnie looked at Ron for help. Her husband shook his head. He was listening to a woman who, as a child, would pick up injured sparrows and take them to her mother crying, "Please do something."

"I mean I can't see putting down a perfectly healthy animal. Where is Oscar now?" Bonnie asked.

"In your garden. He's somewhat wild, being outside the last six months," Jackie warned, "but he waits for the food I leave."

"I see. I guess I'd better go put some out, then."

Evening shadows were just shrouding the frangipani tree when Bonnie and Ron caught their first sight of Oscar. The cat appeared suddenly, prowling openly on their lawn—a large, sleek black panther of a feline whose golden eyes glowed in the dusk.

"A veritable prince of a cat," Ron declared and went to open a can of people tuna.

Every night Oscar would come to eat, eyes ever wary, ready to scoot at the slightest approach. As the evenings got colder—it could get down to fifty degrees at night—Bonnie provided a cardboard box and blankets for the cat to snuggle into.

As the weeks turned into months, Bonnie got closer to Oscar. Once he even allowed her to pet him, then turned and growled a warning. Walter always kept a respectful distance, perhaps in deference to the arched back and loud hiss if he should come within a foot of the intruder. When Walter slunk away dejected Ron would cradle his sheltie in his arms. "There, there," he comforted. "You pay no mind to that bully."

In spite of all that, the couple liked the cat, and Bonnie worried about his nocturnal wanderings. She tried to coax him inside, calling night after night without success. Meanwhile, she got quite friendly with her neighbor, Jackie.

"Amanda used to stand at the back door and hit his bowl with a spoon then call Oscarh! Oscarh! Dinnertime."

"Really," Bonnie said.

The next time Bonnie performed Amanda's ritual. In passing imitation of Jackie's proper Brit accent she called, "Oscarh! Oscarh! Dinnertime." Something flashed by her legs, and the big black cat was inside her house before she could turn around.

"So that's it," she said, following him into the kitchen.

In short order Oscar was an inside/outside cat, courtesy of Walter's doggie door, bestowing his greatest honor on his new persons by sleeping at the foot of their bed. During the day he would often rub against Bonnie's ankles or curl up beside her on the couch. Soon the cat purred contentedly in her arms and she felt an extraordinary comfort in this foreign land from the heavy warmth of his body against hers.

Oscar was now indisputably part of the family. He even deigned to walk between Walter's front legs from time to time, affectionately butting the sheltie's chin with his head as if to tell him he was all right—even though he was a dog.

Bonnie was not prepared for the night Oscar came in matted and torn from what looked like a cat fight, and jumped on her bed. "Hi, Oscar," she greeted, looking up from her book. "What's the matter, baby?"

Like black lightning, Oscar pounced on the hand that fed him, sinking his teeth into the soft flesh between thumb and forefinger. In a second he had torn flesh from the bone. Bonnie screamed; Ron bolted awake from a light slumber. Oscar hissed at both of them, then was gone.

The wound was bad. Ron called an ambulance and Bonnie was rushed to the emergency room at the company's hospital. "You have your choice," the couple were told after she was shot with antibiotics and the gash dressed. "You can put the cat to sleep and we'll take brain tissue to determine if he's rabid. Or, you can quarantine him for ten days but we'll still have to put him down."

Oscar strolled into the duplex the next morning as if nothing had happened. A half-hour later he was in Saudi-Aramco's veterinary clinic.

Dennis Perkins was a Baton Rouge, Louisiana man with small, delicate hands and brown hair cut in straight bangs across his forehead. The veterinarian knew how attached the Heginbothams were to their cat, but there was only one thing he could say to the distraught couple. "Mizz Bonnie, I don't have to tell you, Oscar's time here is over."

"He's had his shots. He's not rabid. He was just disoriented, that's all," Bonnie protested.

Dr. Perkins shook his head. "There's been a report filed. Oscar bit you," he said gently.

Bonnie was inconsolable. Every day she'd go to jail, as she called quarantine, and cuddle Oscar. "Why did you do that?" she asked repeatedly.

One afternoon she walked in to hear Ron on the phone with Dennis Perkins. "He's asking permission to put Oscar to sleep now, isn't he?"

Ron looked miserable. "I said yes. We both don't want you to go through this pain anymore," her husband told her. Bonnie sank down on the couch and couldn't stop crying. Ron sat beside his wife, at a loss how to comfort her. "Honey, let's just make believe Oscar is still alive. There's nothing you could do."

Bonnie lifted her head. "I'd send him to Best Friends." Her eyes widened with disbelief at her own words. "Why didn't I think of that before?" she wailed.

Man and wife stared at each other, both thinking the same thing. Ron scooted to the end of the couch and reached for the phone. "Tell Dr. Perkins to wait. Don't do anything to Oscar. We'll be right over," Bonnie said as she jumped up and ran to the kitchen for the car keys.

Dennis Perkins regarded the anxious couple before him. "I want to help," he drawled soft and slow. "However, the only way I'll sign a health certificate is if this Best Friends will promise me in writing that Oscar will be confined and never adopted out. Is that the kind of life you really want for him?"

Bonnie and Ron nodded in unison. "He doesn't deserve to be killed. Something happened, that's all," Bonnie said.

The silence stretched across the miles as Mrs. Heginbotham finished her tale. Diana had heard similar stories before, but she was touched that this couple were willing to go to all the trouble and expense it would take to save the life of this cat.

Bonnie mistook the quiet. "If you'll take him, we'll pay for any expenses and his upkeep."

"That is very much appreciated, but I'm curious about something. Why did you call Best Friends?"

For the first time in their conversation Bonnie laughed. It was a light, bubbly sound that made Diana smile. "I told you I'm a Delta Airlines flight attendant. My base was Salt Lake. I came off a flight in 1992 and one of your people was sitting at a table at the top of the escalator. He asked if I were an animal lover." She laughed again. "I gave a donation and took the literature. Ron's from back East, and before he went to Dhahran he wanted to see the Grand Canyon. We stopped to see your sanctuary on the way, but I don't expect you to remember us."

"I knew I'd heard your voice somewhere!" Diana exclaimed. She had a sudden vision of a smiling woman who looked to be in her late thirties sporting a chic Liza Minnelli cap of short brown hair shot with gray. She had liked Bonnie's husband too: a solid, kind man with sailor blue eyes like John Fripp's. "I remember you wore a wide-brimmed hat that totally shaded your face. I thought I should get myself one." She paused, then continued briskly. "So what do we need to do to get your prince of a cat out of there?"

Diana Asher had no illusions about what she would find when she picked up Oscar. The cat had been flown from Dhahran to Amsterdam, then transferred to a Delta Airlines flight for Los Angeles, where Bonnie's friends would see him safely through American customs before his final journey to Salt Lake.

The morning of April 12, she loaded her Subaru with a clean carrier for the cat, thick padded gloves to protect her when handling Oscar, and sodas for the road. By 6:00 A.M. she was on the highway to Salt Lake City.

Diana was not surprised by the malodorous smell that emanated from the cat's airline crate, or the coiled tension ready to explode from the animal that had been forcefully caged for so many hours. "Hang loose just a bit longer, and we'll make this all better," she assured as she took possession of the feline. Oscar's answer was to fling his body against his prison with a bloodcurdling yowl.

Even after being moved to the relative comfort of a clean carrier with fresh water, he was in no mood to be placated. Oscar howled the entire journey home. Diana simply turned up the music and sped toward Best Friends as fast as the law allowed.

Diana had filled the shaded area next to the bunkhouse— where so many years before she and Faith had kept the cats from the old Arizona ranch—with toys, treats, and a kitty house for Oscar.

The first couple of days she watched the cat pace his new quarters in obvious agitation. Oscar resisted any overtures of friendship, snarling defiance when she talked to him. Every time she left, Diana could feel those accusing golden eyes at her back—no animal liked being in solitary. She was still fretting two weeks later when a tiny long-haired tabby was brought into the sanctuary.

A member had been feeding some other strays in a park near her house in Salt Lake City, but Heidi was too terrified of her fellow felines to get her share. "I don't know how she survived," the member said after she managed to trap the little scaredy-cat.

Judah saw that Heidi wouldn't eat around the mellow kitties in Catland either, and he had no choice but to keep the scaredy-cat in a crate at feeding time. Even then she ate hardly enough for sustenance, staying hidden the rest of the time.

Diana went into Heidi's room and found the frail tabby, as always, crouched in her kitty house. Diana stared into the darkened interior. "It's worth a try," she murmured. She scooped up Heidi and house and hurried toward the bunkhouse. A half-hour later, her hands and forearms swaddled in padded gloves, Diana sat quietly in Oscar's quarters, ready to intervene if the black cat made one menacing move.

Oscar ignored her as she carefully positioned Heidi's house a few feet away from his fleece bed. When she put down a large bowl of moist kitty food, Oscar devoured as much as his stomach could hold and then lay sated by his favorite toy. Heidi was as silent as a stone within her house.

Diana needed all her patience this afternoon. For two hours Oscar lay staring into the darkness of the tabby's hiding place. Finally, he stretched to his feet and stalked to the food bowl. *Damn, he's going to eat it all.*

Sure enough the big cat took a mouthful of food—but instead of swallowing it, he walked back and laid the morsel under the timid feline's nose. His action reminded Diana of a suitor bringing a bouquet to his lady.

Oscar watched, satisfied as Heidi nibbled tentatively at his offering. He brought another mouthful and again poked it just inside her house, purring loudly. Soon the bowl was clean and Heidi had eaten her first good meal at Best Friends.

It was as if the tabby knew she had found a protector in this Saudi prince of a cat. Oscar, in turn, felt no threat from the timid little female and welcomed her companionship. As Diana watched, Heidi slowly emerged from her self-imposed prison and stared shyly at the proud black male. Oscar gently rubbed his nose against hers.

Chief Cat smiled. There would be no more solitary for these new sweethearts. It was another good day at Best Friends.

CHAPTER FORTY-SEVEN

All Are Beautiful

Amra hobbled forward to greet the afternoon tour. The magnificent malamute's will was as staunch as ever, but the Sheriff no longer bounced forward like a teenager. No more did Amra surprise with a quick duck between unwary legs, and a heady flip from broad shoulders. Dogtown's official greeter never shirked his duties, but now the thinner hips of age sashayed forward with effort, accompanied by a steady panting under the clear shafts of a late-summer sun.

Shy Rhonda, as always, watched and waited for her love a few yards away, anxious eyes never leaving his great frame. Faith could have adopted Amra out many times over the years, but nobody had ever offered Rhonda a home with the malamute.

As time went on, the bonds of attachment between the two canines had deepened into a love as strong and enduring as the Rock of Gibraltar. Ten years later Rhonda still cleaned the eyes and ears of the one that had lifted her out of her doggie depression, still bestowed tiny licks of affection on the great head. The delicate little terrier mutt still eschewed the limelight for herself, but she was never far from the Sheriff's side.

Together plain Rhonda and the glorious malamute patrolled the perimeters of Dogtown, kept recalcitrant hounds in line, confiscated feeding bowls, and slept together, with Rhonda entwined in the protection of the bigger dog's massive paws, her little head beneath his noble jaw. Faith thought it would be like dividing conjoined twins to separate the terrier mix from her beloved.

But life has its own passages, and on this day the Sheriff performed his duty as always, too slowly making his way back to the shade of his favorite juniper. Dr. Allen had diagnosed arthritis in the spring and prescribed pain medication to relieve the malamute's stiffening gait. Best Friends made life as comfortable as possible for Amra over the next few months.

Not one of the Best Friends would inflict any undue suffering on an animal, and Faith, watching the heroic animal's labored movements, sensed something more serious was manifesting itself. She looked into the bewildered golden eyes filled with a pain she had never seen before, and Faith knew Amra was ready to cross over the Rainbow Bridge.

In the cool of the evening, Tyson carried the great canine to the clinic. A subdued Rhonda trotted beside them to where Dr. Allen was waiting. The veterinarian was not his usual jocular self this night. He looked at the valiant shadow of the dog he had known and didn't hesitate. Carefully he eased an injection into Amra's flank to alleviate the distress before preparing the X rays. Dr. Allen needed no tests to know that he was looking at the last hours of a living legend, but there was always the faint chance he could be wrong. Rhonda perched on a chair and stared fixedly at her sedated mate.

"It's bad, Faith," Dr Allen pronounced, holding up the negatives so she could see for herself. "Amra has bone cancer. See these fuzzy areas? That's the cancer eating away the hind legs. That's why Amra's in such pain when he walks. We'd be doing the Sheriff no favor by prolonging this."

Faith turned away. "He's not hurting now, is he?"

"No," the veterinarian assured.

"Give me a few minutes."

Faith walked the familiar lanes of Dogtown. The bustle of the day had given way to the sleepy peace of evening. The dogs still rushed their enclosures to greet Chief Dog, but with less rambunctious energy—their barking more form than content—then returned to their doggie dreams.

She passed over Victor's line in the sand and remembered the respect Amra always accorded the grizzled veteran. Faith stood on the very spot where she, Tyson, Michael, and John had first seen the splendid red creature propel himself into Dogtown. She smiled sadly on Homer's Hill, reminiscing how big and strong the malamute had been to upend the solid 220 pounds of Homer Harris. Most of all, Faith thought on the boundless love between Amra and his Rhonda, and with this thought came the inevitable question: What would happen to the terrier mix when her life's partner was gone?

Faith retraced her steps to the clinic. Her face was clear of tears, stoic with acceptance as she faced Rich Allen. The vet didn't need to ask; he just prepared the syringe. Faith lifted Rhonda onto the table next to her love. The little female whined and sniffed her sleeping spouse, then laid her head against the broad chest that had kept her warm for so many years. Faith cradled Amra in her arms and murmured words of comfort to the dog who couldn't hear, as Dr. Allen sent the Sheriff on his painless journey.

Tyson and the veterinarian wrapped the malamute's body in a white sheet, then lowered it to the floor beneath the table. Without a sound, Rhonda lay beside the inert form.

"Let her stay," Faith decreed. "She needs to mourn, just as we do."

David Maloney met his mother at the clinic the next morning. He and Faith buried Amra at Angels Rest under a juniper tree as the Sheriff would have wanted. Dr. Allen did not accompany them, feeling that he was perhaps too much a newcomer—Amra was part of the fabric of the Dogtown that Faith and David had helped to build from nothing. The vet was waiting outside the gate of the memorial park after their final good-byes. "Rhonda is hiding under the cabinets," he said. "I can't coax her out."

Faith understood. "Leave her be. She'll come to us in her own good time."

For eight days, Rhonda hung around the clinic, meandering from room to room, looking for her mate. For eight days, Faith watched the widow's snuffling and listened to the low, continuous whimpers that would go on for hours. To Faith, the extent of Rhonda's grief was heartbreaking because there was nothing she could do for the bereft little terrier.

For eight days Rhonda broke everyone's heart. Then, on a cool hint-of-fall evening, she dragged out of the clinic and made her way to the juniper that had been the Sheriff's command post. "She's finally figured out he's not coming back," Faith murmured.

Still, Rhonda did not run to greet Big Mama as of old. Rhonda no longer patrolled Dogtown, had no use for the habits of years. Instead she turned inward. Faith fretted. She had always had a soft spot for the loyal, loving mutt, and it was more than she could bear to see Rhonda's heartache. But nothing Faith did could rouse the grieving animal.

November brought days of crisp clarity and chilly nights. David placed a cozy kennel under Amra's favorite tree and Rhonda conceded she needed the warmth. A few days later Faith, at Francis's request, was personally escorting a party from Los Angeles, as part of the L.A. outreach program that devoted hours to the city's shelters. They had been very excited at the prospect of touring Best Friends with Faith.

The director of the sanctuary was explaining how they decided which dogs should be housed with whom, when suddenly a red terrier mix padded hesitantly toward them. With fragile dignity, Rhonda came forward to greet the visitors. She planted four delicate legs beside Faith and gazed into the faces of the enthralled group.

"Oh, she's so darling," a woman exclaimed.

Rhonda immediately gravitated toward the source of the words, standing immobile, allowing herself to be petted, moving into the limelight she had always shunned. Faith stared at the dog that was no longer plain. Rhonda had taken on the mantle of her deceased mate, much as Eleanor Roosevelt had stepped forward in the wake of her President husband's death . . . and she was beautiful.

Something had changed in Rhonda's consciousness. Somehow the dog felt compelled to take over the duties that had always been her gregarious mate's. Still, she kept aloof from the other mutts, and Faith worried at the sight of Rhonda curled up alone under a tree that once had shaded a nest for two.

Michael, too, had been watching Rhonda's mourning. "I'm going to write about that little terrier and her mate," he declared. "Rhonda and Amra are perfect examples of the devotion animals can have for each other."

The love story appeared in the December issue. Within a day of the magazine's arrival in her mailbox, Dr. Sharyn Faro was on the phone from Atlanta. "I want to give that special little being a wonderful home for the rest of her life."

Faith was protective. "We weren't really expecting anyone to adopt her. Rhonda's old, and all she's known is Dogtown. She's run free since she was a pup. She's liable to piddle indoors."

Rich, warm laughter greeted her warning. "I'd have no problem living in a rugless home, Faith. Stuff isn't important to me. I have three senior dogs like Rhonda who all sleep on the bed. I have a huge garden, and every Tuesday we all get to go to my friend's three hundred-acre farm in the country for a really big romp. Rhonda will fit in just fine."

"If you're really serious, there's a two-page adoption application to fill out, and I'll have to interview you."

"No problem. Can you fax it to me? I'd like to pick Rhonda up next week."

Next week! Faith enlisted Tyson and David and the three of them immediately went to work. The terrier had not been in a car since Faith had rescued her from the pound eleven years before. Now she was taken shopping three times a day. Tyson took it upon himself to introduce Rhonda to walking on a leash.

Yet Faith was not to meet Sharyn Faro for another two years. A friend of the psychologist was vacationing in Brian Head, a ski resort two hours north of Best Friends. She arrived with toys, treats, and a fluffy blanket to tenderly escort the new adoptee to Atlanta. Within two weeks a letter from Rhonda detailed her settling into her new home, and Faith immediately replied.

Over the next months, Rhonda wrote Best Friends about her delicious home-cooked meals, the swims in the lake, how her new person, Mama Sha, loved kisses. Rhonda proudly boasted that she accompanied Mama Sha everywhere and she was now the proud greeter of Dr. Faro's patients. "I get so many hugs and loving, if I were the Velveteen Rabbit I wouldn't have any fur."

Faith could only marvel at the twists and turns of fate when Rhonda sent pictures of herself contently sleeping alongside her new doggie companions in the magnificent mansion, filled with antiques and Persian rugs, that she now called home. Rhonda's last days would be the best for which any animal could wish. *And no one deserves it more than you, little one,* Faith said to herself.

The photos reminded Faith of how she had anguished about

letting Rhonda leave Dogtown, just before the arrival of the cat Tyson and his blind brother, Tommy. The memory brought back, once again, the classic tale of the man walking by the ocean, throwing back the starfish beached after a storm, saving them . . . one at a time.

That's the way it had always been for Best Friends. That's the way it always would be. Whether in an alley in Los Angeles or a compound in Saudi Arabia, Best Friends everywhere would forever come to the aid of the furred and feathered creatures with whom they shared the planet . . . one at a time.

It occurred to Faith that, in her way, Rhonda was the archetype for all animals. None are plain. None are common.

Through the eyes of love, all are beautiful.

AFTERWORD

by
MICHAEL MOUNTAIN

ALL GOOD THINGS

May 2000

Tommy and Tyson no longer walk everywhere with their tails intertwined, as they once had to on the mean streets of Los Angeles. Instead, they spend their afternoons snoozing in the sun, high in the rafters of their outdoor porch at the WildCats Village.

The two brothers are still not keen on being approached by people, but the new WildCats Village is perfect for feral cats like them who grew up on the streets but could no longer survive on their own. Their new home was completed a couple of years ago and was largely the gift of a member of Best Friends who lives in Arizona.

Benton's House is still home to the cats with special needs, although it is now under new "management." Benton finally went over the Rainbow Bridge in June of 1999. The old dictator, with his little club foot, kept everyone in line right up to the end, and I cannot begin to imagine what he must be thinking of the fact that we invited members of Best Friends to vote for a new chairpurrson of his TLC Cat Club.

The election was actually won by Julius, a friendly orange kitty with neurological problems, whose back end is never quite sure which way his front end is trying to go. (No matter: He always manages to end up where the treats are!)

But Benton would never have approved of democracy, so I'm sure he's delighted that Patience—an otherwise very polite black-

and-white kitty with hormonal problems and a Charlie Chaplin moustache—promptly stole the election, took over as top cat, and installed herself as chairpurrson. (The other cats seem quite happy with the arrangement and Julius is considered her co-chair.)

Tomato the Cat just completed one of his investigative reports of this scandal in *Best Friends* magazine and concluded that rigging the election was probably the best outcome. Julius, he agreed, is very telegenic, which is important in this media age. "But," he added, "his elevator does not quite go to the top. So a little help from Patience will not be out of order."

(Tomato himself actually went over the Rainbow Bridge, too, a couple of years ago. However, he insists that this was just the first of his nine lives. He sends in a column for every edition of the magazine and seems to be very much alive in the hearts and minds of all of us who appreciate his quirky ways.)

Meanwhile, at the Cat HQ office, Sinjin, the furry, one-eyed pirate who was rescued one Thanksgiving evening back in Part One of this book, still rules supreme, demanding treats at all hours—utterly disdainful of all the media hype surrounding chairpurr-sons, magazine columns, and the like. Real power, he believes, resides in the kitchen. As does he.

Over at Dogtown, Ginger the Chesapeake still does the rounds each day, albeit a little stiffly. She likes to wear a woolly jacket on all but the warmest of days as she continues to keep an eye on the tennis balls and bring any surplus back to her Federal Reserve Tree, the big old juniper that still shades her comfortable dog-house.

Ginger has outlived all the other dogs who were the founders of Dogtown—even her own pups, Cheshire and Mace. When they went over the Rainbow Bridge, a few years ago, two young black spaniel mixes, Francesca and Butterfly, moved in with Ginger. They race around every afternoon, just as Cheshire and Mace did, gathering up tennis balls and issuing the occasional challenge to the top dogs of other neighborhoods around Dogtown.

Since the day Faith rescued her from that dreadful puppy mill all those years ago, Ginger has watched Dogtown grow from its small-town beginnings to something approaching urban sprawl. More fences, more add-ons, a training school, adoption compounds, Old Friends, New Friends, Little Dogs, and an expanding clinic, where Dr. Allen presides over the Big Fix for people from all over the region who need to get their pets spayed or neutered.

Last year, it was becoming urgent to start building a new residential "suburb" for Dogtown. And once again, it was our dear friends Homer and Dolores to the rescue.

"Oh, we just want to do something nice for the dogs," Dolores told Faith and John as Homer put down his pen at a corner table at The Village during staff lunch one summer day when they were visiting. Homer was transferring half a million dollars into a special account to build a new Dogtown—ten sparkling new octagon homes with big outdoor areas for about 300 of the dogs, along with a new clinic and other facilities.

"Do you think our members will put up the other half million it will take to finish this?" Homer asked.

Steven smiled. He could already see the headline in our next newsletter: "Those Doggies Are Feeling Like a Million Bucks!" (Thank you, again, dear members and friends. The builders are just starting work as I write this.)

Every day brings a new round of dogs, cats, horses, birds, and bunnies into the sanctuary. With lots of special care, good food, and a trip to the spay/neuter clinic, most of them are soon able to go to good new homes.

And for those who aren't quite ready for a new home—and, in some cases, may never be—Best Friends will be their home and their haven for the rest of their lives.

Most of the animals who come to Best Friends now come from rescue groups and shelters all over the country. And, with the Best Friends Network operating all over the country too, good fortune works in some remarkable ways.

Take Missy, for example. . . .

Missy's life got off to a rather bumpy start in Kansas City when, as a ten-week-old kitten, she was thrown into the back of a truck. She was rescued and cared for by a local group, but Missy's brain had been damaged and she could no longer walk properly. That was when they called Best Friends.

Faith and Judah reckoned we could find a place for Missy in Benton's House, but then we had to figure out how to bring her here from Kansas City.

Then Carolyn called. Carolyn lives in Wisconsin and used to be a flight attendant with United Airlines, which means she has lots of travel perks with the airline. "If I can ever help out by flying an animal anywhere, just let me know," she said.

"How about right now!" we replied.

The next day, Carolyn flew to Kansas City, picked up Missy, and brought her to Best Friends.

A few weeks later, Sandy, a member of Best Friends from Baltimore, Maryland, came to visit the sanctuary and spent an afternoon in Benton's House. She fell in love with Missy, called her husband, Chris, who agreed that their home would be perfect for Missy, and promptly applied to adopt the little cat. While Sandy and Missy were on their way home, Chris built their new baby a special playpen where she could be safe and happy. And that's what we mean when we say that, thanks to the kindness of members of Best Friends everywhere, dogs and cats like Missy all get to live "happily ever after."

More and more people are going to their local shelter with the idea of adopting a dog or cat who really needs a good home, rather than going to a pet store or breeder to find the cutest puppy or kitten. (Stores that sell pets help keep the puppy mills—like the one where Ginger once lived—in business.) Not long ago, fancy "purebred" animals were very much the pet of choice. But that's all changing now. More and more, it's the dogs and cats who have had the hardest luck, not the best breeding, who tend to find first place in people's hearts!

Also, more and more are getting their pets spayed or neutered so that they're not adding to the problem by producing puppies and kittens at home. And more and more people are coming to understand that once we bring a pet home, he or she becomes a full part of our family.

So, things have come a long way from when Best Friends was still in its early days and "happily ever after" stories like Missy's were few and far between.

Back then, seventeen million homeless cats and dogs were being destroyed in pounds and shelters every year. Most people thought of this appalling carnage as being simply one of those "necessary evils" in life—something terrible that you just couldn't do anything about. (Isn't that exactly what otherwise good, kind, and decent people once said about slavery, child labor, and all the other "necessary evils" of the nineteenth century?)

Today, thanks to the growth of the new "no-kill" movement, only about five million dogs and cats are being killed in shelters each year. That's a whole lot better than it was, but it's still five million too many. So, in communities across the country, this grassroots movement is working to bring an end altogether to the killing of homeless pets.

People often comment on the fact that the love our pets offer to us is unconditional. Animals, they note, don't care how we look or what our problems are. They just accept us the way we are and love us for it. But here at Best Friends, I am even more impressed by the love that people show the animals who touch their hearts. It is an equally unconditional love.

When Sandy adopted Missy, when Lydia rescued Tommy and Tyson, when Homer and Dolores bought the Welcome Center and the horse pastures, when Tom arrived to conduct the Dogtown "orchestra" with his pooper scooper, when Ron and Bonnie Heginbotham shipped Oscar from Saudi Arabia, and when Samantha Glen called me to ask if she could help the cause of "No More Homeless Pets" by writing this book about Best Friends, they weren't looking for anything in return. They just wanted to help the animals.

But, like anyone else who has rescued, helped, or given a home to a cat or dog in need, they discovered that there are enormous rewards in this cycle of love.

Throughout history, prophets and teachers from every culture and creed have taught the simple, universal, and eternal Golden Rule that as we give, so do we receive. This simple rule of thumb is the key to success and happiness in our lives.

There is no better application of the Golden Rule than to help a homeless pet. In doing this, you are giving the gift of life itself. And since there is no greater gift, there can be no greater reward.

That's because in giving life, we receive life. In rescuing an innocent creature, we find a lifeline to our own lost innocence. In offering a helping hand to nature, we discover a connection to our own basic nature.

If, among all of us who care about the animals, we can bring about a time when there are no more homeless pets, this will be a remarkable achievement—but it will be more than that.

At the beginning of a new millennium, in a world that races to embrace new ways of living longer and feeling better in its endlessly elusive quest for human happiness, doing something truly good for the animals would represent a whole new attitude to life.

It might mean that we are not only at the start of a new technological era, but of a new spiritual one, too.

RESOURCES

―――――――

ACHIEVING THE NATIONWIDE GOAL OF NO MORE HOMELESS PETS

How you can be part of the Best Friends network.

The "No More Homeless Pets" movement is growing very rapidly. In communities all across the nation, moves are afoot to bring an end to the killing of dogs and cats that have no home.

If you want to be part of a local "No More Homeless Pets" effort, there are many local groups that you can work with. There are also organizations, local and national, that can help you start a program of your own. We'll be delighted to put you in touch with whichever of them can be most helpful to you.

Indeed, we hear of new efforts that are starting in different parts of the country every week. The best way to keep up with them all, and to be part of what's happening, is through the Best Friends web site at **www.bestfriends.org**. You'll find up-to-date information on "No More Homeless Pets" programs as they're developing, and you can participate directly through the Best Friends Network.

The Best Friends Network connects people and organizations all across the country who are helping animals already or who want to join in. For example:

Perhaps you're feeding some homeless cats in your neighborhood and could use a little help. We'll notify members nearby and ask if they'd like to help.

If you have an afternoon to spare, you might like to help out at your local shelter walking the dogs, grooming the cats, or whatever else is needed. We can put you in touch with a shelter or rescue group that other members have recommended.

Maybe you're an attorney or other professional and would like to donate your skills if there's a problem in your area that involves animals.

If you're good with e-mail or on the phone and have time available, perhaps you'd like to start a community newsgroup or act as a volunteer coordinator for local activities.

Maybe you'd like to organize a get-together with other members. It's always good to know that there are other people who feel the way you do about caring for animals, and we can put the word out to other Network members about your plans.

Or if you'd simply like us to keep in touch with you about network activities near where you live, we'll keep you posted.

And if you're a local organization that's looking for volunteer help, there are probably members of the network nearby who would like to take part.

You can join the Network on the Best Friends web site at **www. bestfriends.org**. (If you don't have direct access to the Internet, it's available in most public libraries, or perhaps you have an animal-loving friend or relative who will be happy to be your technical assistant!)

There are also members meetings, adoption festivals, conferences, workshops, and other gatherings and events, local and national, all through the year. Up-to-date information on these, along with how-to manuals and other resources, can be found in the "No More Homeless Pets" section of the Best Friends web site at **www.bestfriends.org**.

Thank you again, and bless you for caring about the animals.